Consultative Selling

Bryan Dunlop

Consultative Selling

First published in 2006 by: May Publishing,
79 Whinney Hill, Craigantlet, County Down BT16 1UA
Email: b.dunlop@tmti.co.uk

© Bryan Dunlop 2006

Printed in Ireland by Universities Press.

The moral right of the writer has been asserted.

ISBN 10: 0-9553158-0-8

ISBN 13: 978-0-9553158-0-0

CONSULTATIVE SELLING

In ten years of participating in and attending sales meetings as a Coach, Bryan has had the opportunity to study all types of sales behaviours. Drawing on these positive (and negative) experiences has enabled him to produce this book on "consultative selling".

Bryan believes that a salesperson must be able to **proactively initiate new business relationships** on a consistent basis. Consultative selling is the key to being able to do this. The ideas contained within this book are a **proven formula** for creating **proactive** sales success.

Bryan founded Tailor Made Training International (TMTI) in 2001. TMTI deliver bespoke sales and leadership programmes.

"The best way to predict the future is to create it"
Peter Drucker

This book is dedicated to Poppy,
Harry and Tom.

Table of contents

Chapter 1   **ATTITUDE IS EVERYTHING**   1

Chapter 2   **MANAGING YOUR SALES**   31
BUSINESS

Chapter 3   **A VIRTUOUS START**   59

Chapter 4   **"BEING INTERESTED" –**   95
THE PROACTIVE DIAGNOSTIC
SALES MEETING

Chapter 5   **CREATING DOUBT AND**   133
BUILDING CURIOSITY

Chapter 6   **PRESENTING SOLUTIONS –**   157
"BEING INTERESTING"

CHAPTER 1

ATTITUDE IS EVERYTHING

Before we even look into the skills that generate proactive sales success, the first step for most sales people (either new or experienced) is to recognise the relationship between attitude and skill in terms of the extent to which they contribute to success.

So what I would like you to do is take a blank piece of paper, or use the back inside cover of this book, and think about people who have generated outstanding levels of success, either in a sports environment or in the business world and ideally, in the latter, in a sales environment.

The sorts of people you might consider would be Sir Steve Redgrave, Dame Kelly Holmes, Jonny Wilkinson, Alan Sugar, Richard Branson and hopefully a couple of people that you work with as well!

So I am asking you to write down a list of approximately ten **traits** of top performers. Just use one word and create a list.

1

Done?

So your list is complete?

Now that you have completed your list, what I would like you to do is to just look down the list and evaluate whether the traits that you have put down on your list are an attitude or a skill?

If it is an attitude place an A beside it, and if it is a skill place an S.

Finished?

How many of the traits were SKILLS?

How many of the traits were ATTITUDES?

What you tend to find when you complete this exercise is that approximately 80% of the words on your list relate to attitude and that the balance relate to skills.

Now that is not to say that skills aren't relevant, of course they are, especially if the sale that you are involved with is a sale of a technical nature.

What it does say however, is that the difference between mediocre performance and outstanding performance is down to the attitude or mindset of the individual who is using those skills.

What is very clear is that people who are successful in any field must have certain skills but most importantly they also have to be, for example, determined, tenacious, focussed and committed. In order for people to achieve success or achieve their full potential in a sales environment, they have to demonstrate these traits consistently.

Placing great emphasis on having a positive attitude and mindset may seem slightly unusual bearing in mind that this book is devoted to the development of sales skills! Selling does require high levels of skills but it is the ability to access those skills when it really matters that makes people stand out.

What I propose to do later on in this chapter is to cover one or two very simple concepts that are used by top performing sales people across a variety of different industries. We have also produced what we think would be a useful reading list for you in terms of developing your knowledge of some of the areas that we have talked about.

So if attitude is everything in terms of generating sales success then that is excellent news. The reason it is excellent news is that **we** all control our own attitude and mindset.

Once you recognise this you will also recognise that it is **you** that control the level of success that you achieve!

All you need to know is **HOW?**

This book will help with the **HOW.**

In many respects winning business can be likened to a horse race. Even those of you who are not interested in horse racing will have some memories of the Grand National and of one horse in particular, a horse that was a great favourite and who won the event on three occasions.

Most people would be able to identify that it was Red Rum that won the race, however, what most ordinary people wouldn't be able to tell you was by how much. The winning margin becomes far less relevant as time progresses than the fact that the person or individual or in this instance the horse, actually **won**.

This is clearly the case in either transactional or key account selling. A top performing salesperson will do whatever they can on a consistent basis to put themselves in a position where they **win**.

Now the winning margin may be simply by the horse-racing equivalent of a nose or it could be more substantial than that. Top performing sales people are consistently looking for ways to put themselves in a better position to win.

Top sales organisations invest in the success of their people.

BUT

What if this training investment is not available?

What if the training is irrelevant?

Under these circumstances average performers will find numerous reasons for not taking any action.

However, top performers will take action.

What would you do?

A recent survey in the UK identified that the average person reads half a book per annum. Now that statistic applies to all books including any "novels" that people may take on holiday.

So this means that if you are able to read more than half a book a year on a self development subject, sales skills for example, then this is likely to put you ahead of most of the people you are competing against.

The old adage, "leaders are readers" definitely holds true and this is borne out by the number of different self development books you are now able to buy in a variety of different locations on a variety of different subjects.

To put reading into context, if you wish to complete a master's degree then you would be expected to read perhaps thirty or forty books.

I have worked with sales people who read thirty books a year as a **minimum.**

The fact that you have got this far, with this book, is an indication of your commitment to your personal development! Read on!!

We'll look at some simple, peak performance strategies a little later in this chapter.

HOW ARE SALES PEOPLE PERCEIVED?

Let's just take a little time to contextualise the world of sales and sales people in particular. The good news is that increasingly sales people are managing to shake off the negative perception that other "professionals" have of them. Having said that, most people still display a degree of wariness when they find themselves near a "dreaded" salesperson.

Why do sales people attract such a negative press?

There are a number of reasons which I will expand on later in the chapter.

Very few people starting out on a career in sales, when asked what they do at a social function, would happily put up their hand and say **I AM A SALESPERSON**. Think how many other titles there are for a salesperson? We have Business Development Managers, Relationship Managers, Marketing Executives etc etc. Anything but **SALESPERSON**, although they probably all have a sales target!

There must be a number of reasons for this. The public at large, specifically people that do jobs other than in a customer service or sales environment, say that their general perception of sales people tends to be negative.

So still nothing new? When you seek to understand why this might be the case, you get all the usual answers that one would associate with, for example, a stereotypical car salesperson.

Whenever a customer gets anywhere near somebody who is in a "sales" role then their perception is that:

- They are going to be badly treated

- They are going to be sold something that they don't want

- They are going to be put under a lot of pressure

- The whole experience is going to be unpleasant

- It is going to cost them in some way

The risk is that no one (not even a salesperson) wants to be associated with such an unpleasant profession!!!

THE SALES/SERVICE BALANCE?

While some people may be wary of being in **SALES**, they are happy to be in a **SERVICE** role. For some people the definition of **SERVICE** means being **RESPONSIVE**. So when a prospect or client phones up, they are happy to **RESPOND**. Some people like **RESPONDING** because it means that they do not have to **INITIATE** anything. Some people do not like **INITIATING**.

I have included an example of something that happened to me. Read it and evaluate the level of service on a scale of one to ten where one is poor and ten is excellent

I recently asked for some time with one of our professional advisers. Having spent fifteen or twenty minutes discussing some plans that I had for our organisation and their potential impact on this particular gentleman's area of expertise and when we were bringing the meeting to a conclusion and I was in the process of leaving his office my professional adviser said "Bryan, while you are here, I would like to mention X, Y and Z".

He then proceeded to sit me down and talk me through an idea / opportunity that he believed had the potential to be of benefit to us as an organisation.

This opportunity had been created by a change in tax legislation.

We discussed the potential opportunity in some detail. He highlighted the likely benefits to us as an organisation, and he also very clearly articulated what it would cost in financial terms and in terms of our time commitment, to implement this idea.

Having looked at the pros and cons of the proposition it was obvious that this was something that would be of benefit to us.

I made the decision to act on his advice on the spot.

He suggested that we should review it on an annual basis to establish whether or not it was still relevant.

So the question is "Had I received good service?"

Rate it out of ten

All DONE?

Undeniably the professional adviser had brought the idea to my attention. It was something that was of potential value to me and I did ultimately agree to invest both time and money in the acquisition of his idea.

So how did you rate the service I had received?

One could definitely argue that I had received good service **but** one could also argue that I had actually received very **BAD** service.

Or had he actually been selling?

Let's review what happened.

The adviser understood or knew our business and was able to bring something to my attention. He recognised that there would be a good fit between this opportunity and our business. In addition, he was able to articulate why it might be of benefit to me and how it could work within our organisation.

Arguably he had been selling. When I went to see him I had no idea that I would end up with this particular product. In fact I had no idea that it actually existed!

Would I have been worse off without his recommendation? The answer is that **YES** I would have been worse off without the recommendation.

Arguably then he had both provided me with good **SERVICE** and he had **SOLD** me something. So are **SALES** and **SERVICE** inextricably linked?

The answer is **YES**.

You cannot provide good proactive **SERVICE** without **SELLING** to your prospects or customers. The key differentiator is linked to who **INITIATES** the conversation.

Let's review who initiated this conversation.

While reviewing this example of service/sales, there was one element to the whole event that made me slightly uneasy and this is why I only rated it as a three out of ten.

My slight concern was that it was **ME** who had initiated the meeting with this professional adviser.

My worry was that if I had not initiated the meeting with the adviser then I might have missed out on the opportunity.

Arguably he would have raised it at our annual review but the "opportunity cost" associated with not implementing the recommendation at the earliest opportunity is something that would undoubtedly have had a negative impact on our business.

So what would have made this even better?

Well, my adviser could have gone one step further in terms of **INITIATING** the meeting by proactively picking up the phone to me and suggesting that we get together to discuss an important change in legislation. When you proactively pick up the phone to one of your prospects or customers you are actually telling them that you are thinking about them. How often does that happen? Very rarely indeed.

When your prospects or customers know that you are thinking about them, they know that they are likely to get the best service from you.

All he had to say on the phone was that a recent change in legislation had created an opportunity that could be of interest to me and he would have gained my attention.

Why might he have chosen not to **INITIATE** contact with me?

- It could be that he did not have the time

- It could be that he did not want to bother me

- It could be that he had not thought about me

Whatever the reason, I would have been worse off if we had not had the opportunity to have that discussion.

Increasingly as it becomes more difficult to differentiate between products and services it is the **human dimension** that makes the **difference.**

This means that anybody within an organisation who has any contact at all with customers has the potential to positively influence both the service and therefore the sale.

INITIATING contact with the correctly profiled prospect or customer is the key to both successful **SERVICE** and **SALES.**

For those of you that are new to the art of proactive selling, think about it! Your role is to provide a service to your customer by proactively identifying the sorts of things that might be of interest to them. Approach them in an effective, understated and professional manner and then help them to see that the opportunities you have identified have merit. If you can do this, then you will become one of the most successful sales people in your industry.

That is what this book is about, consultative selling and

Helping you to become a great salesperson!

ATTITUDE AND MINDSET

We have touched on the importance of attitude and mindset.

Now there can be days when things seem to go wildly against us and there are occasions when our sales figures for example don't go the way we want them to go.

Conversely, there are days when everything just goes right, everything happens the way we want it to happen. From a sales perspective this sort of performance would usually be referred to as being "on a roll".

The only question is if you are "on a roll" then how do you stay "on a roll"?

And if you are not "on a roll", and your sales performance isn't going the way you want it to go, then how do you get back "on a roll"? All sales people work in increasingly competitive environments. Whether you are selling cars on a transactional basis or managing key accounts for an aircraft manufacturer, when the buyer makes their decision to buy, the days of there being significant difference and competitive advantage between the products on offer are gone.

A little bit earlier we talked about how **WE** control our attitude and how **ATTITUDE** is a key contributor to the success that we achieve.

However, it is possible that, on occasions, circumstances beyond our control have an impact on our day-to-day selling activities. The classic example of this occurred with the stock market crash of approximately 2001. A client we were working with at the time sold stock market based investments to high net worth clients. Customers buy stock market based investment products for a number of reasons but one of the sales peoples' key perceptions was linked to the fact that clients buy stock market investments PURELY because of the investment returns.

The first consideration we had in working with this sales team was trying to understand how they could continue to operate in an environment where all that their customers were doing was complaining about the investment returns that they were receiving.

What we tended to hear was that it was going to be impossible to sell anything to anybody because of the volatility in the returns that people had been receiving in the stock market.

Now, as we choose our attitude, we can choose to become de-motivated about an occurrence such as this. It is however worth understanding the extent to which the Situation (S) is within our control?

An outcome (O) is simply the result we achieve given a particular situation and, most importantly, our **RESPONSE** to that situation:

$$S + R = O$$

Where this stands for situation + your response = the outcome.

In the example outlined above, the situation is the stock market volatility. The response is the salesperson's mindset or approach to managing the volatility. The outcome is being **DEMOTIVATED**.

It is obvious that an individual salesperson working within a sales team has got absolutely no control over what goes on in the stock market. What the salesperson does have control over is how they manage their response to events within the stock market. If the sudden volatility has reduced the value of their investments, investors are likely to want to **INITIATE** contact with their financial adviser.

There is no doubt that when the adviser meets the investor there is going to have to be a discussion regarding the investments in order for any additional sales opportunities a) to be identified and b) to be capitalised on. However, the difference between a top performing salesperson and an average salesperson is that the top performing salesperson will view that situation as an opportunity and they will seek to take advantage of the opportunities that have been created by the stock market volatility.

An average salesperson will sit at their desk and try to avoid answering the phone. They will also make up a variety of different excuses as to why they should not be sitting in front of a customer. So the next time something happens within your sales world that has the potential to impact upon your results, identify whether it is a situation over which you have any control or not.

If you have control, then exercise that control to turn the situation to your advantage. If you have no control, then remember it's your response to the situation that will determine the outcome.

Remember S + R = O

Always look for ways to exploit it!

I was a member of a sales team in 1995 that experienced a similar situation to the stock market volatility of 2001. This volatility in the market meant that our more sophisticated customers were disinclined to make lump sum investments.
The danger of investing lump sums on any given day into the stock market is that it is very difficult to predict where on the volatility curve the market is on that day and your timing can have a huge impact on the number or the amount of investments that your money actually buys.

It was clear was that while our customers were not investing lump sums our business was going to suffer. While our customers had money on deposit, they were possibly missing out on an opportunity. But what sort of opportunity does stock market volatility actually bring?

The solution was a simple return to one of the key principles of creating investment portfolios. Where a customer had a lump sum to invest in the market, we enlightened them to the potential benefits of drip feeding that lump sum into the market on, for example, a monthly basis.

What we were able to do as a sales team was to provide our customers with a means of not only protecting themselves from the stock market volatility but in many instances enabling them to exploit the volatility to their advantage by drip feeding their money into the market.

The example below assumes that the investor invests **£100 a month for three consecutive months.**

In example A, the unit price of the investment is stable. In other words there is no volatility.

	Month 1	Month 2	Month 3
Unit price	£1	£1	£1
Number of units the £100 can buy	100	100	100

So the total number of units bought over the three-month investment period totalled 300.

In example B, the investor is still investing at a fixed rate of £100 per month but the unit price is volatile.

	Month 1	Month 2	Month 3
Unit price	£1	£0.80	£1.20
Number of units the £100 can buy	100	125	83.3

So how many units does the customer get in example B (Tip:

add up the numbers in the bottom row!)

The answer is 308.33 – this is more than 300 is it not? 300 was the number of units the investor received when the unit price was stable?

Does this mean that volatility is good? This example shows that it can work to your advantage if you are prepared to drip feed your capital into the market.

We were able to take this argument to our customers.

An additional feature of top performing sales people is that they will proactively seek out ideas that work. As soon as one or two sales people in the team started achieving success then there was the opportunity for all ten members of the team and the sales manager to sit down and discuss exactly how the strategy was delivered to the customer. The next step was to have the opportunity to practice it before taking it out into the field, with a view to using it to enhance both our customers' position and their perception of our sales expertise.

If you think back to the example of the professional adviser mentioned a little earlier in the chapter, then in essence what the sales team was now equipped with was an opportunity to phone up their customers to discuss the volatility in the market and then to float the concept about having an idea that would actually take advantage of this volatility.

Further on in the book, in chapter three, we are going to look at the use of the telephone with a view to engaging customers for customer appointments.

What was clear was that this underlying strategy of drip feeding was something that could be of interest to most proactive investors and therefore the salesperson had their reason or opportunity for being in contact with that customer. What S + R = O meant in this instance was that by devoting time and energy to managing our **RESPONSE** to the stock market volatility we got a much better outcome.

LEARNING FROM MISTAKES

"If you always do what you have always done you will always get what you always got". This quote suggests that for anybody in any role in any organisation being unprepared or unwilling to change means that the results that they expect to get are very predictable. Those that are more resistant to change might argue that there is no point in changing something that actually works. However, there are examples, particularly in the golfing world, where extremely successful golfers, by embracing change, temporarily reduced their effectiveness in order to take their game to a higher level.

Both Nick Faldo and more recently Tiger Woods have completely reviewed their grips. This resulted in a short term dip in their performance but ultimately led to greater success. It cannot have been a lot of fun for either of them to experience that dip in their performance. However, both people realised that this was a necessary step in order for them to move their performance to a higher plane.

The one thing that generally stops people from taking action towards the pursuit of any particular goal, whether it is a business goal, a public speaking goal or a sales goal, is fear of failure. When people undertake something new their perception is that they are going to get one of two results. They are either going to **WIN** or **LOSE**. Because of the way that we are brought up and conditioned from an early age our inclination is to avoid areas where we might **LOSE**.

If, however, we were to take the "lose" out of the relationship and ensure that no matter what we did we would generate a beneficial outcome, then there would be no reason to stop anybody from taking action in any area. So all that one has to do in the win / lose relationship is simply replace the word lose with the word **learn**.

So **WIN/LOSE** now becomes **WIN/LEARN**.

This simply means that every time we undertake something, even if we don't get the outcome we are looking for, if we actually learn something from it then that will take us one step forward. If we were able to enhance our efficiency by 1% a day then within just over three months we would have increased our efficiency by 100%.

Having coached a variety of different sales people it is interesting to note that when one approach doesn't work there is a lack of inclination to sit down and try and understand **why** that approach didn't work. The next time you have a fly trapped in your house watch it trying to get out of the window. The fly consistently bangs its head against the pane of glass.

What can happen in the sales environment is that once we have our "pitch" or our "approach" we don't sit down on a consistent basis and evaluate how effective it is.

Are we therefore guilty of "fly mentality"?

Top performing sales people will seek out opportunities to test their skills in front of a third party, a sales coach or a colleague, and will accept feedback in order to be able to improve their sales skills.

When you look at a premiership football team or a top performing rugby team and evaluate the relationship or ratio between the time spent in preparation and the time spent performing, what you tend to find is that the bulk of time is devoted to preparation.

In the sales coaching roles that I have undertaken, I have tended to find that the relationship is very heavily orientated towards performing. We are going to look at sales preparation in the next chapter; however it is very important to recognise the requirement to consistently devote time and energy to enhancing or honing both our skills and our mindset.

Chapter key learns:

1. It is **attitude** and not just skills that contribute to top performance.

2. Most sales are increasingly won by small margins of either service or product performance.

3. The professional salesperson must consistently seek to provide themselves with these additional factors that contribute to success.

4. The sales/service balance. Service is not just being responsive. There is a requirement to be an **INITIATOR** in order to deliver exceptional performance or service to customers.

5. Remember **S + R = O**. More often than not it is the situation that we seek to control, when it is something over which we have no control. What we need to focus on, is our response to that situation.

6. Finally don't think **WIN/LOSE**, think **WIN/LEARN**. If we are able to take learning from everything that we undertake, then we are increasing our effectiveness on a daily basis.

CHAPTER 2

MANAGING YOUR SALES BUSINESS

As we have seen from chapter one, attitude is everything when it comes to top performance in any environment; this is particularly true in a sales environment.

In this chapter we are going to look at managing **YOUR** sales business. The first and most obvious place to start is with your goals or the targets that you have either self generated or are generated by your sales manager.

When we have looked at the sales cycle in greater detail further on through the chapter, we will be able to further evaluate the impact of targets.

If you are in a sales related role then you have got to have a goal or target to aim for.

The extent to which you can influence your target or goal is dependent on your remuneration system. We have worked with companies where the sales people were rewarded solely on the basis of what they sold. The better sales managers were able to identify what earnings the individual sales people wanted to receive and then were able to link this back to the number of products that they needed to sell in order to achieve that salary and therefore that level of lifestyle.

Clearly what this means is that the target that is linked to the income requirement is a far more personal thing for the salesperson. It is therefore something that they will tend to pursue with a greater degree of determination and tenacity.

However, we have also worked with organisations where the remunerative system did not lend itself to this "personalisation" of the goal setting system.

In this case, as in most cases, the sales people have their targets imposed. The reality was that there was no better way of implementing the targets than by imposition.

This is a classic example of **S + R = O** because the **SITUATION** is that we have our targets imposed. There might be some sort of opportunity to influence the size of the targets; however the reality is more likely to be that they are imposed without a lot of debate and that it is our **RESPONSE** to those targets that will dictate the **OUTCOME** that we get.

The salesperson who is preoccupied with day-to-day selling activities can overlook the fact that business goals are ultimately linked to the overall desired performance of the business and, therefore, debate with the immediate sales manager is of little value.

On the assumption that the goal has to be achieved within a defined period, and it's usually anything from a week up to twelve months, then obviously the salesperson needs to know how long it actually takes them from the **INITIATION** of a sale through to the where the deal is closed.

THE SALES CYCLE

Whether you are selling a product or a service, what we have found is that there are six or seven clearly defined stages through which a sale tends to go. The sale might be the lending of a substantial amount of money or it might be as simple as the sale of a piece of crystal.

The sales cycle is outlined below; what we will do now is go through each of the stages in some detail just to explain the key points. Thereafter, we will devote a chapter to each of the key stages in order to give you the opportunity to further develop your skills in each of the key areas.

THE SALES CYCLE

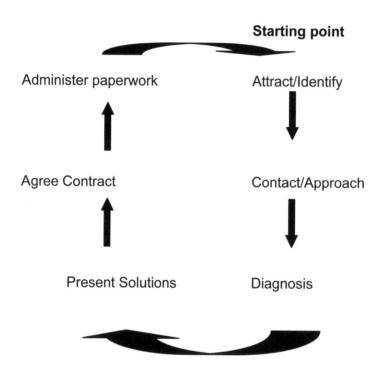

Starting point

Administer paperwork   Attract/Identify

Agree Contract   Contact/Approach

Present Solutions   Diagnosis

The first thing to say about the sales cycle is that it is either a **VIRTUOUS** cycle or a **VICIOUS** cycle.

If you **INITIATE** the sales cycle with the right sort of prospect, then you have the potential for it to run through to a successful conclusion. Clearly, if you are seeing the wrong sort of people consistently, you are not going to get the sort of outcomes you are looking for.

ATTRACT/IDENTIFY

The sales cycle can be initiated either **PROACTIVELY OR REACTIVELY**. The focus of this book is proactive consultative selling. This means that we are more interested in our having initiated the sales cycle, rather than having the sales cycle initiated for us.

The **identify** element of **Attract/Identify** is the proactive approach to starting the sales cycle. What this actually means is that the salesperson sits down and profiles the perfect prospect as far as their products or services are concerned. Your ability to do this is obviously based on your knowledge of your product or service and also an understanding of the market in which you are operating.

If you are unable to complete this task effectively, then you have just learnt that either your product knowledge or your market knowledge is insufficient. Great opportunity to embrace the **WIN/LEARN** concept!

The next obvious step is to improve your product or market knowledge.

The **attract** element of **Attract/Identify** simply refers to initiating the sales cycle reactively. Depending on the organisation that you work for, you may or may not have a market presence. If you work for Coca Cola, you work for one of the most well recognised brands in the world.

If however you are working for Woodside Widgets of Waterford, then there is an argument that says that your potential prospects will not have heard of you. The **attract** element applies to the fact that your brand or your position in the market place has the potential to **attract** new prospects to consider using your products or services.

This means of course that the potential customer has initiated the sales cycle. The potential risk associated with this **"reactivity"** is that you have little or no control over the quality of the opportunity. We will develop this a little bit later.

CONTACT/APPROACH

THE SALES CYCLE

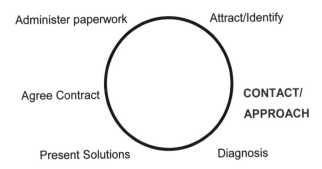

Administer paperwork | Attract/Identify

Agree Contract | **CONTACT/ APPROACH**

Present Solutions | Diagnosis

So, if you are undertaking proactive consultative selling, once you have identified a prospect with which you want to do business, the next step is for you to **contact** them.

Your potential prospect is sitting in blissful ignorance of the potential benefits of either your product or service offering. Your obvious challenge is to get in touch with that prospect with a view to getting the opportunity to meet them face to face.

These skills are something we will develop in a later chapter; however, it is possible, even if we have profiled our prospect accurately, that when we try to make contact we will actually be rejected. The way we manage this rejection will also be developed later on in the book.

The **approach** element of **Contact/Approach** refers to the fact that once a prospect has been **attracted** to either our product or service or to our brand, the prospect will then **approach** us.

This could be as simple as an inbound telephone call or somebody walking onto your premises.

Clearly our ability to manage this reactive inbound sales inquiry is something that will dictate whether or not the initial inquiry leads to business.

It is possible that due to the nature of what you offer, there may be seasonal considerations, where at certain times of the year large numbers of prospects are attracted to your organisation. This could equally mean that at other times during the year prospects do not tend to pick up the phone to you. In terms of the management of your sales business, recognising these seasonal peaks and troughs of inbound or reactive opportunity will have a bearing on your sales strategy.

DIAGNOSIS

THE SALES CYCLE

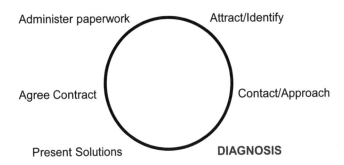

Administer paperwork

Attract/Identify

Agree Contract

Contact/Approach

Present Solutions

DIAGNOSIS

Regardless of whether the sales cycle was initiated **reactively** or **proactively**, when we are sitting face to face with a prospect we have obviously got to ascertain the extent to which the product or service that we are offering will actually meet their business needs.

Traditionally when people came into a sales role, one of the reasons that they came into sales was because they were perceived to have the "gift of the gab".

This tended to refer to the fact that sales people were perceived to be people who came in with a "pitch". All that the salesperson needed to do was to deliver a slick pitch then manage the prospect's objections effectively and this would lead to a sale.

While some of these skills still have relevance, this is directly at odds with the "consultative nature" of proactive consultative selling.

In the **diagnosis** phase it is the salesperson's challenge to gain a genuine understanding of the prospect's business. Where the business is now, where it has come from and most importantly where it is going to in the future. This is vital if you are to be able to recognise to what extent your product or service will meet that prospect's business requirements.

If you have profiled or **identified** the prospect effectively then this meeting should be a validation of the work that has gone previously. It may be that during the **diagnosis** phase you recognise that this prospect doesn't actually meet your desired profile and at this point you have two options:

1. It is unwise to try and push a losing position. You might seek to take advantage of a referral opportunity from the person that you have met, on the assumption that they

recognise that there is value in your proposition but that there is simply no value for them at this stage.

2. Alternatively you might just seek to bring the meeting to a conclusion and go back to the drawing board, making sure to extract as much learning as possible from the investment of your time.

We will develop a model for use in **diagnostic** meetings in a later chapter.

PRESENT SOLUTIONS

THE SALES CYCLE

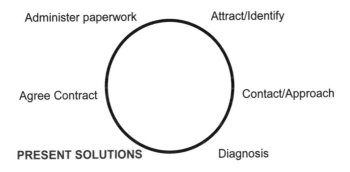

Administer paperwork   Attract/Identify

Agree Contract   Contact/Approach

PRESENT SOLUTIONS   Diagnosis

Once we have understood the prospect's business to an appropriate level of detail, it will then be necessary for us to

41

present our solution. This may take place at that particular meeting or possibly at a subsequent meeting.

Clearly, the complexity of the product or service that you are offering will dictate whether or not you need to have some thinking time between the diagnostic meeting and the presentation meeting, in order not only to formulate the solution but also to start thinking about how you are actually going to present the solution.

In a simple transactional sale like, for example a credit card sale, it is perfectly conceivable that an element of diagnosis will take place swiftly, followed by a presentation that is linked to the outputs of the diagnostic element.

The key challenge to the salesperson is to be "deft". They have to be able to follow a structure while recognising that they will have to include and exclude the elements that are inappropriate for that particular sale.

AGREE CONTRACT

THE SALES CYCLE

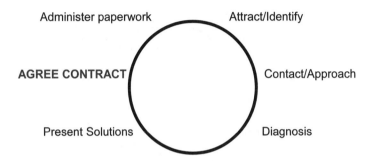

Administer paperwork — Attract/Identify

AGREE CONTRACT — Contact/Approach

Present Solutions — Diagnosis

Once the prospect has bought into the solution that you are offering, the next step is to **agree the contract.** Depending on what you are selling, this could be as simple as either signing a form or possibly the start of the negotiating process which will ultimately define the terms on which the business will be completed.

The key is to make this stage as painless as possible. Some people will sweat the detail; some will have teams of people to sweat the detail on their behalf.

Preparation is the key. Getting it right is the only outcome. The last thing you want is for a deal/sale to fall through because this stage gets unwieldy.

ADMINISTER PAPERWORK

THE SALES CYCLE

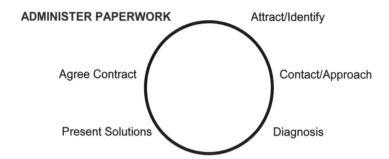

ADMINISTER PAPERWORK — Attract/Identify

Agree Contract — Contact/Approach

Present Solutions — Diagnosis

The penultimate step is taking all the paperwork on which the deal has been agreed and administering that within the requirements of your employer.

If you sell a regulated product, this can be a lengthy part of the sales cycle, but the bottom line is that the paperwork needs to be done so you might as well be as efficient as possible.

ATTRACT/IDENTIFY

The fact that we refer to the sales cycle as a cycle indicates that the process should continue seamlessly.

It is generally recognised that the best time to ask for a referral opportunity is when you have just completed business with somebody and you have a satisfied customer.

Later on in the book we will look at strategies for taking advantage of this opportunity with a view to your being able to proactively identify additional prospects with whom to initiate a further sales cycle.

So what are the key learns then from the sales cycle?

KEY LEARN 1.

Time versus targets.

The first consideration is the length of time that it takes you to go through all of the steps of the sales cycle.

We talked about targets at the outset of this chapter and whether you are targeted on a weekly, monthly or annual basis.

Depending on the complexity of your offering, it is possible that you will have pieces of business that "drop" during your targeted time period that were initiated either in the previous reporting period whether that was a week, month or year, again depending on how you are measured.

Sales people often overlook the length of the sales cycle. It has a huge bearing on your ability to deliver your targets within the time frames required by your employer.

The first training company that I worked for had an annual **target** of £1,000,000 of new business. This equates to £250,000 per quarter or £83,000 per month. We were measured on a **quarterly** basis. At the end of month one in quarter one, we had booked business of approximately £70,000 for that quarter. This meant that we had a **deficit** of £180,000 for the quarter with two months to go.

The first step was to work out the length of the sales cycle. We were able to establish that, no matter how efficient we were in the sales cycle, it was going to take us approximately **thirteen weeks** from the initiation of a sales cycle through to any revenue starting to appear from that customer.

If it was a new prospect, then the sales cycle was going to take longer.

The harsh reality from that particular example was that we already knew that we would significantly under perform our target and we were only a third of the way through the quarter!

The company's cash flow was dependent on our business performance. So we were able to proactively go and speak to the Chief Executive and the Chief Financial Officer and explain our sales position and the logic behind our expectations. This wasn't a particularly enjoyable meeting!

We were also able to make plans for delivering enhanced business figures for the remaining three quarters of that financial year.

While the Chief Executive was clearly not happy with the early performance, he was more impressed with the fact that we had been honest, sat down and given some thought to the actions we needed to take to rectify the problem.

Clearly the next step was to initiate sufficient sales cycles to be able to deliver the business that was required in each of the subsequent quarters.

Similarly, I was being prospected by a mobile phone selling organisation.

On a Friday lunchtime, having given initial agreement to buy a new phone I then started to receive numerous texts and telephone calls from the selling organisation. I paid no attention to the texts and very little attention to the same number appearing in the LCD on my existing phone.

Ultimately at four in the afternoon, when I did have some time, I answered the telephone and the salesperson told me that if I wanted to have the phone by Monday then I had to make the commitment there and then.

It was obvious that her behaviour was being driven by a requirement to have that particular piece of business closed on that Friday.

Given my knowledge of the sales world, her strategy was therefore understandable. The flaw in her strategy was that at no stage in the conversation that we had had together did I ever say to her that I had **a requirement** to have that phone by Monday.

In this instance the reporting timeline for that particular salesperson was forcing them into a position where she was starting to appear pushy. This might even have led to the loss of the sale. If the company had recognised that the sale was as good as done, and if the company had agreed to a relaxation of that particular timeline for her, then the salesperson would still have got the order. However she would have got the order on **my** terms.

KEY LEARN 2.

Quality.

So if the length of the sales cycle is a key consideration for the salesperson in terms of their being able to deliver a target against specific reporting times, then an additional consideration is the ratio between the business that walks in the door and the business that you have to **INITIATE**.

49

Most sales people enjoy receiving a few sales inquiries and a lot of sales people don't like to have to **INITIATE** sales cycles.

What most sales people, who have worked for different organisations, will tell you is that the one thing that they can't control in terms of the inquiries that they get is the **QUALITY** of the inquiries.

In certain organisations you tend to find that the top performing sales people actually make a request to be taken **OFF** the list of people for receiving inquiries.

One bank that we worked with was run off its feet with borrowing requirements for new property developments in a certain geographical location.

The core objective for the corporate lenders within this organisation was to grow the size of their "lending book" (the money they had already lent out). This meant that their ideal client was somebody who would come along and actually borrow money for between five, ten or fifteen years so that they would be receiving an income stream from the interest that the borrowing generated.

Due to their location, they had a client bank of short-term property developers whose sole objective in life was to borrow money for the **shortest** amount of time possible.

The Corporate Bankers had to go through the **whole** lengthy risk management and credit application process, which was taking up a lot of their time and energy, simply in order to be able to lend the money for as little as nine months in some cases.

When one building project was complete, the property developers would be back for some more short-term borrowing.

It is clear that this organisation needed to try and move to a position where they were less reliant on this type of **short term** lending opportunity.

As this short term lending had been going on for some time the obvious question was why the organisation hadn't made any effort to move away from this short term lending?

What was clear was that in order for that organisation to move into other sectors they would have to **INITIATE** the sales cycle more proactively. They were so heavily immersed in all of the ongoing applications and additional inquiries that they were processing that they didn't have the time to move their business to a more proactive footing.

KEY LEARN 3.

Pipeline Management.

When you sit down and evaluate how a salesperson uses their time then you tend to find that they spend time:

- On the phone
- In the car
- With prospects/customers
- Preparing
- Undertaking diagnostic meetings
- Presenting to clients
- Attending networking events
- Post sale administration of paperwork

There are certain activities that sales people undertake that make a direct contribution to their performance against target.

If the product or service that you sell takes one meeting with a prospect or a series of meetings, then the time that you spend face to face with prospects is obviously of great value to you. The preparation that you undertake ahead of these meetings is also going to be of considerable value.

When you sit down and evaluate the activities that a salesperson undertakes each week, and why they undertake a particular activity or the order that they do them in, you occasionally find that there tends to be little reason or rationale behind what they do and when they do it.

This rather unplanned approach to their key activities is going to have a detrimental impact on their bottom line.

The sales cycle allows you to recognise the key stages in the sale and to plan the activities that you will undertake each week.

A simple diagram like the one below helps you to monitor the progress of each piece of new business as it travels down the sales cycle.

Prospect Name	Deal Value £	A /I	C/ A	D	PS	AC	AP	Next Steps
Darwin Inc	125,000	X	X					Meeting in 1 week
Derby Ltd	34,000	X	X	X	X			Adjust terms and re-submit

I hope that by now you can recognise the key steps in the sales cycle, albeit in abbreviated form! Just in case you don't yet, they are, to recap, Attract/Identify, Contact/Approach, Diagnosis, Present Solutions, Agree Contract and Administer Paperwork.

This simple pipeline management format not only allows you to track each piece of business, the **NEXT STEPS** column does actually provide you with a **TO DO** list that should complement your time management strategy. (You do have one don't you?)

Recognising that it takes time for your sale to progress through the sales cycle would also seem to indicate that you need to be:

- Identifying new prospects
- Speaking to new prospects
- Meeting new prospects for diagnostic meetings
- Presenting to new prospects
- Agreeing contracts with new prospects

on a weekly basis.

Some of the most successful sales people that we have worked with have got very clear ideas and methodologies about what they do and when they do it. The classic example of this is linked to how people use their Monday mornings.

One organisation that we have worked with knew that on Monday mornings the relationship managers were likely to have to field high volumes of inbound telephone calls from existing customers. In order to be both responsive and also to identify the potential sales opportunities that these inbound calls could generate, there was an obvious requirement for the relationship managers to be available on a Monday morning.

What the most effective relationship managers did was identify some additional activity that they could complete during that Monday morning that would still be of value to them from a time management perspective on the off chance that the phone didn't ring.

What the exceptional performers tended to do was to spend the very early part of Monday morning acquainting themselves with the various activities/events that had happened over the weekend in order not only to be able to build rapport with customers but potentially to have some understanding of what those activities/events might actually mean to their customer's business.

Attached below is an outline of what we call a **MODEL** diary. The theory behind the model diary week is that it has identified the optimum times for the certain activities that the salesperson selling this particular product would undertake.

As this chapter has been a contextual scene setting chapter each of the activities has been identified below in the model week, in other words the telephone session, the diagnostic meeting and the presentation meetings will be covered in much more detail in the chapters that follow.

THE MODEL WEEK

	MON	TUE	WED	THU	FRI
Morning	Meet PA Respond to inbound calls	2 Client meetings (D or PS)	Administer paperwork 1 Phone session 2 (C/A)	Office all day Planning	2 Client meetings (D or PS)
Afternoon	2 Client meetings (D or PS)	Phone session 1 (C/A)	2 Client meetings (D or PS)	Weekly team meeting Complete Head office returns	Administer paperwork 2

Chapter key learns:

1. Successful selling is the result of **structured** and **meaningful** sales activity based on the key stages of the sales cycle.

2. Sales targets define the type and quantity of activities that we undertake in order to achieve them.

3. The sales cycle can be initiated either **reactively** or **proactively.**

4. While **reactive** selling is initially less challenging for the salesperson, the issue is that we have **NO CONTROL** over the quality of the potential client.

5. The sales cycle provides a workable pipeline management tool.

6. In order to be able to manage your pipeline effectively, you need the skills to be able to manage the **LENGTH** of your sales cycle.

7. Whether you report on a quarterly or annual basis you should have an understanding of the implications of seasonality to your business.

8. There are optimum times during the week that must be for the customer, facing events that **really** contribute to your sales success.

CHAPTER 3

A VIRTUOUS START

In the previous chapter we looked at the sales cycle. The sales cycle is simply the series of predictable stages through which a sale progresses. We said during the chapter that we would break down each of the stages involved in the sales cycle in order to look at them in more detail.

One of our core objectives when we initiate a sales cycle is a face to face meeting with a new prospect. For this reason, the **Attract/Identify** and **Contact/Approach** elements of the sales cycle have got to be **VIRTUOUS**. By this we mean that we have got to ensure that we only initiate sales cycles with the right types of prospects.

As this book is focussed on the proactive side to consultative selling we are assuming that it is our responsibility as a salesperson to **"identify"** a prospect with whom to initiate the cycle. As we will see when we break down the diagnostic meeting later on in the book, customers will ultimately buy for one of two reasons:

59

Either the product or service that you are offering takes them **AWAY** from a situation that is currently unacceptable to them, (in other words a faulty or defective product or service); or possibly that what you are offering has greater benefits than what they currently have, or perhaps in the ideal world from your perspective, what they don't have.

The essence therefore of the diagnostic meeting is going to be to identify:

1. Something that they **DON'T HAVE** but should **HAVE**
   OR
2. Something that they **DO HAVE but** that you can **ENHANCE**

In essence a "GAP".

It's logical therefore that if you are in the identification phase of the sales cycle, it is the ability to look for and find this **"GAP"** that is going to form the fundamental part of your research.

What you sell of course will dictate where you do your research. If you are truly proactive and do not rely on an existing client bank, then there will be a variety of different prospects with whom you want to be having meetings. With a view to getting as much leverage as possible on the time and energy you invest in initiating new relationships, one obvious strategy is to identify people who have a long term potential ability to **REFER** you on a consistent basis.

Those banks that fund the development of property need to work with property brokers who are in turn consistently looking for banks with whom to develop a lending relationship. It is obvious that once a relationship with the broker has been established, you then have the potential to benefit from a constant stream of referrals.

Be aware however that you are creating a series of reactive sales cycles and again the key consideration that might come into play is the potential quality of those referrals.

On the assumption that you do have a customer portfolio, then you will be using the technology that is available to you through your organisation to identify gaps in customers' current product or service holdings.

In the financial services world sales people are trained to recognise the different "life stages" that people go through. In its basic form, people move from being:

- Single   **(LAGER)**
- Through to being dependent with children   **(AGA)**
- Through to having grandchildren   **(SAGA)**
- Through to old age   **(GAGA)**

It is obvious that as each person moves through these different "life stages", the requirements they have for financial services planning change.

Therefore during the identification process the financial services salesperson will in the first instance look at the age of the person they are seeking to prospect. Again, the quality of the information that the organisation holds on the people within their customer portfolio determines whether this is an effective or ineffective step.

Ultimately the salesperson has got to generate a list of potential prospects that they then want to contact.

On the assumption that you have no customer portfolio into which to prospect, then your creativity in terms of identifying new prospects has an opportunity to express itself!

When working with a well known Irish Crystal manufacturer, the key criteria that the national account management team had for qualifying a new prospect was the extent to which that organisation or retailer was **CURRENTLY** selling crystal.

This may seem slightly unusual.

The key account manager's rationale was that if the retailer already had some understanding of the methods and benefits of selling crystal, then all that the national account manager had to do was to persuade the retailer that it was worth their while to carry one **additional** supplier.

What they had learnt to their cost was that retailers with no experience of selling high quality crystal became very dependent on the account manager in an attempt to develop their sales expertise.

While one could argue that the time invested with these new retailers would be time well spent, the evidence of research undertaken by that organisation suggested that this was not the case.

For this reason a number of existing crystal retailers in their target area that were currently not holding their product line became the focus of their short-term sales strategy.

In essence, we are looking at the pre telephone call element to this particular stage of the sales cycle. One question that gets asked repeatedly is to what extent a pre approach letter of some variety should be used during this part of the sales cycle.

It is worth remembering at this stage that the key objective of the **Attract/Identify** and **Contact/Approach** elements of the sales cycle is for the salesperson to get a face to face meeting with their prospect.

The only circumstances therefore when any investment of your time beyond the telephone call is worthwhile, is when it makes a proven contribution by ensuring that when you pick up the phone you stand the best possible chance of getting the meeting you are looking for.

PRE APPROACH LETTERS

There are two views regarding the value of pre approach letters:

1. They are of value
2. They have no value

I have no firm view either way. One of the perceived benefits of using a pre approach letter is that it acts as context for the telephone call:

"I am calling in relation to the information I sent through last week..."

I know sales people who have used this **PEG** without ever having sent a pre approach letter!! Decision makers get so much junk mail that they lose track of what they have had from whom.

A **must** for any pre approach letters is the inclusion of your business card. On the off chance the letter gets opened by the decision maker or an assistant there is some possibility that your card might be retained. The letter may well be discarded.

TIPS for the pre approach letter:

1. Address it to the decision maker using his/her full name and title.
2. Use a **bold** title that generates immediate interest in your product or service offering.
3. Compose a paragraph that establishes both your and your company's credibility in the market.
4. Another paragraph should contain details of your intention to telephone, specifying whether it will be a morning or an afternoon call and identifying the potential duration of the telephone call.
5. Include your business card.

Finally the letter should always provide the prospect with the opportunity to contact you in case what you are offering has created immediate interest. An example of a pre approach letter is at the end of the book.

MANAGING THE GATEKEEPER

Depending on the position of the person you are prospecting, they may have an executive assistant or a personal assistant who are referred to as "gatekeepers" in the sales profession.

It is one of the gatekeeper's objectives to ensure that the prospect (who is usually a decision maker) isn't pestered too frequently by people who are selling products or services that are of no value.

Equally, it is the gatekeeper's role to ensure that anybody who does telephone out of the blue offering something that might be of value to the decision maker is actually **FILTERED IN** to the decision maker.

Although attitudes are changing, sales people view gatekeepers negatively in the main because they can create an additional layer of resistance or an additional barrier to reaching the prospect. For a salesperson to be effective when proactively prospecting customers on the telephone, the salesperson has to be effective at managing the gatekeeper. So how do you **MANAGE** the Gatekeeper?

There are several strategies for managing gatekeepers.

The pre approach letter can be used to generate an initial level of interest not only with the decision maker (prospect) but also with the gatekeeper. Before you start creating gatekeeper related pre approach letters, what you need to know is whether your prospect has a gatekeeper!

What has worked effectively for a number of prospecting sales people in the past is a simple telephone call to the receptionist at the organisation they are prospecting.

The size of the organisation will dictate if there is a receptionist or if the telephone system is answered by one and all. If there is a receptionist, then all that you need to tell the receptionist is that you want to send some information through to (name of the decision maker) but that you would like to know if the decision maker has a personal assistant to whom you could also send a copy. For example:

Receptionist: "Chelmsford China, Gilly speaking, how may I help you"?

You: "Hello Gilly, this is Bill Bales from Superior Sand calling. I was wondering if you might be able to help me. I would like to send some information directly through to your sales director but I do not know his or her name"?

Receptionist: "The sales director is Nigel Southill".

You: "Thank you; does Nigel have an executive assistant"?

Receptionist: "He does, it is (NAME).

You: "Thank you Gilly, that has been very helpful – goodbye".

At this stage the receptionist might offer to put you through to the gatekeeper or even the decision maker so you should be prepared to seize the opportunity. If you are not completely prepared then obviously you should decline the opportunity at this stage. What you have now learnt is that you should have no objections or barriers to getting through to the gatekeeper further down the line.

BYPASSING OR ENGAGING THE GATEKEEPER

For many years sales people have used all sorts of tricks and methods to try and bypass the gatekeeper. For example, simply phoning outside "normal" office hours means that someone who is less able to manage the call than the gatekeeper might pick up the phone. Though simple enough, this is often very effective.

What is obvious is that when relationships are "the difference that makes the difference" it is up to the salesperson to start to create or to initiate some sort of relationship with the gatekeeper.

On the assumption that you want to stand out for positive reasons and that gatekeepers still get treated badly by some sales people, it would seem reasonable when making contact with the gatekeeper that the first question we ask them should be:

"Is it convenient for you (the gatekeeper) to speak at this time"?

In addition when you think about the time that we make the telephone call you should put yourself in the gatekeeper's shoes. The wrong time to phone the gatekeeper is when they are up to their eyes with lots of other tasks. The best time to phone the gatekeeper is when they are less likely to be under pressure, though this is always a best guess.

The structure for the telephone call with the gatekeeper is the same for the prospect and is as simple as:

- An introduction
- A peg – the context to the call
- A hook – the fact that will interest the prospect
- Managing objections – the obvious objections
- The close – what happens next, especially if no appointment is made

THE INTRODUCTION

In terms of the introduction, once we have made contact with the gatekeeper or prospect, the introduction should simply contain:

- Your name
- The name of the organisation you represent
- The question relating to the convenience of the timing of your call

If the gatekeeper has answered the telephone by using their name then it's fair and reasonable to use the gatekeeper's name in your introduction. Example "Hello Andrea this is Bill

Bloggs from Wexford Widgets in Waterford, is it convenient to speak at this time"?

If you have been put straight through to the prospect, be prepared to use their name without trying to find your copy of the pre approach letter on your cluttered desk!

A good tip is to consider the use of a mini **HOOK** between your name and the question regarding the convenience of the call.

A financial services company was calling clients who had not been contacted for any reason for between five and eight years.

What the sales people who were making the calls learnt very quickly was that they were being rejected very early in the call because the clients could not remember that they had pension plans with this Company! Added to this, the company only had the home telephone numbers of their clients, so the majority of the phone calls were being made in the early evening. Every prospecting company's preferred time and every prospect's least preferred time!

Using the **WIN/LEARN** principle, the sales people started using a mini hook as follows:

"Hello is that Mr Bill Perry? This is (name of salesperson) calling from Retirement Life about **the retirement plan you have with us**. Is it convenient to speak for about five minutes"?"

If Mrs Perry answered the phone, then the conversation is as simple as:

"Hello is that Mrs Perry? This is (name of salesperson) calling from Retirement Life about the retirement plan that Mr Perry has with us. Would it be convenient to speak Mr Perry for about five minutes please"?

It is unusual for it to be inconvenient for you to speak to a gatekeeper, but should that be the case what you clearly need to evaluate at this stage is when it would be a better time to speak. Once you have received that information your obvious challenge is to put it in your diary and to ensure that it is followed up on. On the assumption that the gatekeeper agrees that it is a convenient time for you to speak to them, then the next step is for you to "peg" the telephone call.

THE PEG

The purpose of a **PEG** is to give some context to the call. In this instance the peg might simply relate to your pre approach letter and may be simply along the lines of "Andrea I am phoning in relation to the letter I sent through to you regarding our new widget". I would then move seamlessly into the "hook". This **PEG** would be equally applicable to the prospect. The **PEG** is not designed to invite any response; it is designed to bring the recipient's attention away from what they have been doing before they picked up the telephone and to focus their attention on you.

I don't want to get into a conversation as to whether or not they can remember the content of my letter, what I am trying to do is open the door to my being able to "hook" the gatekeeper and ultimately the prospect.

THE HOOK

A hook is something about either your product or service that will appeal to the prospect. If a hook works well, it will make a big contribution to your achieving your objective – a face-to-face meeting.

The ideal hook will create **DOUBT** and/or **CURIOUSITY** in the prospect's mind.

Earlier we talked about the fact that people take action for one of two reasons or a combination of both.

People either want to move towards something that enhances their position **(PLEASURE)** or they want to move away from something that is unacceptable **(PAIN)**.

The doubt that we are seeking to create, is emphasising the motivator away from **PAIN**:

"Am I currently doing the wrong thing"?
"Do I really have the right product at the moment"?

The curiosity that we are seeking to create is linked to the motivator that encourages us to move towards something we may find to be of **PLEASURE**:

"Maybe what he is offering has more advantages".

So a good **HOOK** creates both **DOUBT** and **CURIOUSITY**. To take the development of a hook even further, a hook can be either:

- Very specific

OR

- Of a general nature

What do I mean by this?

Let's put ourselves in the prospect's shoes. The prospect has been engaged in a completely different activity when your telephone call arrives. Your call is therefore an interruption. By the time you have got to your **HOOK**, you will have been speaking to the prospect for about forty seconds. During this time, the prospect will be tuning into you, your voice, your tonality and your words. If you hit the prospect with a very specific **HOOK** at this stage, you run the risk of:

- Being misunderstood

Or

- If you play your biggest card first and receive an objection, you have nowhere else to go

We therefore recommend that your initial **HOOK** is of a general nature – that is not to say that it is wishy washy or that the benefits are not clear. If you lead with a general **HOOK**, you know that you will get one of two responses:

- The prospect's agreement to a meeting

Or

- A request for more detail

Both are very positive outcomes!

The meeting is what you set out to achieve and if the prospect asks for more information they are demonstrating some interest – a good result at this stage.

All top performers will be prepared for both outcomes. If the prospect says **YES** they will close to a meeting – if the prospect asks for clarity then they are in a position to respond.

Remembering that the objective of the telephone call is to gain a face to face meeting with a customer, then the **HOOK** should be as effective and as tried and tested as possible.

My personal view is that a good **HOOK** will create **CURIOUSITY**. If you can make the prospect curious, they will definitely be encouraged to want to find out more.

Let's look at an example:

A good hook used by a training company that I worked for was one focussed on sales directors as opposed to Human Resources, who had been the usual targets.

Having got through to the Sales Director, the **HOOK** was as follows:

"We have worked with a number of sales organisations and have evidence of our ability to make their sales teams as much as 30% more effective. What I am asking for is thirty five minutes of your time to come and explain how we achieved that outcome".

Clearly the **HOOK** was focussed on what the Sales Director wanted as an output – enhanced sales results. The salesperson did not focus on the "input" – sales training, nor the detail of how they achieved what they had achieved.

Remembering that people take action either to move them away from pain or to move them towards pleasure or a combination of both - the most effective hooks tend to appeal to both of these motivators.

One customer we were working with was proactively phoning customers in their customer portfolio with a view to talking to them about taxes that have to be paid by people when they die. The sales people had identified that there was an opportunity in the customers' wills that their solicitors had overlooked.

The salesperson's strategy was to gain a face to face meeting to raise the subject of inheritance tax and to introduce the customer to this concept. Having gained the customer's trust the next step was to then develop the solution using additional relevant financial services products.

The telephone calls that generated the appointments went along the following lines.

"Hello Mr or Mrs Customer this is Mike Brewer from your bank, is it convenient to speak? **(Introduction)** The reason for my call is that I have been undertaking a review of some planning opportunities with some other clients who fit a similar profile to you. **(Peg)** **(Hook)** I have discovered that a lot of my customers are <u>not currently</u> taking advantage **(Doubt)** of an opportunity by the way their wills have been structured." **(Curiosity)**

As we'll develop in more detail later, people talk to themselves – though usually not out loud!

A good question will start an "internal conversation" in your mind. You will start to ask yourself questions. A good **HOOK** simply gets you to ask yourself the sort of questions that the salesperson wants you to ask yourself!

If you were the recipient of this phone call you are likely to be asking yourself the following questions:

1. What is it about my profile that made me interesting to this person?
2. I have a will. I wonder if is set up the best way?
3. What if my will is not set up the right way?
4. What am I missing out on?
5. Assuming what this person says is correct, have I been given bad advice?

There are enough questions here to have raised both **DOUBT** and **CURIOSITY**.

The telephone call is now ready to be closed by the salesperson.

THE CLOSE

We are going to talk about managing objections in a moment, but at this stage, having delivered your hook to the customer, the next step is to close, by telling the customer what you want from them in very clear terms.

The close should contain:

- What you want – to meet – and gain agreement to the meeting

81

- The location – your office or their home or office
- The date
- The time
- Anything else that would add value to the meeting

The final step is to **SUMMARISE** the arrangements.

The key at this stage is to make it easy for the prospect to put you in their diary.

To continue our telephone call from before:

"So I would like an opportunity to meet for approximately fifteen minutes, either at your home or possibly here in town, to review your existing wills and to see to what extent you are currently taking advantage of the opportunities that the Inland Revenue allow people in your circumstances. Does that seem reasonable"? (A non threatening close)

(If you get an objection here – then manage it here – more detail later)

"How are you fixed next week? (Very open – allows them lots

of choice)

Friday? Fine – morning or afternoon (Very open allows them choice – again!)

What time would suit you?

Thank you – so I shall see you at your home on Friday of next week at 11am. It would be very useful if you could have your current wills to hand. Do you think that would be possible"?

When you have delivered your **HOOK** and asked for the opportunity to meet, the customer/prospect should be clear about what you want. You will get one of three responses:

- Yes
- No

or

- Somewhere in between

On the assumption that you get a yes then the next step is just to **CLOSE** as we have discussed.

If you get a no, then the next step is to try and understand why you have had a negative response, (though this tends not to happen that often) and if you get a response that is between yes and no, then the customer is telling you that they require additional clarification.

CLARIFYING OBJECTIONS

In sales training, when a customer doesn't immediately take you up on your initial offer, then the expression that is given to the skills that are used at this stage is **"managing objections"**.

However, we believe that this gives this particular phase of the telephone call a negative connotation. In most cases the customer hasn't **objected** in the true sense of the word.

What has happened is that the customer has misunderstood either:

- What you are seeking to achieve

or

- The benefit to them of what you are offering

It is obvious at this stage that there needs to be additional clarity in terms of why you are seeking to meet with the customer and the benefits to them of that meeting.

Objections tend to fall into one of two camps:

- Specific
- Vague

Let's look at each in turn.

SPECIFIC

As it says this is specific.

Prospect: "I don't have any time right now".

This is good as we know what their objection actually is. The tip for this type of objection is to have a couple of responses pre-prepared:

"Mr Prospect, I am just asking for fifteen minutes, entirely at your convenience. My experience with other prospects is that they have found this to be time very well spent. When we meet is entirely up to you but I wouldn't like to leave it too long".

Prospect: "I am very busy at the moment".

You: "I appreciate that and that is why I am phoning. My experience with other prospects is that they have found this to be time very well spent. When we meet is entirely up to you but I wouldn't like to leave it too long".

The key is to be prepared and not to panic; have rehearsed your responses and be able to deliver them clearly and calmly.

VAGUE

As it says the objection is vague.

Before you start answering an objection that you possibly don't understand, you need to clarify what the actual objection is.

The model we use for this is **APIAC**.

- Acknowledge
- Probe
- Isolate
- Answer
- Confirm

So if a prospect delivers a vague objection along the lines of: "Sounds interesting **but** (the use of BUT is always a sign that they are going to object!) when we set up our wills our Solicitor talked about some options for us but they didn't seem to meet our requirements".

ACKNOWLEDGE – "that's interesting".

PROBE – "just for my benefit, could you give me an insight into what exactly your solicitor was suggesting"? Your challenge here is to ask as many questions, as you need to, in order to be sure that you have **ISOLATED** the objection. Once you know what the objection is, you can then **ANSWER** it: "Actually Mr Prospect, the idea we are considering is not a discretionary will trust, it is actually much simpler than that which is why so many of our clients are taking advantage of it". In outline, what we are recommending is that you consider.......

CONFIRM: "Does that seem sensible"?

If the answer is **YES** then move to the close.

We talked about **SPECIFIC** or **GENERAL HOOKS** a little earlier. In many respects the objection handling process is simply moving from a **GENERAL** hook through to a **SPECIFIC** hook **but** taking the time to ensure that you have understood precisely what the objection actually is.

TOP PERFORMER / AVERAGE PERFORMER

If an average performer is met with resistance at this stage, the average performer's slightly negatively focussed mindset will mean that they apologise to the customer for disturbing them and terminate the call.

A top performer will recognise that the research they did before the telephone call is still valid and therefore that the customer still has an unmet need. The top performer will then seek to understand why the customer is not agreeing to the meeting and try and answer those queries using the APIAC model.

If you spend enough time on the telephone there will be certain objections or questions that get raised on a fairly consistent basis.

The obvious solution is to reflect on those questions and prepare answers to them. Your challenge thereafter is to deliver your response as if it is the first time you have been asked the question so that the customer doesn't feel as if they are being delivered a script.

Either way, if you have done your identification correctly or you know that this prospect does have a need, then it is your responsibility to politely work your way through any initial resistance, in order to re-emphasise the benefits to the customer of meeting with you.

AFTER THE TELEPHONE SESSION
In order to consistently improve, we need to know how effective we have been. The simple contact sheet will tell you at the end of a thirty or sixty minute telephone session how effective you have been.

In the first example you will see that the salesperson has dialled ten prospects, only actually managed to make contact with one but has made one appointment.

TELEPHONE SESSION SUCCESS EVALUATION FORM
Dials: 1 2 3 4 5 6 7 8 9 10 11 12 13 14 15
Contacts: 1 2 3 4 5 6 7 8 9 10
Appointments: 1 2 3 4 5 6 7 8 9 10
Self evaluation comments:

This tells you from a coaching perspective that whatever this salesperson is saying on the phone to their prospect is good because they have made one contact and secured one appointment. However you need to look at why the salesperson is dialling so many people but actually only making contact with one?

In example number two you will see that the salesperson has dialled six customers, has made six contacts but has only got two appointments.

TELEPHONE SESSION SUCCESS EVALUATION FORM
Dials: 1 2 3 4 5 6 7 8 9 10 11 12 13 14 15
Contacts: 1 2 3 4 5 6 7 8 9 10
Appointments: 1 2 3 4 5 6 7 8 9 10
Self evaluation comments:

The positives here are that the salesperson is making contact with the prospects but you need to look at the success of the hooks. If I have spoken to six prospects and only made two appointments, then there is something that I am saying on the phone that isn't working quite as effectively as it might.

I may need a coach or mentor to help me develop this skill. The key learns with this are that there are three stages to a telephone session. There is what I do beforehand, there is what I do during the session and there is what I do after the session.

I must consistently evaluate my effectiveness at every step.

Chapter key learns:

1. The sales cycle is either **VIRTUOUS** or **VICIOUS.**
2. Spending time identifying the right prospect should lead to a sales cycle that is **VIRTUOUS.**
3. If you decide to use pre approach letters, use my "TIPS" and seek advice from colleagues.
4. Develop a strategy for managing the gatekeeper.
5. When developing your **HOOK**, ensure that you create **DOUBT** and build **CURIOUSITY.**

6. Be prepared for prospects to have both **VAGUE** and **SPECIFIC** objections – manage them without becoming flustered.

7. Use **APIAC** to manage vague objections.

8. Evaluate your telephone success. Be equally curious about your successes and failures so that you can repeat the successes and reduce the number of failures.

CHAPTER 4

"BEING INTERESTED" – THE PROACTIVE DIAGNOSTIC
SALES MEETING

Following on in the sales cycle from the **Contact/Approach** stage our assumption is that you have successfully spoken to the prospect and they have agreed to a meeting at their premises.

THE SALES CYCLE

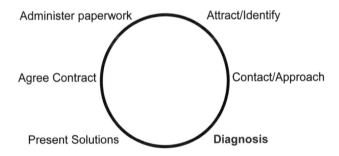

THE DIAGNOSIS/PRESENTING SOLUTIONS
RELATIONSHIP

The point that has to be emphasised at this stage is the

relationship between the **DIAGNOSTIC MEETING** and the **PRESENTING SOLUTIONS MEETING**.

Average sales people can allow these two stages to become inappropriately intertwined. For example, they start to **PRESENT** their solution before they have completed the **DIAGNOSIS**. There are obvious risks associated with doing this.

If you remember nothing else from this book, remember this:

- DIAGNOSIS – BE INTEREST**ED**

- PRESENTING SOLUTIONS – BE INTEREST**ING**

A subtle but important difference.

As with the telephone session, we will break down the activities associated with the diagnostic sales meeting into three areas:

- What happens before the meeting
- The meeting itself
- What happens after the meeting

BEFORE THE MEETING

Gone are the days when a salesperson was able to walk into a sales meeting without any preparation whatsoever.

The obvious information you are going to need ahead of the meeting is the location of the meeting and some understanding of how to get there in good time. In addition to this, knowing where to park is important.

Be under no illusion that punctuality still counts for a lot with the buyers that we have spoken to. It is never going to be a deal breaker however if you are late for a sales meeting, you are telling the customer that you are sloppy, possibly badly organised or even worse, that you are arrogant. Is this the sort of person they are going to want to do business with?

In addition to knowing where you are going and how to get there, there is an obvious requirement to have done some research on the company. Clearly, during the **Attract/Identify** stage of the sales cycle you have been searching for companies with whom you want to do business.

This will have involved gaining an understanding of the company in order to "qualify" them as a prospect.

Obviously a website, if one exists, is a great starting point. Websites are a great source of information about a company. There are the "Meet the Team" and "Press Release" pages that can provide valuable information not only about the organisation but also about the person you are going to meet. If you work in an area that has a local newspaper, it is often worthwhile looking up the archives of the paper to try and find articles that have been written about the organisation.

This information is extremely useful in the early parts of the meeting where you have the opportunity to demonstrate that you have done some research and you have started to develop an understanding of their business. Don't overlook the fact that it is the small things that combine to make a big difference when buyers make a buying decision.

Search engines can also be used to run a search on the person you are going to see. Clearly if their name is a popular one you may have to trawl through a huge amount of information. Occasionally, with a focussed search you can gain a direct reference to that person.

If you are attending the meeting on your own (and not with a colleague) then obviously the final preparatory steps are to ensure that you have all the equipment that you need, including basic things like:

- Business cards
- A calculator, if you anticipate using one during the meeting
- Copies of any presentation you may have prepared and
- Any sales aids that you might wish to take to the presentation

Finally, depending on the type of briefcase or folder that you are using, there is merit in ensuring that all the documents are to hand and that they are easily findable. There is nothing more off putting in the early part of a meeting than watching a salesperson digging around in an enormous battered briefcase trying to find a business card.

This demonstrates that you are disorganised and this has obvious implications for the sale further on down the time line.

If there are two people attending the meeting then you have the opportunity to take advantage of the benefits of having two sets of eyes and two sets of ears.

We could devote an entire chapter to the preparation that could be undertaken for the two person sale. For the purposes of this book we are going to focus on the fact that the salesperson is attending this initial meeting on their own.

SETTING MEETING OBJECTIVES

In order to be in a position to evaluate how successful you have been at this proactive diagnostic sales meeting, you need to have some clearly understood objectives which give the meeting focus.

I believe that you need to take this one step further. I believe that if you have taken the time and energy to qualify the right prospect onto your list and therefore into the meeting, then you should have the clear objective of keeping the sales cycle alive.

Any diagnostic meeting that comes to a conclusion without any clearly identified and agreed next steps is a diagnostic meeting that has not been effective. So my bottom line objective is to leave that meeting with a clearly understood and mutually agreed next step.

There will be several elements that will help you to achieve this and I break them down into the following:

- Sell yourself
- Sell the company that you represent
- Sell an opportunity

Bringing a structured approach to any activity, whether it is a proactive telephone call or a proactive diagnostic sales meeting, has the potential to add enormous benefit for a salesperson. A structure ensures that you are consistently able to meet all of your specific objectives. Any structure that is used in a sales meeting must have a degree of flexibility, therefore the three objectives listed above do not necessarily have to be achieved in the order laid out.

At the end of the meeting it is necessary to evaluate the extent to which the customer has bought into:

- You as an individual

- The company that you represent

and

- The extent to which you are able either to

a) reveal a need

Or

b) exploit an opportunity that existed with the prospect

So all of your preparation has been done, you know exactly where you are going and where you are going to park. The next step then is to undertake the diagnostic meeting itself.

BEING INTERESTED – THE PROACTIVE DIAGNOSTIC SALES MEETING

Most people think that a sales meeting starts the minute that they walk through the door of the office of the person that they are meeting. This is not the case.

You should aim to arrive at the client's premises a good ten minutes before the meeting is due to take place. The most successful sales people we have worked with travel to the sales meeting in silence.

The reason for this silence is that these sales people are using the final ten or fifteen minutes to clearly picture in their minds how the meeting is going to go, where the key elements of the meeting are and in particular what "key" questions they plan to use with this particular customer. We'll develop the concept of "key questions" later on in chapter five.

Similarly, the most disorganised and unsuccessful sales people turn up late, at the wrong address, with the wrong equipment, are flustered and have not thought through the sales meeting when they meet the decision maker.

Is it conceivable that people still run sales meetings in this way? The good news is that the answer is yes. The bad news is that fewer sales people are as badly organised as this.

We talked about punctuality a little bit earlier in the chapter. There is still a requirement to be five minutes early for your sales meeting. This may mean that you are left in reception for some time however this is a great opportunity not only to build rapport with the receptionist, if there is one, but also to further develop your understanding of the organisation based on any company reports/brochures that are on display in reception.

THE RECEPTIONIST

When you meet the receptionist for the first time you have an opportunity to create an excellent impression. These people sit at front desks all day signing people in and signing people out. They are chosen for a variety of different reasons but if you are able to make a difference to that person's day it can stand you in good stead.

One of the sales teams I worked for recruited new talent three times a year.

One of my sales managers used to hold a short screening meeting with potential new recruits.

When the hopeful person had left the building, the sales manager would walk down to reception and ask the person on reception for their view of the candidate.

A negative view from the receptionist was not necessarily the end of the recruitment process, but if the view had been negative, it was a "worry" in the sales manager's mind.

Similarly, if you create an excellent impression, there is a possibility that the receptionist might mention you to the person with whom you had the meeting. Small things that add up to make a big difference.

So the receptionist has told your prospect or your prospect's PA that you are waiting in reception, the tip at this stage is **DO NOT SIT DOWN.**

The reason for this is that when your host arrives you don't have to try and extricate yourself from a low sofa. An ungainly attempt to rise from the sofa is a poor way to greet a new prospect.

Stand up, regardless of whether there are other people in reception, so that when you are met by the person that you are meeting, you are able to walk straight towards them with your hand outstretched, keeping good eye contact and able to greet them in a professional way.

As with punctuality, the importance of a firm handshake and strong eye contact at the first time of meeting is vital. Again, while this is not a deal breaker, many of our clients have told us that a loss of eye contact at this stage is a possible demonstration of a lack of integrity.

If you find it difficult to make eye contact with people when meeting them for the first time, come up with some sort of plan which ensures that you are able to look straight at them as opposed to looking away or down. If you are not able to overcome this, then you will have to recognise that this is going to be a disadvantage for you throughout your selling career!

We have not yet touched on the importance of appearance.

I have worked with companies whose sales teams used to devote a considerable amount of time and energy to trying to evaluate what sort of attire would be most appropriate for the sales meetings they attended. Occasionally this led to meetings taking place, where our team were dressed down and the team from the buying company were in suits. We had clearly anticipated this incorrectly!

The best advice is to dress in an appropriately conservative fashion at the initial meeting with a view to ensuring that any offence that might be caused through your choice of attire is minimised. This will allow you to gauge the appropriate dress going forward. Navy blue suit, white shirt and red or blue tie is classic, if possibly too classic. A (non reflective) grey flannel suit, with a light blue shirt and a conservative tie should not offend anyone. Shoes should be good quality and clean, it is amazing how many people consider this an indicator of quality.

A shiny blue suit, with a purple shirt and tie combo and cowboy boots is a bit of a risk. Do people really dress like this?

Being smart is one thing, being vain is another; vanity is not an admired trait. If your appearance suggests that you habitually devote a huge amount of time and energy to yourself, then your commitment to others might be called into question by somebody who is contemplating using your services on an on going basis.

I worked with one sales manager in a large financial institution who was permanently tanned and always impeccably turned out in the latest fashions. While this obviously creates an impression, the impression that it created for me was that this sales manager spent more time focussed on himself and his appearance than he actually did on the development of his sales people.

As I developed my knowledge of his team and his approach to managing his team, it became clear that everything he did **was** for his own benefit.

So you have met your host and created a good first impression. You now have the opportunity of the journey from the reception area to the prospect's office to "break the ice".

ICEBREAKING

Icebreaking is simply defined "as some informal chat that is designed to break down a degree of formality between people who have never met before". What you decide to talk about is entirely up to you.

Two subjects that we would recommend that you avoid are your journey, which has usually been through heavy traffic, and the weather, which is usually bad.

We will be using a simple model for finding out about the customer's business - the model is the PPF model.

THE PPF MODEL

PPF stands for:

- Past
- Present
- Future

The model is a simple approach to asking questions that are aligned to three different time frames.

Past questions are good questions to ask during icebreaking and at the outset of a sales meeting because you are asking about events that have already occurred. The aim of an icebreaking question is to get the other person to talk to you. The recommendation would therefore be that you avoid asking questions that are difficult to answer!

Questions you might consider asking would be:

- How long have you been with the company?

- How long have you been in your current role?
- How long has the company been in this building?

These types of question will often create an opportunity for you to ask a **"branching question"**.

A **branching question** is simply a question that you can use to develop an initial line or thread of information with a view to gathering either more information or breaking the ice further. When you have exhausted that line of questioning, you simply "follow the branch back" to the point in the conversation from which you developed the "branch".

So you are at the prospect's office – tea or coffee has been served – informalities are complete and it is now clearly time to get down to business. Let's remind ourselves of a basic rule:

IN THE FORMATIVE STAGES OF A BUSINESS RELATIONSHIP - WHO NEEDS WHO?

For you the salesperson, it is worth recognising that as you asked for the sales meeting, the prospect has every right to sit behind their desk with an expectation that you are going to drive the meeting and that you are actually going to demonstrate something of value to them.

When you phoned and asked for the sales meeting you may have asked for twenty minutes. This is not a ploy to get a foot through the door and take up more of the prospect's time. If you do not have the ability or skill to have identified an opportunity after twenty minutes then you need to re evaluate your ability to sell effectively.

The ice has been broken. It is now time to move on to the core of the meeting.

SETTING THE SCENE

Some sales people use either a verbal or written agenda at this stage. Some people may have enclosed a written agenda with a meeting confirmation letter once they have made the appointment on the telephone. Both options are perfectly valid and the question is which of these works for you?

Regardless of which of these approaches you are using, the first step is to bring the agenda to life. Remember the reason that you are there is to gain an understanding of the customer's business and future business objectives and to see if your product or service offering is likely to be of interest to them either now or in the future.

It doesn't matter whether you are a service or product provider, it is worth remembering what underpins your future relationship with the prospect.

Providers of products or services are called in to a prospect's environment in order for the prospect to make their own business either more profitable or more efficient. While banks lend money, the entrepreneurs, who take advantage of the fact that banks lend money, spend twenty three hours of the day focussed on trying to get **their business** to work.

The provider of their working capital is somebody that they perceive as one of their suppliers. If you are the banker who is managing the relationship with the customer, it is worth remembering that the customer has chosen to use your product for a number of different reasons but that the reason that you are there is because <u>you</u> work <u>in support of their business</u>. It is amazing how many people forget this.

I remember speaking to someone I knew in an Estate Agents office. A relative of mine was receiving terrible service from this well known company. When I called the person I knew in that Estate Agents office and expressed my surprise at the poor level of service being delivered, I was told that it was worth remembering that it is vital to build up a good relationship with the Agent as this would help the sale/purchase proceed smoothly!

The arrogance.

It implied that if the agent's view of the relationship with the customer was less than favourable, that the standard of service would diminish.

This person had clearly forgotten who was paying whom. Would you pay for a service where the service provider was dictating the terms to you?

It is worth reminding ourselves of the three objectives for the meeting at this stage. We are trying to achieve a clearly defined "next step"; an opportunity to present a solution to the prospect.

The key steps that we need to take in order to get to that position are to:

- Sell self
- Sell our company

and to

- Sell an opportunity

The first step is to start to develop your knowledge of the prospect's business. We talked earlier in the chapter about the past, present, future model and there is a great opportunity to use that model at this stage. We also talked about "branching". Great sales people have an ability to ask great questions and to listen effectively. The salesperson is effectively probing around the company to find areas of opportunity.

Some people are uneasy asking a stranger a lot of questions so early on in the new relationship. Consider this:

Imagine that having spent fifteen or twenty years working in a hot climate one day when you are looking in the mirror you see a dark blemish on your neck. What do you immediately think the blemish might be? Whatever you think it might be, the first step is to go and see your doctor. You are at the doctor's surgery, imagine two different scenarios.

Scenario 1

You walk into the doctor's consulting room; the doctor takes one cursory glance at your neck, writes out a prescription in their indecipherable handwriting, hands it to you and says "nothing to worry about, rub this on your neck and everything should be fine".

What might you seek?

Scenario 2

The doctor asks you to sit down, loosen any clothing you may have in that area and starts to ask you a number of questions:
"Where you have worked"?
"How long did you work there"?

"To what extent were you exposed to direct sunlight"?

"To what extent did you use any form of sun block"?

"To what extent did you use any form of suntan oil"?

"Have you have seen anything like this before"?

"Has there been any discharge"?

"Has there been any irritation"?

The second doctor, who you may not have met before, is asking you a lot of probing questions. As this is happening, this doctor is building trust and rapport based on their determination to understand your situation correctly.

Lack of understanding at this stage could be very detrimental to your future. The same is true in consultative selling.

In this instance, it is clear why the doctor is asking those questions.

In the business world, even though you have asked for the opportunity to meet and find out about the prospect's business with a view to adding value, you may need to reiterate at the outset **what** you want to do and **why.**

If you have used an agenda of some sort, this should have helped, if not use a **SIGNPOST**.

What is a **SIGNPOST**?

Cast your mind back to 1940, the German invasion force has reached the coast of France – all that stands in their way is the English Channel. The German High Command would dearly love to know what is going on in England, but they can't see from where they are.

So what did they do?

They used spies and agents to report what was going on. Some of those spies were there at the outset of the war; others had to be placed in England. The spies got there in many ways, by parachute, by boat etc.

The British Government knew this would happen so what action did they take to ensure that someone who was not familiar with the area had trouble navigating around it? They took down the **SIGNPOSTS**.

If you are not sure where you are going, this can lead to confusion and frustration and you're actually getting **LOST**.

This can be the same in a sales meeting - so use a **SIGNPOST**.

A signpost has four components:

1. Where you have come from
2. Where you are going to
3. How you are going to get there
4. Why you are going there

Here is an example of a signpost used at the outset of a sales meeting.

So Mr Prospect, thank you for your time, as I said on the

phone **(FROM)**, what I would like to do is find out about ABC Limited **(TO)** by gathering as much information as possible at this stage **(HOW)** so that we are in a position to see if we are going to be able to add value to your business **(WHY)**.

So the prospect knows how the meeting is going to proceed, the next step is to start finding out about the business.

THEIR BUSINESS

As with the doctor, great sales people ask lots of great questions.

The good news is that there aren't that many great sales people about; so when you go and see a new prospect for the first time, it may be the first time that they have been asked lots of searching questions about their organisation so use a SIGNPOST.

Starting with the "past" questions, one might ask a customer questions along the lines of:

1. When was the business set up?

2. Who set it up?

3. When did the individual you are talking to join the company?

4. From which company did they join?

5. How has the company changed since it was set up?

And so on.

Good open questions will give you the opportunity to "branch". As we said before this is simply picking up on a train of thought or a line of questioning which has obvious potential benefit to you as the salesperson. Once you are reasonably comfortable that you have gathered a good understanding of where the company has come from, then the next step is to understand what is happening in the company right now.

SEEKING OPPORTUNITY

I have come across numerous examples where the customer has been using one provider of a service for thirty years.

By asking the prospect how long **they** have been with the company you may be able to establish if they inherited the relationship. If this is the case there is a possibility that the relationship may not now be as strong as it was before. This can be perceived as positive as it demonstrates that your prospect wasn't necessarily the person that managed the initial tendering process.

This "present" line of questions can easily merge in to the "future" line of questioning. Future questions should deliver the greatest opportunity for you. However, the benefit of using a structured approach at this stage is that you are able to cover a lot of information in a very short period of time.

A company that we worked with had a very innovative solution for helping prospects and customers with their working capital requirements.

A manufacturing company represented the perfect client profile for this product. The most effective salesperson in the team had a structured approach to understanding not only the nature of the product that the client manufactured but also:

a) Where their raw materials came from and

b) Where the final product went

In addition, for both the pre manufacturing process and the post manufacturing process, the salesperson had a model for understanding the "terms of trade" that the prospect was getting from their existing suppliers and providers.

The use of this structured approach made it very obvious to the prospects that this salesperson was running through their business in an extremely logical fashion.

Prospects are likely to appreciate logic from the person who is going to put together their working capital solution. It also means that questions that need to be asked don't get asked twice.

It is worth reiterating that having had a lot of experience of sitting in sales meetings, there is nothing that demonstrates a lack of effectiveness and efficiency, and breaks rapport more consistently, than a salesperson that goes over the same ground again and again.

So we now have a better understanding of their business, how it has performed in the past, what is happening at present and what plans they have for the future.

The next step is to focus on the product or service that we are seeking to sell. In order to do this we need to develop our understanding of what solutions they currently have in place and why they have what they have.

DON'T HAVE

It is obvious that if the organisation you are with **do not** have the solution that you are offering, then the first job that you are going to have to do is to convince them that there is a benefit to them of having your product or service.

DO HAVE

The alternative is of course that they do have your product or service offering in place. This is interesting, because if they have a similar product or service in place and they have agreed to the meeting, then they have subliminally told you that they may be open to an alternative.

Let's consider the world of sales training for a moment. Our experience is that companies who do not have sales training in place at the time of our meeting, are companies who pose a greater challenge for us. The reason for this is that if an organisation doesn't see the value in developing its sales people, then the first sale that we are going to have to make is to try and get them to value the concept of developing their people. This could take time.

Companies choose not to invest in their people for a number of reasons. Some company's sales teams experience a high level of turnover. Why invest in someone who is going to leave anyway!

Ultimately, if you are successful in getting this customer to value sales training, then you stand a very good chance of being the provider of that sales training. It is also possible that having recognised the value of the sales training, they put the whole process out to tender.

The concern with this is that your sales cycle is now starting to lengthen. If cash flow is a consideration for your business, then a lengthy sales cycle is not what you want. It is important to try and minimise the length of the sales cycle where possible.

Alternatively, if the company that we are prospecting into already have an external provider who is delivering sales training then we know that:

a) They value sales skills development
b) They have a budget in place

It is clear at this stage that our only concern is that the budget is going to somebody else!

Whether you are selling a product or service, you should never overlook the fact that you are selling an **input**. Remember the prospect or customer is going to be far more interested in what the product or service is actually going to do for their business, **the output**.

For that reason, during the questioning around what the customer currently has in place, it is important to try and ascertain how well the product or service is performing and how satisfied they are with it.

This will provide you with an opportunity to evaluate the competitive situation. You should be able to see if you have a competitive advantage because the product or service **you** are offering has additional features that will be of benefit to the customer and which set you apart from your competition. Equally it could be that you as an individual, with your expertise in that area, will be the "difference that makes the difference" in convincing the customer to switch provider.

RECAP

So let's recap:

- We have broken the ice
- We have started to develop our understanding of the client's business using the PPF model with the occasional branching opportunity
- We have also started to gain an understanding of what they currently have and why they have it

So gathering information **(BEING INTERESED)** is the key to being able to identify potential opportunities for your product or service. The key skill for a salesperson at this stage is to recognise the opportunity that is being offered to them but not necessarily to "pounce" on that opportunity at this stage.

PARKING

The reason for not "pouncing" is that it is at odds with the agenda you established at the outset of the meeting. You said that your aim was to understand their business before seeing whether your product or service could be of value. "Parking" is a skill that effective sales people use consistently. They identify an area of the prospect's business that has the potential to yield a business opportunity and they wait for the appropriate moment to develop that opportunity.

Through **being interested** you now have an understanding that an opportunity exists.

Our original objective in terms of finding the opportunity has been achieved at this stage and one would hope that you are also starting to build rapport with the prospect.

BAITING THE HOOK

Just before we start to **sell** our company and ourselves, it is excellent practice to "bait the hook". The best examples I have seen are very simple but create instant interest.

The information that may have been "parked" is alluded to but not specifically mentioned. The salesperson does impart the fact that they think there is an opportunity to "add value".

The hook is baited as follows:

The Salesperson:

"Thank you for all of that information (pause while the salesperson reviews their notes) I think there are a couple of areas where we may be able to add value. What I would like to do is just give you an insight into who we are and what we do before we develop those ideas further, is that okay? Now tell me........."

SELLING YOUR COMPANY

Depending on the extent to which the organisation that you represent is known in the market place, the next step is for you to impart a couple of your company's unique selling points (**USPs**).

It is too late at this stage in the sales meeting to start inventing **USPs**. This is something to which you need to have given consideration ahead of the sales meeting. If you represent

Coca Cola, it is more than likely that the customer will know who you are. However, if you represent a less well known organisation, you should be using one or two **USPs** to let the customer know that you are a credible organisation with whom an ongoing business relationship would be beneficial.

It is also possible that the prospect may have done some research on the organisation that you represent.

Rather than coming across as a salesperson and just "hitting" the prospect with a series of what you perceive to be **USPs**, it is worthwhile at this stage asking a question in order to qualify the prospect's understanding of who you are.

This question is a simple:

"Could you tell me Mr/Mrs Prospect, what do you know about our company?"

If the customer says "Well actually I know nothing at all", you have then just received an opportunity to deliver a couple of punchy **USPs** that will help to start developing the prospect's understanding of who you are.

As we have said the aim at this stage is to establish your credibility.

If, in response to your initial "What do you know about our company" question, the prospect gives you chapter and verse on exactly who you are, then again the prospect has told you that they have either done some research or they have already got some understanding of who you are. This also helps you to clarify what type of buyer you are dealing with.

SELLING SELF

It is useful thereafter to give the prospect a brief insight in to who you are. It is worth remembering the old sales principle "that understatement sells quality" and therefore this is not the time to give the customer your full curriculum vitae. Think about the type of information that is likely to be of interest and to add value and deliver it succinctly.

We are now at the key stage in the meeting. So far, the passage of information has resulted from the salesperson asking questions and the prospect delivering responses to those questions.

At this stage, control of the meeting is still firmly with the prospect. We now need to move the control not necessarily away from the prospect but more towards ourselves/the salesperson. The way that we are going to do this is by raising doubt or by creating curiosity in the prospect's mind – this is something we will look at in considerable detail in chapter five.

Chapter key learns:

1. Preparation is everything. The right sort of preparation in advance of a sales meeting will contribute to the overall success of that meeting.

2. This includes mental preparation time ahead of the sales meeting. A quiet ten minutes where you have the opportunity to shut out any distractions that may have been occurring in the office or on your journey to the sales meeting and focus on exactly what you are trying to achieve in the meeting and how you are going to achieve it.

3. Before you meet your prospect, if you come into contact with anybody else in the organisation, take the opportunity to **"break the ice"** and start the rapport building process.

4. **Never** sit down in reception! In greeting your prospect shake their hand firmly and look them straight in the eye.

5. Some form of verbal or written agenda at the outset will give the meeting direction and provide clarity for both you and your prospect.

6. Use the **PPF model** and **"branching"** to develop your understanding of where the business has come from, where it is currently and where they see the business going in the future.

7. Use **PARKING** to maintain the focus on being **INTERESTED** NOT **INTERESTING**.

8. **Bait** the hook, before selling self and company.

9. Use proven and relevant **unique selling points** to sell the credibility of your company.

Finally, once you have fully understood their business, start to develop their knowledge of the product or service that you provide.

CHAPTER 5

CREATING DOUBT AND BUILDING CURIOSITY

In the last chapter we looked at the proactive diagnostic sales meeting up to the point where you as a salesperson have:

- Clearly understood both the prospect's business and their business objectives

and

- You have had the opportunity to impart a number of USPs about your own organisation and a brief introduction to yourself

To reiterate, the aim of understanding the prospect's business objective at this stage is to try and identify opportunities for you to successfully sell them your service or product offering.

It is worth reminding ourselves at this stage that people are motivated for one of two reasons or possibly a combination of both. People in the main tend to be motivated away from pain or towards pleasure. What do we mean by this?

The dentist is a good example.

For a lot of people the six monthly letters (now annual letter) requesting them to attend for a check up was something that got overlooked. People knew that their teeth were working reasonably well, they were in no discomfort and they tended to put it off. This was particularly so if the person was busy.

This means that, regardless of the population or audience that are receiving these letters, when this letter comes out there is no **guarantee** that people will take action.

If, however, an individual person has a toothache, then taking action becomes a different matter.

All of a sudden, the person **wants** the services of a dentist whether it is 9pm on a Friday evening or 3am on a Saturday morning and the fact that the dentist has taken the weekend off is something that the individual now views as being entirely unreasonable!

Sales people in the main have tended to appeal to the pleasure motivator.

We referred in the book a little bit earlier to the concept of a salesperson's "pitch". If you had "the gift of the gab" you were well equipped to be a salesperson. Having the **"gab"** would enable you to deliver your **"pitch"** with some style, apparently!

This **pitch** tended to focus on all of the benefits of the product or service offering. It is possible that if your product is as good as you think it is, then you may have a significant competitive advantage. In this case, **pitching** the benefits is all that you may actually need to do. If it is the first time that you have met a customer, then structuring your proposition to appeal to only one of the two motivators is taking a risk.

So if in the dentist's example the motivation away from the pain of the toothache is the motivator to get the person to take action right **NOW** then the question is how do we weave this into a selling scenario?

The first principle to recognise is that **"people buy"**, they are not "sold to". This means that it is actually very difficult to impose your product on somebody. This largely negates the traditional salesperson's skills of assertiveness and influencing and the "hard sell".

As we alluded to a little earlier, a good question to ask is:
"Do you talk to yourself?"

On the numerous occasions that we have posed this question in the training room you tend to get one of two responses. You can get people who immediately put their hands up and say "yes I do". The alternative is that you suddenly get people who become quite reflective, start looking around and are probably internalising the question along the lines of:

"He is asking me do I talk to myself, I'm not sure, do I talk to myself? I might, I suppose, on occasion but definitely not out loud but yes I do talk to myself"!

I believe that everybody talks to him or herself and that it is this feature of "internal conversations" that is at the heart of consultative selling.

When we make a decision to buy something of value, it is often a decision that is considered for some time, possibly with the advice of others. We refer to this as our internal buying line. As we go through the process of making the decision, so we move from a low position on this imaginary line to a high position. Many factors can influence the move.

The fact that it is a proactive sales meeting means that our buyer is low on our **BUYING LINE.**

1   10

Not buying   Buying

Our challenge is to facilitate the movement of the prospect from low on the buying line to high on the buying line.

We could tell them what to do or -

The alternative is that **THEY** tell **THEMSELVES** what to do. If **they tell themselves** to take action, they **will** take action.

The concept that we will use to our advantage at this stage is what we will call a "key question".

So what is a key question?

Well, if you imagine a flat pool or pond of water and you imagine somebody dropping a stone into the water, you will initially get a splash and once the splash has subsided then you'll get a series of ripples.

A key question will have the same effect in a prospect's mind as the stone did in the flat pool of water. It will create an initial thought followed by supplementary thoughts. Let me talk you through an example.

Think about a product as basic as a life assurance product. In its most basic form, a "term assurance" product simply promises to pay out an agreed lump sum if the holders of the plan die within a specified time period.

Now the producers of these products recognise that in a husband and wife relationship there is a requirement to protect the financial lives of both the husband and the wife. What has traditionally been sold in the past is what is called a **"joint life"** assurance policy.

This means that when the company providing the life assurance assesses the risk to determine the cost (premium), it looks at both Mr and Mrs and tries to establish the likelihood of who will die first.

So if you have your average Mr and Mrs Couple, a joint life policy will cover both lives but only pay out in the event of the first death. So if Mr Couple predeceases Mrs Couple, then the plan pays out. However, Mrs Couple is now without any cover even though she may still have financially dependent children.

> **MR AND MRS**
> **Couple**
> **£100,000**
> **Paid out on the**
> **first death**

A company that I worked for had a life assurance product that had a competitive advantage in this situation.

The competitive advantage was that rather than putting one plan in place on two lives, we were able to put two plans in place on the two lives. One plan for Mr Couple and one plan for Mrs Couple.

This effectively meant that because we had put two plans in place both Mr Couple and Mrs Couple were covered.

MR Couple £100,000	MRS Couple £100,000

And this was at no extra cost to the prospects!

In the event of the unhappy circumstance that one of the clients were to die, then the plan that had been put in place on their individual life would pay out. The additional benefit of having set up two plans was that the surviving member of the family, the husband or wife, would still have a plan in place and in the event that both people were to die together, this meant that our solution paid out **double** that of the competition, **but at no extra cost** to the prospects.

So why was it then that the bulk of the prospects that we met with for the first time had "joint" life plans when setting up two single life plans was clearly the better option?
Well there were a number of reasons for this:

1. Some advisers didn't recognise the added value that existed from two single life plans

2. Some company's pricing models for two single life plans were more expensive than a joint life plan

3. Some advisers just couldn't be bothered

While there was no guarantee that a prospect that we met would have a joint life plan, our experience was that eight or nine out of ten did. This created opportunity for us.

Even if the adviser had recommended two plans – they never took the next step which was to put the plan into a trust. So even if the prospect had two single plans – we still had an "angle". The angle being created through a lack of product knowledge on the part of the person we were competing against.

Ask yourself this question:

Do you have any joint life assurance plans and if so WHY?

What type of trust was used?

Do you think that you need to contact your Adviser?

So how does this example then weave into our "key" question approach? Well a "key" question is designed to be a number of things and a good **key** question would tend to be:

Assumptive
Prepared
Rehearsed
Delivered with care

Let's talk you through an example of this in the life assurance business.

I am with a prospect who I have never met before. We have had a general discussion about his family and about the objectives that he has for them, when the conversation switches to the arrangements that he already has in place.

Salesperson – "So Mr Prospect I see that you have a term assurance policy covering both you and your wife"?
Prospect – "Yes that is correct. We have £150,000 of cover running until the children are over eighteen."

Salesperson – "Excellent stuff – that is exactly the sort of thing you should have in place. One question if I may Mr Prospect – was your term assurance plan set up on a joint life basis or a single life basis"?

Prospect – Thinking? – "I think the plan was set up on a joint life basis".

Salesperson – looking quizzically at the prospect and delivering this in a reflective tone "You set it up on a joint life basis (pause) – may I just ask one question of you Mr Prospect - **Why** did you set the plan up on a joint life basis"?

We talked earlier about the ripple effect of a key question being the same as the effect you get when you drop a stone

in to a pond of water. In the example above the "**why** did you set it up on a joint life basis"? is the stone being dropped into the pond. Let's evaluate the ripples that might be occurring in the prospect's mind assuming that the prospect is having an "internal conversation".

I appear to be a professional salesperson representing a well known company. I have asked the prospect about one of his plans and then I have challenged him on the structure of that plan. What's the prospect thinking? For some reason, because of the way we think, what tends to be going through the prospect's mind is "What is wrong with my plan"?

In this instance, there is no reason why the prospect should have the appropriate depth of technical knowledge to be able to answer that question for himself. He might even come back and say "well we did consider two single life plans but it was too expensive".

If this is the case, and we know that our solution is inexpensive, then clearly we have got an angle.

But let's assume that we are back with the customer to whom we have posed the question: "Why did you set it up on a joint life basis"?

He is standing or sitting there thinking:

- "What have I done wrong"?
- "What is the alternative"?
- "Was I given poor advice"?

These three questions that have formed in the client's mind are the ripple effect associated with being asked a "key" question.

Let's think about the balance of interdependency that we talked about in the last chapter. Until this stage in the meeting all of the control has largely rested with the prospect. However, the balance of interdependency has now started to shift.

In essence, the prospect has now got an element of **doubt** about how their existing plan is structured and they are developing a degree of **curiosity** about the alternative that I might be able to offer. If I keep quiet at this stage, then the next person to speak will be the customer. What sort of questions are they going to ask me?

145

The sorts of questions that they tend to ask are:

- "Is there a better way"?
- "Is there a better option"?
- "What have I done wrong"?
- "What do you think I should do"?

At this stage, the balance of the relationship has now shifted. The prospect is now dependent on me, the adviser, for an answer to these questions.

I have two options at this stage.

But let's just remember what my key objective was coming into this meeting.

The objective was to ensure that we had a definitive next step with a view to keeping the sales cycle alive, assuming that the opportunity is mutually beneficial.

If this opportunity is mutually beneficial then I have achieved my objective. If I were to answer the prospect's questions completely at this stage, then I run the risk of removing or reducing the impact of this "interdependency".

So the skill that I must now apply is the skill of providing the prospect with just enough information to **"whet"** their appetite, while confirming with them that there is an opportunity for us to consider this together in more detail.

In the financial services industry, this would have meant my taking down some additional relevant information in relation to things like the prospect's age, state of health etc. This in itself is a demonstration of commitment from the prospect.

Once I had this information then I would have been able to run some premium comparisons to demonstrate to the prospect what the potential benefits actually were. This work would have to have been done back at the office and therefore I have just bought myself another opportunity to meet with this prospect and to present and explain my solutions **(BEING INTERESTING)**.

We will talk about managing objections in a later chapter but it is not inconceivable at this stage that a prospect might just have said: "Why can you not just send me the information out in the post"?

The prospect could be motivated to say this for a number of different reasons. Usually at the core of their request was a desire to minimise the inconvenience to me. As we will see later on, the best way to overcome an objection is to pre-empt it. For that reason you would have had a number of explanations as to why that was not the best way forward.

In this specific example we would have consistently added a trust document to any life assurance recommendation, in order to make the plan as tax effective as possible.

Explaining to the prospect that there was a requirement to come back and discuss the suitability of the trust document created the opportunity for the salesperson to return and close.

So let's just re-emphasise one key point.

The balance of this meeting in terms of the interdependency between the salesperson and the prospect shifted when the salesperson asked the **key** question which in this instance was simply:

"**Why** did you set the plan up on a joint life basis?"

At this stage the internal conversations that we have talked about have kicked in and the customer is wondering:

"What have I done wrong"?
and
"What does he know that would be of benefit to me"?

What we are not saying, is that if your product is sufficiently well structured, it won't sell itself. What we are saying is that if you are in a truly proactive diagnostic sales meeting then you have to have the ability to create this level of **doubt** or **curiosity**.

It is this doubt and or curiosity that will ensure that the prospect gives you another opportunity to come back and discuss your potential solution. This in itself keeps the sales cycle alive.

When we considered the sales cycle at the outset of this book, one of the key learns was that managing the length of the sales cycle was fundamental to cash flow management and managing your sales figures. For this reason, our intense focus on keeping the sales cycle alive within our own time frames is key.

Another simpler example using banking for illustrative purposes is a situation where cashiers consistently see customers who they know have got money on deposit. Clearly all banks are trying to provide the best possible financial planning advice in terms of opportunities like the investment of lump sums of money. It is therefore the cashier's responsibility to gain a referral to an investment specialist.

What tended to happen in the past is that time after time after time after time the cashier has said to the customer: "You know you have got lots of money on deposit. I think you should speak to one of my colleagues".

For a number of reasons, customers may or may not be in favour of this. The challenge therefore, was to identify a **key** question that would engage that customer and create this **doubt** and or **curiosity**.

Having asked the cashiers to evaluate why customers might keep money on deposit, the main reason was that people were looking for "safety". Now in the investment world "safety" means a variety of different things.

What was important was that when the cashier, who had a fifteen to twenty second time frame to complete this exercise, said to the customer:

"I am curious Mr Customer, why did you put such a substantial sum of money on deposit"?

That when the customer came back and said:
"Well I was looking for **safety**."

This was an **expected response**.

What is now required of the cashier is a key question that will create **doubt** or **curiosity**.

Having conducted a number of workshops with the cashiers, one simple but very effective question that the cashiers created for themselves was along the following lines:

"That is interesting Mr Customer, **safety** is what you were looking for. May I ask one question, when you made the decision to put the money on deposit, what other **safe** investments did you consider"?

Now nine times out of ten the customer hadn't considered any other type of investment. The fact that the cashier had asked an open question which linked back to the customer's requirement for "safety" and introduced the concept of options created a degree of both **doubt** and **curiosity**.

When this question is posed, the likely response from the customer is:

"Well I didn't consider any others".

The "close" at this stage is for the cashier to say:

"Well I have a colleague who has access to a variety of different secure investment options which may provide better returns and which may be appropriate for some of the funds you keep on deposit. I would strongly recommend that you spend fifteen or twenty minutes with them to see what they have to say".

YOUR KEY QUESTIONS

The question that you have to ask yourself is, are there any features of your product or service about which you can ask key questions?

SUMMARY

In a truly proactive sales meeting, not only is the salesperson trying to get the prospect to consider their product or service offering, the salesperson is also potentially trying to wrestle the relationship away from another salesperson or account manager.

The approach for building new relationships by breaking existing relationships is well illustrated in the following example:

For many people the famous Dam Busters Raid of 1942 was all about blowing up some dams. The bouncing bomb was required to blow up the dams due to the presence of nets across the reservoirs that would stop torpedoes had they been dropped from planes.

The **actual** objective of the raid was to use the water that was contained within the reservoirs behind the dams to flood the industrial heartland of Germany and greatly reduce their industrial manufacturing capacity. So the reality was that the weapon that would be used to deliver the primary objective was the **water** that was contained within the dams.

Now anybody who has walked across a dam will tell you that there is a lot of concrete involved in its construction. If you were to use TNT or another explosive to blow up the dam you would need a lot of TNT or explosive. On the assumption, as in this case, that the bomb is to be delivered by air then this places an immediate restriction on the amount of explosive that can be contained in the bomb.

It is obvious that when you have huge weight of water pressing against a concrete wall, all that the bomb needs to do is crack the wall. Once the wall is cracked, once the integrity of the structure is in question, then the weight of water behind the wall will do the damage.

In a proactive sales environment when you meet a new prospect for the first time, you must be looking for an opportunity to "crack the dam".

You will achieve this if you are able to identify areas where your product or service offering and knowledge are superior to that of your competitor.

If you are able to get your prospect to start questioning themselves (another internal conversation!) about the value of the relationship that they have elsewhere, then you are moving yourself into a position where you can become the preferred provider.

If all that you do is demonstrate that your product is slightly better than the other person's then you are winning a short term battle.

As a salesperson's time is their most valuable commodity, you have to be seeking to achieve not only a short term sale but also the creation of a long-term relationship.

Chapter key Learns:

1. Nearly all of us go to the dentist as soon as we have a toothache. The motivation **away from pain** is a stronger motivation in some instances than the motivation towards pleasure.

2. What we have to seek to deliver in our proposition is something that enables us to harness both of the two motivators to **create doubt** and **build curiosity**.

3. People talk to themselves. It is taking advantage of these **internal conversations** that enables us to sell consultatively.

4. Having gathered all of the information that you need and identified some opportunities, you then have to use a **key question** to create doubt and to build curiosity.

5. If it is a truly proactive diagnostic sales meeting with a new prospect, then being able to identify one simple area where you, through your expertise, are able to add value, will bring into question the benefits of their relationship with their existing provider.

CHAPTER 6

PRESENTING SOLUTIONS – "BEING INTERESTING"

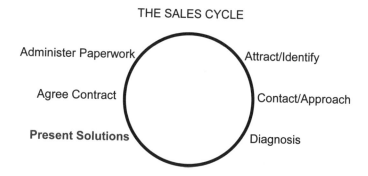

THE SALES CYCLE

Administer Paperwork — Attract/Identify

Agree Contract — Contact/Approach

Present Solutions — Diagnosis

In the previous chapter we looked at creating doubt and building curiosity using **key questions** during the diagnostic sales meeting.

On the assumption that you have closed the meeting successfully and gained the prospect's agreement for you to come back with a solution, then obviously the next step is to look at the presentation of that solution.

As with the subject matter covered in the previous two chapters, we are going to look at it in three stages; what you do before you come back to present, the presentation itself and what you do after the presentation.

Before the presentation there is an obvious requirement for you to pull together quotations, figures and your actual proposal. This will be done based on your own individual technical expertise. What you also have to start thinking about is **HOW** you are going to present the information that you have pulled together.

PREPARATION IS EVERYTHING

During the creation of your solution, you will be able to identify how effectively you have completed the diagnostic meeting. It is sensible to have pre-agreed with the prospect that if you need any additional information, it is okay for you to be in contact either with them or with somebody from their organisation in order to gather that information.

Depending on whether you are selling in a transactional world or whether you are selling five or six key contracts on an annual basis, will dictate the amount of time and energy that you can devote to the creation and rehearsal of your presentation.

Obviously if you are pitching for a huge contract, then the preparation for this event will take up the bulk of your time and energy. However, even sales people who deliver sales presentations on a weekly basis or several times during the week should give consideration to the use of some sort of model which will keep the presentation meeting tight and will enable them to **build value**.

BUILDING VALUE

Towards the end of the last chapter we looked at the possibility that even when you have created doubt or built curiosity and gained the customer's agreement to a next step it is conceivable that a customer will say something like "Just send it to me in the post".

If all that your presentation consists of is a discussion around a quotation document, then you might just as well have sent it in the post.

The "difference that makes the difference" is the individual salesperson and their expertise. Therefore, when you return to a presentation meeting, you have to ensure that you:

a) Enhance the relationship

b) Ensure that you build value through your presentation

The simple triangular model below provides any salesperson with a three step process to building value.

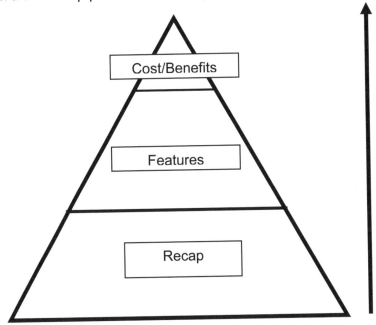

We said that preparation is everything.

Use the presentation model format to initially build your recap.

The objective of the recap is to prove to your prospect that you have clearly understood their business and their business objectives.

In the features section, what factors or features of your product or service are the ones that are most relevant based on the recap?

Finally, you will need to cover the cost at some stage. The best time to do this is when the prospect has clearly seen the suitability of your recommendation and you have articulated the benefits of taking action.

It is worth remembering that:

$$Value = \frac{Benefit}{Cost}$$

Sales people occasionally get hung up on cost, trying to fashion the cheapest possible alternative. Customers want quality and most are prepared to pay for it. You should therefore not be preoccupied with cost.

THE MEETING ITSELF

As with the initial diagnostic sales meeting, the requirement to mentally prepare before you deliver the meeting is paramount. You should also ensure that you have all the various documentation that you will need in case the customer decides to do business with you!

You also need to ensure that you are fluent in the delivery of the presentation. The creation of the presentation model during the preparation phase will help to provide you with this fluency.

In terms of the structure for a presentation meeting it is as simple as:

- Rebuilding rapport
- The use of the presentation model
- Managing any objections or questions that the customer might have
- Gaining the customer's agreement

In the previous chapter we talked about the internal buying line. At the end of the diagnostic meeting, our objective had been to move the prospect up the buying line towards ten.

The amount of time that has elapsed between the diagnostic meeting and the presentation meeting will dictate where the customer is on the buying line right **NOW**.

You must assume that they are back down to a low position i.e. towards one. Assume that they are at the point they were when you met them for the initial diagnostic meeting.

Obviously our objective is to move them back up towards the ten on the buying line.

The recap and features elements of the presentation triangle are designed to do this. In addition, they are designed to provide you with an opportunity to demonstrate to the prospect that you have genuinely understood their business, and that knowledge was at the forefront of your mind while you were developing your solution.

This may be the most important prospect in the world to you and you may have thought about nobody else for the last two weeks. However, it is likely that the prospect stopped thinking about you the minute you walked out the door. The prospect will probably be distracted with something else right up to the moment that you walk **back** through the door for the presentation meeting.

REBUILDING RAPPORT

Put yourself in the prospect's shoes. They are interested in your solution, they have met you before and the fact that you are back there presenting again means that they have started to see some potential benefit in the relationship with you. Keep the rapport bit short and simple.

Recognise that at this stage the bulk of the talking that will be being done in the meeting, particularly during the presentation, will be done by you. The obvious benefit of having committed the bulk of your presentation to memory is that this will enable you to observe the prospect and to gauge the extent to which your presentation is hitting the mark. This is far more effective than simply reading documents or facts from a sheet.

So rapport has been rebuilt, let's look at the recap.

RECAP

The type of prospect you are with will dictate what level of detail they require. You must be prepared to deliver the level of detail that is required for the person who is most detail conscious. By observing the prospect as you run through the recap using the PPF (Past, Present and Future) model, you should be able to gauge the extent to which your level of detail is causing **agreement** or **frustration**.

Even for those prospects who just want you to get to the bottom line in terms of the cost, it is still **absolutely necessary** to **build value**.

What if you are consistently interrupted with "What is the cost"?

Your way of managing this particular objection is to ask the prospect to wait. They will wait if you give them a reason. The reason is that you need to re-confirm your understanding of their needs before making your recommendations.

So you have recapped your understanding of the organisation using the PPF model, the next step then is to start talking about the prospect's specific requirements for the product or service that you are offering.

If you are offering a bank lending product then at this stage you have to be able to feed back to the prospect the features of the lending product that are going to be most important for that prospect.

Let's assume that the prospect is involved in the development of residential housing. The building project, in other words the amount of time that the money is required by the prospect could be fifteen months. What might also be the case is that the prospect has their greatest cash requirement at the outset of the project. Now the prospect knows this but what they want to know is do you know this and does your proposed solution actually reflect the importance of this?

Therefore in the presentation you should identify this by linking back to the recap and demonstrate that your solution meets their specific objectives.

Again, it is worth bearing in mind at this stage that their business will continue **whether or not** you are there! They view their banker as somebody who **supports** their business, as opposed to being the person who actually **drives** their business. For this reason, you have to show a desire to be the person who works **alongside** them in their business.

Once you have completed the presentation of features in full, then the next step is to tell the prospect what this is going to cost them.

All sorts of books on selling come up with ideas of how to dress this up with a view to minimising the impact of the cost. If you have genuinely understood your prospect's objectives and if your product genuinely fits their requirements then, on the assumption that your costing is reasonable, they will do business with you.

If you think of the game of golf, closing is like putting. If your approach shots are bad and you are left with a long putt, you will struggle.

If your approach shots are good and the ball is left eighteen inches from the hole, you should be able to sink the putt easily.

So in sales, focus on your approach shots. Understand your prospect and their objectives and tailor a solution that really helps them grow their business.

That is not to say that every prospect that you meet won't try to negotiate with you on a reduction of cost!

With some products there is no room for negotiation. There may, however, be room to negotiate on peripheral features that cost little to you but are of significant value to the customer. Delivery time is an obvious consideration.

In the sales training world, conducting "field based follow up" at the end of a major training rollout, at no cost to the prospect, is of immense value to both parties. The prospect has "transfer training to the field" activities and the Training Organisation has the opportunity to identify successes and "learns" for the Training Effectiveness Report.

Once you have delivered the cost to the prospect you also need to focus them on the benefits of not only your product or service offering but of an ongoing relationship with you. This puts the cost into perspective and enables the customer to see the obvious benefits of taking action.

CLARIFYING OBJECTIONS

Unfortunately, not every presentation will go as smoothly as you hope. Prospects will object.

During chapter three we looked at "clarifying objections" in some detail.

Now for the average salesperson an objection is viewed in a negative light.

So when a prospect objects, the risk is that the <u>average</u> salesperson will view this negatively. This can cause them to become defensive or even confrontational. This will obviously be of no benefit to either the salesperson or to their embryonic relationship with the prospect.

Alternatively, objections can be viewed in a positive light.

The prospect hasn't said **NO!**

The prospect has said that there are some areas within your presentation on which they require greater clarity. If this is the case, it is worth remembering that the person who caused the lack of clarity is **YOU**, the salesperson. It is therefore up to you to provide the clarification the prospect requires.

At this stage of the sales cycle, objections tend to need to be clearly understood before you try to answer them.

As with the prospecting telephone call, the most appropriate model to use is **APIAC**.

The first step is to evaluate precisely what the prospect is objecting to. The **A P** and **I** of the **APIAC** model will enable you to do this:

A – Acknowledge that there is something that requires clarity

P – Probe, using open questions as to what the objection might actually be

I – Isolate the objection. Confirm that you have understood the objection and ask if there are any additional objections. Once you know what the objection actually is, then you can answer it.

A 43-year-old male prospect had agreed to buy some health insurance. As he was completing a medical evidence questionnaire, he asked the salesperson:

"Will I have to have a medical"?

Now there was a distinct possibility that he might have had to have a medical but it wasn't definite.

In terms of trying to interpret his question we could come up with a number of reasons why he might have asked the question: "Why does he want to know if he has to have a medical"? "Is he hiding some sort of medical condition from us"? "Has he failed a medical before"?

If the salesperson had simply answered/asked any of the questions above, there was the possibility that it might cause offence. Fortunately the salesperson used the **APIAC** model as follows:

Salesperson: "Will you have to have a medical"?

(Acknowledgement) It's possible; may I just ask what has prompted you to enquire about the medical"? **(Probe)**

Prospect: "It's nothing really, it's just the last time I thought about taking out health insurance, I did have to have a medical and the problem was that I had to travel across town at lunchtime to the doctor's surgery which was very inconvenient".

Salesperson: "So the consideration is the location of the medical, if you have to have one, is that right"? **(Isolate)**

Prospect: "You are right, it's not that big a deal, but if I could see a Doctor near where I work, and ideally at lunchtime, it would be far more convenient".

The next step in the **APIAC** model is to **ANSWER** the objection and then **CONFIRM** that you have answered it satisfactorily.

On the assumption that you clarify, and then manage the objections successfully at the face to face meeting then you have the opportunity to close and complete the paper work. It could be that the prospect has raised some objections which you cannot actually address at that meeting.

Obviously, with a view to keeping the sales cycle alive we need to write down the objections that we are unable to answer at this stage in order to be able to address them at a third meeting.

If this happens consistently you are learning a lot about your approach to the diagnostic meeting. You are learning that it needs to be developed!

If you are not gathering enough information at your diagnostic meetings, this will be reflected in the poor results you achieve at your presentation meetings.

AFTER THE MEETING

You will know based on the product or service you sell, what needs to take place after the meeting but, in terms of the sales cycle itself, there is an obvious requirement to administer any paperwork that the sale has generated.

There is also a requirement depending on the type of person you are dealing with to now start the account management element of the relationship. Recognise that people are different. Don't assume that every prospect wants you all over them every week either by phone, email or on a face to face meeting basis.

When the first piece of business is closed, you need to sit down with the new customer and ask them how they want the relationship to be managed. Your interpretation of the answer you get back at this stage will give you an understanding of whether the person is a task orientated person, a people orientated person or an analytical type of person.

Task orientated people in the main only want you to be in touch when you have something of value for them. They don't appreciate ad hoc meetings for a cup of tea or coffee that add no value.

People orientated customers expect you to be in touch on a pretty consistent basis. They would be disappointed if the only time you got in touch with them was when you actually had something for them or wanted something from them. They want the relationship to **develop** and to be **nurtured** and they expect this to be driven by you.

Analytical people prefer to have information sent through to them ahead of any meeting. If you simply turn up for meetings with huge amounts of data then the first thing that an analytical person will want to do is to digest and understand that data.
For that reason, there is a requirement for you to be in touch with the data, and the reason for the meeting, well ahead of the actual meeting itself.

Before we move on and look at gaining **"qualified name referrals"**, it is clear that we need to revisit one or two of the features of the sales cycle, now that we have reached the end of the presentation.

In an ideal world, the proactive salesperson has the ability to execute all of the component parts of the sales cycle with new prospects. In practice, the number of sales people who are able to do this effectively is very small indeed. This is due to attitudinal reasons, skills shortages or both. If you develop the ability to:

- Consistently pick up the phone to somebody you have identified as a good prospect and make an appointment with them
- Execute an effective diagnostic meeting where you genuinely understand the prospect's business and are able to create doubt and build curiosity
- Put together a meaningful presentation and deliver it in an enthusiastic and professional manner leading to business

then you have become an incredibly valuable resource.

What the sales cycle allows you to do is to evaluate your success at each stage in the cycle.

Once you know what you are good at you are able to recreate that and when you know what you are bad at then you are able to do something about it. Choosing not to reflect on the success or failure that you achieve in each of the sales cycles that you initiate is setting yourself up for failure.

The outstanding salesperson takes complete responsibility for everything they do, including the analysis of their sales performance. If you rely on a sales manager to identify what you are not good at, then you are missing out on self development opportunities on a daily basis.

As the cycle is a cycle, it is obvious to take the opportunity to springboard from a satisfied customer to a new prospect. During both the proactive diagnostic sales meeting and the presentation meeting, you have had several opportunities to look for potential referrals.

These might be within the group of companies that you have prospected in to or possibly through colleagues or associates of the prospect that you have been working with during the presentation design stage.

In simple terms there are two approaches to asking for referrals:

- Reactive

- Proactive

REACTIVE

This is essentially just asking a prospect if they are satisfied with what you have done for them and if they would be willing to pass your name on.

The most sophisticated form of "reactive referral" involves the salesperson handing over a couple of business cards and leaving the responsibility with the prospect. Some people favour this approach because it is unthreatening and has the potential for multiple benefits. The disadvantages, however, outweigh the advantages.

The responsibility clearly lies with the customer and while they may be very satisfied with what you have done for them, they are unlikely to devote their valuable time and energy to thinking about people to whom they could pass on your business card!

As with the reactive element of the sales cycle, the concern with any referrals gained in this way is the quality. Even if the referral is poor quality, you have a huge obligation to deliver an exceptional customer experience in order not to offend the person who referred you.

PROACTIVE

It would seem, therefore, that the proactive approach to gaining referrals has the potential to have more advantages and this is the case.

By proactive referral generation I am referring to **"the qualified names approach"**. By "qualified names" we mean the actual name of an individual that you have identified during a sales meeting, the person with whom you want the opportunity to meet.

During the preparation phase for the presentation meeting, you have identified the fact that as well as closing business, you want to gain a referral. At this stage you should know precisely who you want to gain the referral with. Thereafter all you have to do is ask!

What tends to stop people from asking is their perception that if they do ask they will be turned down. Fear of failure and fear of rejection inhibit a lot of people from taking action in areas where they are uncomfortable.

I certainly have had experience of being in a two man sale with a customer with whom we had an excellent relationship, and from whom we had asked for some **reactive** referrals. Our customer very firmly said: "No I never do that". Rather than being embarrassed, my colleague said: "Well, you appreciate that we have to ask"?

Our customer said that he did appreciate that. The learning for me was that if being turned down was as painless as that then there was nothing to be worried about. (He later referred a colleague to us).

In chapter one we talked about $S + R = O$, the situation plus the response equals the outcome. If you are to ask for a referral (the situation) and the customer says no, then it is your response which will affect the outcome and the extent to which you ask for referrals again.

If you are prepared to ask, then all you need to have is a form of words, which you are comfortable with, that explains what you want from the customer and why you want it.

Having done a lot of research into trying to understand what the most successful referral generators asked of their clients, we consistently came up with the following approach:

"Mr Prospect, I hope you have been satisfied with the business we have done together. Now, as you will appreciate my remit as a proactive business developer is to meet new people who we believe have the potential to benefit from the products and services that we offer.

On several occasions you have mentioned Mr A as being somebody who is in a similar sort of position as yourself. Now I have never met Mr A but he sounds like the sort of person we would like to do business with.

What I would obviously like to do is meet him in order to give him a brief insight into who we are and what we do in order for both of us to ascertain whether or not there is any potential for us to work together in the future.

Would it be possible for you to mention me to Mr A, and say that we have done business together and to explain that I would like to contact him?

I appreciate that he may not be in the market for our services at this stage, but when he is next in the market then he'll know enough about us to consider our proposition".

Let's look at this script in some detail. The first point is that you have identified a reason for asking for a referral to the specific person that you have mentioned. This is based on what the customer has told you and is almost guaranteed to ensure that the potential for rejection or objections at this stage is minimised. All you are asking for is the opportunity to meet the prospect or referral in order for you both to **mutually evaluate** whether your offering is of value to them.

The final point is that you are **clearly asking** for your new customer's advice or assistance in going about asking for the referral.

Outstanding sales people are constantly on the look out for referrals. They take full responsibility for generating the right sorts of leads for themselves and never make excuses about the lack of opportunities being generated by their employer.

Chapter key learns:

1. Use the simple presentation model during your preparation phase and if necessary **rehearse**.
2. At the presentation meeting, devote a small amount of time to rapport before moving into your presentation.
3. Be able to engage the client with **eye contact** by having committed the bulk of your presentation to memory.
4. Recap fully in terms of the client's business before then identifying the elements of your product which are directly linked back to the objectives that they have for their business.
5. **Value = Benefit over Cost.** Conclude your presentation with the cost. Be positive about the cost, be convinced that it represents excellent value to your customer and deliver the cost without any apology. Support this with the benefits of your solution.
6. If the customer objects, recognise this as a positive thing. Use the **APIAC** model.
7. Always evaluate **why** you were successful so that you can **recreate** those habits.
8. Equally, evaluate when you lose business so you can learn from those experiences too.

In relation to referrals:

- Be **proactive**
- If you **don't** ask you won't get
- Develop your **own** approach and **remember** to ask
- Even if your client says **NO**, continue to ask others – the benefits far outweigh the cost

SAMPLE PRE APPROACH LETTER

Here is a sample pre approach letter.

These letters are simply designed to get the salesperson's business card and some simple information in front of the prospect and to act as a **PEG** during the telephone call.

If the prospect decides to phone the sender, that is an unexpected bonus.

Dear Prospect

UP TO 30% INCREASED SALES PERFORMANCE FROM YOUR EXISTING TEAM

We have a proven track record in being able to consistently increase the ability of any sales team to proactively generate more sales both from your existing client bank and also from new prospects.

We have completed this with the sales teams of –

Three existing client names and logos here (with their permission of course)

I would like the opportunity to meet you for forty minutes to give you an insight into how we achieved this success and to see how we might deliver the same results with your Team.

I will call you early next week to arrange to meet. I am enclosing two copies of my business card for your files. If you prefer to call to make an appointment please do so.

Yours sincerely

RECOMMENDED READING

The 7 Habits of Highly Successful People   Stephen R Covey

Get Everything Done and Still Have Time to
Play   Mark Forster

Think and Grow Rich   Napoleon Hill

Feel the Fear and Do It Anyway   Susan Jeffers

The Greatest Salesman in the World   Og Mandino

Unlimited Power   Anthony Robbins

Natural Born Winners   Robin Sieger

BRYAN DUNLOP

Bryan Dunlop graduated from the Royal Military Academy, Sandhurst winning a commission in 2nd King Edward VIIs Gurkha Rifles.

After military service all over the world, Bryan worked in both the adventure travel industry in Nepal and the diamond mining industry in Angola, West Africa.

Bryan started his selling career with a major financial services company in January 1994. His role was the provision of tailored financial advice to high net worth clients.

Bryan has over ten years' experience of selling, coaching sales people and designing and delivering effective and inspirational sales and leadership training.

Bryan founded Tailor Made Training in 2001.

Our clients include The Royal Bank of Scotland, Standard Life Assurance Company, The Bank of Ireland and HBOS.

www.tmti.co.uk.

TER

ON FOOT IN
SOUTHERN
SCOTLAND

40 WALKS IN THE
SOUTHERN UPLANDS

David & Charles

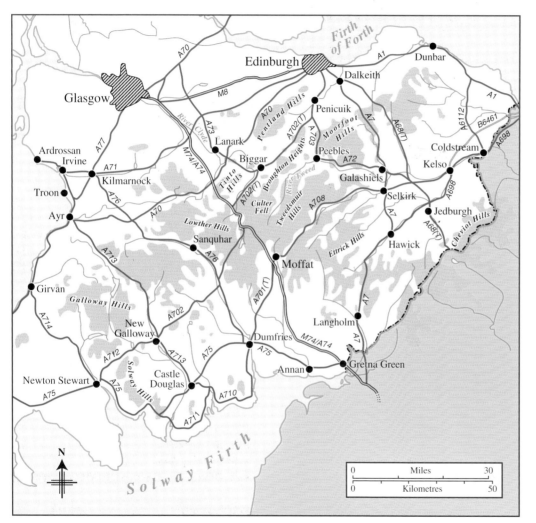

(Title page) Tinto Hill, popular with walkers from
Glasgow, viewed from the Culter Fells

**All photographs and maps by the author, except
map on this page by Ethan Danielson**

A DAVID & CHARLES BOOK

Copyright: Text, Photographs and Maps
© Terry Marsh 1995

First published 1995

Terry Marsh has asserted his right to be identified
as author of this work in accordance with the Copyright,
Designs and Patents Act 1988

A catalogue record for this book is available from
the British Library

ISBN 0 7153 0160 8

Typeset by BLANC VERSO
and printed in Italy by Milanostampa SpA
for David & Charles
Brunel House Newton Abbot Devon

CONTENTS

INTRODUCTION 5
EXPLANATORY NOTES 11

1 THE GALLOWAY HILLS 15
THE AWFUL HAND
Walk 1 The Merrick 19
Walk 2 Shalloch on Minnoch 22
Walk 3 Tarfessock and Kirriereoch 24

THE DUNGEON HILLS
Walk 4 Mullwharchar by Gairland Burn 27
Walk 5 Craiglee and the Rig of Jarkness 30

THE KELLS RANGE
Walk 6 Meikle Millyea, Little Millyea and Darrou 33
Walk 7 Corserine and the Rhinns of Kells 36
Walk 8 Coran of Portmark, Meaul and Cairnsgarroch 41

THE MINNIGAFF HILLS
Walk 9 Loch Dee, White Laggan and Curleywee 44
Walk 10 Millfore and Cairngarroch 47
Walk 11 Larg Hill and Lamachan Hill 50
Walk 12 Loch Trool to Clatteringshaws 53

THE SOLWAY HILLS
Walk 13 Cairnsmore of Fleet 56

Walk 14 Cairnsmore of Dee and Benniguinea via the Raiders' Road 59
Walk 15 Criffel 62

THE CAIRNSMORE RANGE
Walk 16 Cairnsmore of Carsphairn and Benniner 65

2 THE LOWTHER HILLS 69
Walk 17 Lowther Hill and Green Lowther 73
Walk 18 Rodger Law, Ballencleuch Law and Wedder Law 77

3 THE PENTLAND HILLS, MOORFOOT HILLS AND THE BROUGHTON HEIGHTS 81
THE PENTLAND HILLS
Walk 19 The Pentland Ridge 84
THE MOORFOOT HILLS
Walk 20 South Esk Watershed 86
Walk 21 Windlestraw Law 88
THE BROUGHTON HEIGHTS
Walk 22 Broughton Heights and Trahenna Hill 90

4 THE CULTER HILLS AND TINTO 93
THE CULTER HILLS
Walk 23 Culter Fell and Chapelgill Hill 94
Walk 24 Culter Watershed 96

THE TINTO HILLS
Walk 25 Tinto and Scaut Hill 98

5 THE TWEEDSMUIR HILLS 103
THE MANOR HILLS
Walk 26 Broad Law, Cramalt Craig and Dollar Law 107

THE MOFFAT HILLS
Walk 27 Hart Fell 110
Walk 28 The Blackhope Burn Round 115
Walk 29 Grey Mare's Tail and Loch Skeen 119
Walk 30 Mid Craig and White Coomb 123
Walk 31 Talla Water and Lochcraig Head 127

6 THE ETTRICK HILLS 131
Walk 32 Bodesbeck Law 134
Walk 33 The Ettrick Round 136
Walk 34 The Bodesbeck Ridge 138
Walk 35 Loch of the Lowes and St Mary's Loch 141
Walk 36 From Ettrick to Yarrow 144

7 THE CHEVIOT HILLS 147
Walk 37 The Cheviot 150
Walk 38 The Schil 152
Walk 39 Windy Gyle 154
Walk 40 Mozie Law, Beefstand Hill and Lamb Hill 156

BIBLIOGRAPHY 158 **INDEX** 159

Appearances, we are led to believe, are deceptive. While I had long known that to be true of people, it took some time before I realised it applied equally to landscapes.

Like many walkers, I had all-too-often hastened car-bound northwards, mentally blinkered against the palpable attractions of the soft, rounded landscape that flanked my route as I sped by Gretna, Lockerbie, Moffat and Abington.

There seemed to be nothing here that would interest a serious walker: I followed the clarion call of the high mountain lands of Britain and Europe, only slowly coming to hear the soft, insistent voice of the Southern Uplands that whispered every time I sped by, bound for Skye or the Highlands.

Most of the great tract of country between the Anglo-Scottish border and the Forth–Clyde corridor is know as the Southern Uplands. Beyond this lie the Central Lowlands (though not all the Central Lowlands are low, and not all the Southern Uplands are high).

I love the mountains of the Scottish Highlands, the superb contrasts of Skye, the fells of Lakeland and the summits of Snowdonia, the ridges and lofty heights of Ireland, the Alps and the Pyrenees,

Culter Waterhead Reservoir, concealed in the heart of the Culter Fells

the Yorkshire dales, but I shall be eternally grateful that I found my way into southern Scotland.

Soft, flowing, heather-purpled, bracken-gold hills fill the autumn landscape, bright waters and green mark the spring; snow-clad domes proclaim winter's grip, far views, and dark, shady hollows the height of summer. Southern Scotland exhibits simplistic beauty at every turn, even at its most rugged – space, wide, spreading miles of it, wood-cloaked hills, blue-eyed lochs, white-water cascades and lazy meandering streams where trout and salmon slip among the river shadows and the curlew calls from afar.

If that seems a lavish feast leave room to digest the turbulence of a history that is now hard to believe, of bloody border battles, religious ruin, murder and mayhem, of a time when loyalties were formed and betrayed, and the seeds of hatred deeply sown. That benign landscape conceals many secrets; southern Scotland is a tapestry woven from a thousand strands, a creation that is unique, a land of wonder, a place of discovery.

The Lie of the Land

The foundations of southern Scotland were laid during Ordovician and Silurian times, 500–440 and 440–395 million years ago, respectively. In those distant times, Scotland lay south of the equator, and England, part of the European land

mass, still further south. Slowly, the two land masses came together, raising southern Scotland into the Southern Uplands, later to be shaped by wind, water and ice, a process that, imperceptibly, continues still.

Scotland is divided into three distinct regions: the Highlands, the Central Lowlands and the Southern Uplands, each separated by geological faults. Between the Southern Uplands and the Central Lowlands lies the Southern Upland Fault, extending from just south of Ballantrae on the west coast to Dunbar on the east. With the odd exception, much higher land lies to the south of this line, grouped into a fine collection of hills.

Within this vast region there are two sub-regions, separated geographically by the valley of the River Nith, and rather more prosaically by the M74/A74. But there is a more natural, less conspicuous, divide: the British watershed, which, near Moffat passes between the source of the Tweed, flowing to the North Sea at Berwick, the Annan, meeting the Solway Firth at Annan, and the Clyde.

To the west rise three important granite masses, at Criffel, Cairnsmore of Fleet and around Loch Doon, giving the landscape a rather more rugged form, and here the rivers tend to flow either into the Clyde or south to the Solway Firth. To the east, the hills are more rounded, with fewer

outcrops of rock, greater abundance of grass, and a wide spread of rivers, many captured by the Tweed.

The initial shaping of the landscape in southern Scotland was done beneath great ice sheets, the main centres of glacial activity being around Loch Doon and the Moffat Hills. The glacial period, which ended about 10,000 years ago, lasted for some 60,000 years, compressing the land beneath an enormous weight of ice. Huge quantities of rock debris were carried away by glacial torrents and dumped in the valleys, flattening them and providing a base for the human settlement that was to come. In many places, unimaginably huge chunks of ice became stranded by the debris cast up by torrents, and in time these formed lochs.

There are few natural lochs in southern Scotland, the most notable being Loch Trool, Loch of the Lowes and St Mary's Loch, though these last two were a single loch 10,000 years ago. Many lochs, such as Clatteringshaws and Daer, are man-made, and drowned communities in their formation. Man-made, too, are the forests which cover large tracts of southern Scotland, grown commercially, but in a balanced way, with immediate replanting following felling. Studies of pollen and plant remains have revealed that much of southern Scotland was once covered in deciduous forest, a dark and dank mass of trees

The new forest track alongside Birnock Water provides a fine view of Swatte Fell and Pirnie Rig

and undergrowth, fallen timber and deadwood, a landscape of alder, ash, birch, elm, oak and willow.

The First Settlers

It is from scattered finds of microlithic implements that we derive evidence of earliest habitation in southern Scotland. With little tangible evidence available, it is not surprising that we cannot agree over when our prehistoric ancestors first reached Scotland. Some suggest that hunters and fishers travelled and lived along the Solway Coast from as early as 8000 BC, following the elk, deer, ox, beaver and brown bear north as they extended their range. Other authorities speak of hunter-gatherer groups in what is now the Borders Region from 4000 BC. With large, swampy areas to contend with it is certain that early settlers found it easier to travel by sea than by land, and so the coast and river valleys were the first sites of habitation and exploration. Many of the earliest dwellings were *crannogs*: lake dwellings built on artificial islands of logs in shallow lochs as defence against wild animals and enemies.

The discovery and mastery of metals brought technical advances, enabling the Celtic people, or Gaels, of central Europe to venture from the Euphrates valley northwards, conquering England in the process and continuing over the Solway into Galloway. Various names, Picts, Gaels, Scots and Britons, were taken by different tribes, but it is with the Picts that the early history of Scotland is associated. Indeed, not until the

ninth century was Scotland known as such. Before then it was called Alba, a Pictish kingdom. Some authorities suggest that all the people of Scotland are descended from the Picts. As a race, they claimed the most ancient origins in Christendom, and gave the genealogy of their kings going back to the time of Noah, and the Flood. No one is certain when the Picts reached Scotland, but it was probably around 500 BC. Nor do we know why the Picts, who represented about 95 per cent of the population, started calling themselves 'Scots', and their kingdom of Alba, 'Scotland'.

Nigel Tranter explains the history of Scotland in an enlightening and entertaining way in his book *The Story of Scotland*, where the minutiae of this turbulent and difficult tale may be found, but a few key moments are worth mentioning here. As elsewhere, the Romans came, conquered, built walls and roads, and went home, around AD 400, leaving the tribes of Scotland (Alba) to fight for domination. In southern Scotland there were four main tribes, the Novantae in Galloway, the Damnonii in Strathclyde (which was then much larger than present-day Strathclyde), the Selgovae around the Solway basin, and the Votadini in Lothian and the Merse.

In medieval times, English and Norman landowners found their way into Scotland, and many of them, like Robert the Bruce, came to play a critical part in the country's history. During these times, too, religion played an important role in fashioning the land and its

people, and many religious houses were founded during the time of David I (1084–1153), giving rise to the early development of sheep farming and the introduction of many features of the feudal system established south of the border in the late eleventh century.

From then on, Scotland experienced troubled times. Centuries of war with England and the activities of robber barons did nothing to ease the already arduous life of ordinary people. During the Middle Ages, virtually the whole of southern Scotland and northern England experienced a period of theft, violent death, and wanton destruction of property, for this was the time of the Border Troubles, most interestingly recounted in George MacDonald Fraser's excellent book *The Steel Bonnets*. By the sixteenth century, robbery and feud were almost systematic.

In time, the feudal system was eroded, and social order came to be based on a system of extended families. Border raiding (stealing your neighbour's cattle), was a most lucrative way of making a living, and those who could do it best, gained at the expense of weaker families. The recipe was one for unmitigated violence, theft and destruction of property. Most dominant families lived in fortified houses, 'peel' towers, the remains of which still dot the landscape of southern Scotland.

For centuries the land on both sides of the border was a lawless tract. Nowhere are present-

The River Tweed flows sedately through Peebles

day appearances more deceptive than in a pleasant, green, quiet stretch of farmland only a few miles north of Carlisle. From the River Esk at Metalbridge the land extending northwards as far as Langholm and Liddesdale used to be known as 'The Debateable Land', the very hub of border country. It was once the toughest quarter in Britain, and in MacDonald Fraser's view 'belonged in the same class as the Khyber Pass, the Badman's Territory, the Barbary Coast, or even Harlem, Soho and the Gorbals'. The problem was that neither side would admit ownership by the other side, so no one could be held responsible for the activities of those who lived there. Many opportunists were quick to seize on this lack of rule.

No matter how territorial the Scots were they could not move the border far into English territory. The border issue had to be resolved for the sake of peace, north and south, and this occurred in 1603, with the Union of the Crowns, when James VI of Scotland became James I of Great Britain. Then it was that the authorities, under the King's order, clamped down on the activities of the border clans.

James's reign was very much a watershed, though peace was yet some way off. Part of the problem was that James decamped to London, leaving Scotland subject to long-range government, via chosen minions, who increasingly acted on their own discretion, effectively distancing themselves from London. James only returned to Scotland once, in 1617, though by shrewd management he ensured that

no one of great ambition ever wielded influence in the north of his united kingdom.

From the point of view of lowland Scotland, the main concern of James's rule was to impose episcopacy, the rule of bishops, though he was far from religious himself. This was to lead to another period of unrest as the Scottish kirk rebelled. That the resultant struggle outlived James, into the reigns of Charles I and Charles II, gives some idea of the virulence between Scotland and the distant power base of London. James was succeeded in 1625 by his son, Charles I, whose endeavours to impose Anglican-style worship on Scotland made matters worse. By 1638, a great National Covenant, a declaration of religious freedom, had been drawn up, and when the King, seeing this as a plot against himself, sent the Marquis of Hamilton to Scotland to curb the protesters, it initiated a series of events that led to the 'Wars of the Covenant', another unhappy episode in the history of Scotland. The Covenant, contrary to the beliefs of some (including Charles himself), was not set against the King, but against religious dictatorship from London and the introduction under royal decree of an alien form of worship. Many Covenanters were persecuted and dealt with brutally, and throughout much of southern Scotland there are constant reminders of these struggles.

After Charles I was executed in 1649, Cromwell's Commonwealth prevailed until his death in 1658. When Charles II returned from France, the restoration of the monarchy in 1660 heralded a dour period of reaction that came to be known as the 'Killing Times'. The Covenanters were eventually victorious, hence the existence of the Presbyterian Church of Scotland.

Approaching the Present

Before the industrial age, rivers were the main sources of power and communities were seldom found far from one. Many of the mills founded during this time were the seeds from which the larger towns of southern Scotland flourished.

Significant changes were to come during the eighteenth and nineteenth centuries, arising from the wealth that flowed from the Industrial Revolution. Rich merchants came north and enclosed large tracts of countryside with walls, known as 'drystane dykes'. During the nineteenth century in particular the populations of the main towns and villages grew, leaving many smaller, isolated settlements to decay.

Today while the whole of southern Scotland is well equipped with roads, the paucity of public transport has polarised populations, and made them dependent on private cars. Visitors to much of southern Scotland will find a car is essential to tour the region, and without one, few of the walks in this book are easily accessible.

Driving along the quiet back-roads, or walking across the hills and glens, it is hard to imagine the scale of violence that once beset the land. Everything, it appears, is at peace.

The remains of Sweetheart Abbey, founded by the wife of John Balliol

EXPLANATORY NOTES

The Walks

Many volumes of this size would be needed to do justice to the magnificent mountain heritage of a region so vast and richly varied as southern Scotland. The walks here cover most of the principal mountain ranges, but some are unavoidably omitted. I hope that the reader will be inspired by those I have included to seek out the Lammermuirs, the Eildon Hills, and the quiet corners of all the other ranges that have equal merit to those I have described.

The given walks are either circular or linear, to maximise each one's rewards. Obviously, linear walks will require transport arrangements. Some of the walks, notably those in the wilderness areas of the Galloway heartland, cover extremely rough and untracked country, far from outside assistance. They might also involve burn crossings, which in spate conditions are dangerous. In addition, the absence of clear paths across many stretches makes route description difficult. For these reasons only experienced and strong walkers should venture into this terrain, preferably accompanied. Where problems of this kind are likely they are mentioned in the text.

Maps

The maps with the walks are purely indicative, and are no substitute for conventional maps.

The Ordnance Survey Landranger Series, at a scale of 1:50 000 (2cm to 1 km), will be found adequate for most purposes, though Pathfinder maps at 1:25 000 (4cm to 1 km) give much greater detail, and are more useful where walks go through forests. The Pathfinder maps, however, do not cover as large an area as the Landranger maps, and while a dozen or so Landranger maps will suffice, many more Pathfinders would be needed to cover all the walks described.

Harveys Walker's Maps, produced on a waterproof material known as 'Duxbak', cover parts of southern Scotland, and will be found useful in the Galloway Hills, the Lowther Hills, and the Cheviots. Originally produced for orienteering purposes, they are at a scale of 1 : 40 000 (2.5cm to 1 km).

Length

The stated length of each walk is for the *complete* walk, be it circular, up-and-down, or linear.

Walking Times

These represent a realistic allowance for a walker of average fitness but it must be stressed **they make no allowance for stops**, other than perhaps a brief halt to take pictures.

The Sensitive Walker

All visitors to the magnificent hills and glens of southern Scotland should recognise and respond to the sporting and proprietary rights of landowners and farmers. During the stalking and shooting seasons in particular, people walking through deer forests and across grouse moors can do irreparable harm.

Throughout Scotland the deer stalking season is usually from 1 July to 20 October, though the culling of hinds may continue until 15 February. In southern Scotland there are fewer red deer preserves to worry about. The grouse shooting season, however, is from 12 August until 10 December, and grouse moors form a significant part of the countryside covered in this book. These activities are not merely sporting, but form a vital part of the economy of many of Scotland's estates. It is also important to avoid disturbing sheep during the lambing season, which in Scotland runs from March to May. During this time dogs should not be taken on to the hills, and must be kept under close control at all times. Walkers may be interested in a book published by the Scottish Mountaineering Trust, called *Heading for the Scottish Hills*. This gives the names and addresses of factors and keepers who may be contacted for information about access to the hills. Write to Cordee, 3a DeMontfort Street, Leicester, LE1 7HD.

Walking in any mountainous region calls for expertise and a clear understanding of the techniques and responsibilities involved. The walks contained in this book are given on the understanding that they will be followed by people who have those techniques, and comprehend and observe the responsibilities. If you lack these attributes you should learn them elsewhere, in more populous areas, where the likelihood of attracting attention in the event of an accident is considerably greater.

One of the greatest aggravations is the amount of litter found scattered about our hillsides. Why people carry full containers up a mountain and then can't be bothered to bring them down empty defies explanation. Please don't be one of them.

Rights of Way

Many of the longer and most spectacular rights of way in the United Kingdom are found in Scotland, but rights of way here are not distinguished from other paths on Ordnance Survey maps, nor on the Harveys Walker's Maps which cover part of the Galloway Hills, the Lowther Hills and the Cheviots.

For a right of way to exist, it must satisfy four criteria:

1 The track must run from one public place to another (and here a 'public place' might simply be a public highway).
2 The track must follow a more or less defined route.
3 The track must have been used openly and peaceably by members of the public, without permission, express or implied, of the landowner.
4 It must have been used without substantial and effective interruption for a period of 20 years or more.

Of course, walkers are not in a position to verify all these requirements before venturing along a track, but fortunately considerable and very welcome tolerance of access to many areas of land, particularly to moorland and mountainous areas, has been shown by landowners over the years. This is not a concession, it is a privilege, and as such must not be taken for granted.

The walks described in this book follow rights of way, existing paths that are not established rights of way (but are obviously used by walkers), other paths and tracks where access appears to be tolerated, and, quite often, untracked ground. Given these conditions, it is important to exercise care and attention at all times to help maintain the good relationships that exist, and to preserve the freedom to explore Scotland's fine heritage without hindrance. ***None of the routes described in this book is intended to imply that a right of way exists.***

Many people believe there is no law of trespass in Scotland; there is, and the fact that the author has been able to follow these walks should not be taken as proof that there is any automatic right to do so. Wherever feasible, a courteous enquiry at the nearest farm will generally elicit the consent needed to continue with the walk, and will do much to promote goodwill.

Anyone wishing to explore further the whole question of rights of way in Scotland should contact the Scottish Rights of Way Society, John Cotton Business Centre, 10/12 Sunnyside, Edinburgh, EH7 5RA for a copy of their booklet: *Rights of Way: A Guide to the Law in Scotland.*

However, rights of way and pathways are subject to change, and can be altered by forestry work, fires, changes in land ownership, etc. Every effort has been made to ensure the accuracy of the information contained in this book, but readers are advised to be alert to the possibility of changes, and requested to notify the author, through the publisher, of any noted changes.

Walls and Fences

Dry-stone walls in Scotland are known as dykes, and many of the high ridges of the Southern Uplands have dykes, frequently found in a dilapidated condition, running along them. Apart from their obvious value as guides in poor visibility, they often represent regional and district boundaries, but because the art of building these walls is a dying one, many of them are being echoed by post-and-wire fences, some topped with barbed wire.

The use of electrified fences in southern Scotland is becoming commonplace. Most carry only low voltages, and will give no more than a mild shock, but some, in Galloway especially, carry much more, and should be treated with the utmost caution. Unfortunately, there is no sure way of knowing which is which!

Munros, Corbetts and Donalds

Throughout the book, I have described mountains as Munros, Corbetts or Donalds, where appropriate. These titles reflect a grouping of mountains in Scotland according to the practices of their eponymous compilers.

Munros, named after Sir Hugh Munro, are Scottish hills of 3,000 feet (914 metres) and above. There are no Munros in southern Scotland.

Corbetts were identified by J. Rooke Corbett, and have altitudes between 2,500 and 3,000 feet (762 and 914 metres), but have the added complication of a minimum of 500ft (152m) of re-ascent on all sides. All seven Corbetts in southern Scotland are visited in this book.

Donalds are confined to the Scottish Lowlands, and were listed by Percy Donald. They are hills over 2,000 feet (610 metres) in height, of which there are 82 in the current edition of the publication listing all these summits: *Munros Tables.* Not all of the Donalds are included in this book, but their 'conquest' will provide many a happy day for those prepared to seek them out.

Ram monument, Moffat town centre

1
THE GALLOWAY HILLS
MOORS AN' MOSSES MANY, O

Galloway is a compact region, of immense beauty, formed around mighty hills, laced with myriad streams and lochans. Beyond the hills the land falls gently to a seaboard that never fails to attract, while the rivers continue their timeless task of fashioning the landscape, the Nith, the Urr, the Dee, the Ken, the Fleet and the Cree. Very soon you come to realise that here is a place that knows little of overcrowding, of noise and clamour, of urgency, a place where peace, tranquillity, and solitude are available in great quantity.

For the walker, the Galloway Hills must seem like a corner of paradise, far from the bustle of the Highlands, or the weighty tread of visitors to Cumbria's summits beyond the Solway Firth. From lofty heights to forest trails, from the warm welcome of its people to the romance of its legends, its history and culture, from purple-heathered moorlands to brightly-flowered glens, the charms of Galloway are manifold.

Galloway lies far to the west of the main thoroughfare of southern Scotland, the M74/A74, but has always been by-passed by travellers. Prehistoric remains abound along the coasts of the Solway Firth, but they become fewer and fewer as you progress inland. Nor is there much

Autumnal colours fill the landscape around Loch Dee

evidence that the Romans found the region to their advantage, though traces of a 'Deil's Dyke', reaching from Loch Ryan in the west to the Nith valley, are thought to date from Roman times, possibly to protect the coastal plains from the fractious tribes of Strathclyde.

Although the southwest part of Scotland is renowned as the country of Robert Burns, he had surprisingly little connection with Galloway. Burns was born in Alloway in Ayrshire, and died in Dumfries, and has become, with good reason, the national poet of Scotland. Yet he wrote little about the beauty of his land, partly because eighteenth-century Galloway was only just losing its Gaelic tongue, but principally because the pens of Scott and Hogg, and their contemporaries, flowed at their evocative best, awakening the Scots to the beauties of their own country, only after Burns's death, or late in his life.

Nevertheless, Burns could not have gazed upon the hills of Galloway without some stirring in his breast, and from time to time we are permitted a glimpse through the window of his mind, as in

'Behind yon hills where Stinchar flows,
　'Mang moors an' mosses many, O,
The wintry sun the day has clos'd,
　And I'll awa' tae Nanie O.'

Hugh Douglas in his *Portrait of the Burns Country* suggests that 'Galloway can get along quite well without Burns for it has its own sons and daughters of whom it is proud', for this is the land of Crockett, the novelist, of St Ninian, who brought Christianity to southern Scotland more than a hundred years before St Columba, of saintly Devorgilla, of William Wallace and Robert the Bruce, King of Scotland. The battles of Scotland's efforts for independence may have been fought on some distant killing-field, but it was among the Galloway Hills that the English were tormented and held at bay, and it is here that many regard as the Cradle of Scotland.

Geologically, the whole of Galloway lies to the south of the Southern Upland Fault which separates the hills of southern Scotland from the Central Lowlands. At its centre is a band of Ordovician rock, that lies around the Merrick and Kells ranges, though much of the area has been intruded with other sedimentary rocks, and by igneous upthrusts that have produced metamorphic rocks in the process. The result is a geological wonderland. The scenery is at its most rugged between the former counties of Ayrshire and Kirkcudbright (now Strathclyde, and Dumfries and Galloway), where mile after mile of troubled landscape rolls on across hill and glen, moor and loch.

Much of the land now forms part of the Galloway Forest Park, and has a rich and colourful heritage, a mix of wildlife habitat and recreational opportunity, where visitors are welcomed and encouraged to enjoy what the hills have to offer.

For the purposes of this book, the Galloway Hills have been divided into sections, and extended beyond their natural boundaries by the inclusion of fringe ranges to produce a more composite whole. This is purely an action of convenience.

To the north and west rises the range of the Awful Hand, reaching down to Loch Trool. To the south are the Minnigaff Hills, forming the base of an elongated U, that leads northwards again across the Dungeon Hills. Further east are found the smooth-flanked hills of the Rhinns of Kells. Reaching not far north from the Solway Firth are the Solway Hills, and beyond them the delightful summits of the Cairnsmore range. Enough walking country to occupy a good part of a lifetime.

Inmate, Goat Park, Galloway Forest Park

The Awful Hand

The name, the Awful Hand, derives from the shape of the range, particularly when viewed from the west. Benyellary, a satellite of the highest summit, The Merrick, is the thumb of this fanciful hand, The Merrick the index finger, and so on, across Kirriereoch Hill, and Tarfessock, to the 'little finger', Shalloch on Minnoch. Two of the summits, Shalloch on Minnoch and The Merrick are Corbetts, indeed The Merrick is the highest mountain in southern Scotland. Kirriereoch Hill used to enjoy Corbett status, but those who determine such things have long since demoted it from the ranks of the elite, the accuracy of modern surveys showing that it fails to achieve the 500 feet of re-ascent on all sides, by a mere few feet.

The southern limits of the range slip into Glen Trool, one of the most outstandingly beautiful parts of southern Scotland, and popular with walkers and casual visitors alike. Not without good reason does the Southern Upland Way, that long-distance, coast-to-coast trek, steer its 202-mile course through Glen Trool.

The Minnigaff Hills

Bounded on the north by Glen Trool and the Dee trench, the Minnigaff Hills extend east as far as Clatteringshaws Loch, and west to the River Cree. Unlike the hills of the Awful Hand, the Dungeon range or the Rhinns of Kells, those of Minnigaff orientate east–west, as if forming a base on which the Galloway Hills as a whole might rest.

The group contains four summits in excess of 2,000 feet (Donalds), including one Corbett, Lamachan Hill. The remaining hills, Larg Hill, Curleywee and Millfore, can be combined with Lamachan Hill in one long and strenuous day, but give greater pleasure if explored at a more leisurely pace. They can be accessed both from Glen Trool, with the exception of Millfore, or from Craigencallie, beyond Clatteringshaws Loch.

The hills are a mix of rock outcrops, grass and bracken, and all have far-ranging views, in some respects better than the higher summits of the Awful Hand.

The Dungeon Hills

Lying at the heart of the Galloway Hills, the Dungeon range is not exceptionally high, but contains some of the roughest and wildest scenery in southern Scotland. The hills lie in a roughly north–south line, sandwiched between Loch Doon and Loch Dee.

The centre of the range lies around the glacial hollow occupied by Loch Enoch, and for the geologist there is abundant evidence in the corries, moraines, lochs and numerous erratic boulders of the movement of the ancient glaciers that used to occupy the region.

The main summit of the range is Mullwharchar, along which, as elsewhere in the range, there are long stretches of granite slab, making progress on the tops rather easier than in the surrounding valleys. The valleys act much as a barrier to progress, wet and boggy moorland

at its tiring worst, coated in a deep vegetation of tufted grass, and with wide clutches of heather on the adjacent hillsides to molest those who escape the glens. Once on the tops, however, the sense of relief is wonderful, and the walking then of the highest order. The Dungeon Hills provide rough and tough walking, with a quality that will appeal to strong, determined walkers.

The Rhinns of Kells

Although only called the Rhinns of Kells from Corserine southwards, the name, and its more customary title of simply the Kells range, tend to be interchangeable. For me, the 'Rhinns of Kells' has a tremendously evocative ring about it. The range is rather higher than the adjacent Dungeon range, and indeed, in Corserine, contains the second highest mountain in the Galloway Hills.

In essence, the range is one long ridge that stretches from Coran of Portmark overlooking the expanse of Loch Doon, southwards, across Meaul, Carlin's Cairn, Corserine, Millfire, Meikle Millyea to the River Dee. Both flanks of the ridge are heavily afforested, but permit access to the hills at a number of points.

The Solway Hills

Unlike hills described previously, those of the Solway region are not arranged into a convenient group, spreading instead over a far greater area of upland and lowland. As a result, there is a fine contrast between the dramatic landscape of hill country and the pastoral scenery of the coastal plains, between forestry and farming, between

urban settings and rural communities.

Only three walks from this vast region are included in this book. One, set close by New Abbey, south of Dumfries, takes in the Solway sentinel, Criffel; another, much nearer to Newton Stewart, visits one of the three 'Cairnsmores', Cairnsmore of Fleet, while the third tackles the rough terrain of the Cairnsmore of Dee, overlooking Clatteringshaws Loch. Visiting all three summits will take the walker through some of the most appealing scenery in southern Scotland, where town and country are tastefully blended. All three are granite, and represent a major appearance of the rock in the region.

The Cairnsmore range

The final section of the 'Galloway Hills' looks beyond the village of Carsphairn to a fine group of summits clustered around Cairnsmore of Carsphairn, not only the highest summit in the range, but the highest of the three 'Cairnsmore' summits, which some extremely fit walkers have managed to complete in one outing. Such feats of endurance are not for most of us. The shapely Cairnsmore of Carsphairn is more usually combined with its neighbour, Benniner.

For walkers the hills of Galloway are as fine a collection of summits as may be found anywhere in so compact a region. Your efforts will be rewarded with spectacular views, wildly extravagant and exciting walking, moorland expanses highlighted by numerous lochs, streams and rivers, and outstandingly beautiful glens.

THE MERRICK

Higher than any other mountain in the whole of southern Scotland, The Merrick is a worthy monarch, and commands the attention of most walkers sooner or later. The name derives from *tiu meurig*, the 'Finger' of the range of the Awful Hand. It is, not surprisingly, a popular mountain with experienced hill-walkers and casual visitors alike, and a good path ascends all the way to its summit as a result. The route described here gives double value, for the ascent unavoidably takes in Benyellary (*being iolaire*, the hill of the eagles).

The walk starts from the road end in Glen Trool, one of the most beautiful glens in Scotland, flanked by rugged grey-brown hills that give so much Highland flavour to the scenery hereabouts, described by Scott:

Land of brown heath and shaggy wood,
Land of the mountain and the flood.

The Merrick, seen across Loch Neldricken, near 'The Murder Hole'

Along a minor road people come in droves to visit Bruce's Stone. Splendidly sited on a bluff overlooking the loch, the memorial is to Robert the Bruce's victory in 1307 over an English force. From the steep-sided Mulldonach opposite the monument, Bruce's men are said to have rolled great boulders on 2,000 advancing English troops, under the command of Sir Aymer de Valence, Earl of Pembroke and then Guardian of Scotland, who were following a narrow track beside the loch shore. The flat land at the head of Loch Trool is known as The Soldiers Holm, from its association with this Battle of the Steps (steeps) o' Trool. Before that date is was known as Ringielawn, from the Gaelic *roinn na'leamhan*, the point of the elm trees. The inscription on the stone reads:

IN LOYAL REMEMBRANCE
OF
ROBERT THE BRUCE
KING OF SCOTS
WHOSE VICTORY IN THIS
GLEN OVER AN ENGLISH
FORCE IN MARCH 1307
OPENED THE CAMPAIGN OF
INDEPENDENCE WHICH HE
BROUGHT TO A DECISIVE
CLOSE AT BANNOCKBURN
ON 24TH JUNE 1314

The stone was erected in 1929 on the 600th anniversary of Bruce's death.

The start of the ascent of The Merrick is signposted at the road end: 'The Merrick Climb. 4 miles to 2,784 feet'. The '2,784 feet' is the height of the mountain, not the amount of ascent, though the figure comes from an outdated map. The metricated height, 843 metres, roughly converts to 2,766 feet, but because Benyellary is taken in first you will have to climb almost 2,500 feet in a lateral distance of a little under four miles; quite a haul.

A good path sets off from near the car park, but soon degenerates into a bouldery path leading towards Buchan Burn, which it finally reaches at a gate. The burn flows through a hanging valley created by a side glacier more than 10,000 years ago that flowed into the main east–west flowing glacier in the valley below. A short way on, take a higher, signposted path, above the burn, running on to another gate at a forest boundary. Benyellary is as yet out of sight, but across the burn, the rugged slopes of Buchan Hill, a modest elevation, are characteristic of this part of Scotland, where, to quote Hamish Brown's *Climbing the Corbetts*, you will find 'the wildest scenery and the roughest landscape south of Rannoch'.

Enter the forest and follow an undulating path that leads to an old shieling (summer cottage),

Culsharg **(1)**, still in use as late as 1947, but since then fallen into disuse, other than as a rudimentary bothy. Keep left at Culsharg and climb to meet a broad forest track, turning right along it to cross an incongruous concrete bridge and immediately left (signposted: 'Merrick') for a tiring pull to the upper edge of the forest. The blanket of trees, and the climb from Culsharg do nothing to lift the spirit until they are both left behind. Then the windswept open hillsides take over, and suddenly the swelling slopes of Benyellary are in view. The path leads to a gate in a fence, beyond which it heads for a dyke **(2)** that will now escort you to the top of Benyellary. The summit of the hill is marked by a large cairn.

Across a neck of land, the Nieve of the Spit, the on-going dyke leads to the corrie of Black Gairy, from where its rim can be followed to the summit of The Merrick. But there is a prominent path now, lower down, that launches from the end of the Nieve of the Spit **(3)**, and brings you close to the summit cairn-shelter and trig, and the attendant scattering of erratics. The view is outstanding, reaching from as far as the Lake District and the Mountains of Mourne to the mountains of the Southern Highlands, around Crianlarich. Much closer the landscape is one of

confusion, as if the Almighty in the process of creation had been called away on urgent business and not yet returned to finish the task. Some regard this awesome scene as a wilderness of stones, other as the 'riddlin's of creation', while Samuel Crockett describes the view as a 'weird wild world, new and strange, not yet out of chaos – not yet approved of God'.

Immediately below the summit stands Loch Enoch, one of the numerous glacially carved lochs that glitter the countryside to the west, while beyond, the undulations of the Rhinns of Kells throw down a challenge to any red-blooded walker. It is all rough, tough, magnificent walking country of the first order.

The simplest return to Glen Trool is to retrace your steps, and in misty conditions this is the only safe route. On a clear day try descending The Merrick's east ridge, aiming for the southern edge of Loch Enoch (4), and from there following a fence/dyke to a gate in a forestry fence (5). Along this stretch, a profile of rock, where the fence is closest to the wall, has been given the name 'The Grey Man of Merrick' for fairly obvious reasons. From the gate go right for 200 metres/yards and then follow a fire break to a ford across Gloon Burn (6), continuing through forest to a path leading down to Culsharg, where the outward route is joined, and followed down to Glen Trool.

Benyellary and The Merrick viewed from Buchan Burn

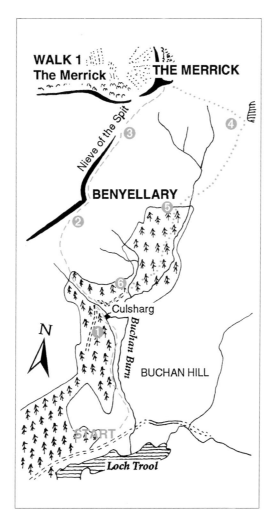

FACT FILE

Map OS Landranger 1:50 000 Series Sheet 77: Dalmellington to New Galloway
Harveys Walker's Map: Galloway Hills
Start/Finish Glen Trool GR 415805
Length 12 km (7.5 miles)
Walking time 5 hours
Difficulty Moderate, but plenty of uphill work

The Route in Brief

Start GR 415805. Signpost 'The Merrick Climb'; good path worsens and reaches Buchan Burn at gate. At next gate enter forest. Follow path to Culsharg shieling.
1 Keep L, climbing to broad forest track. Go R across bridge then L (sign.'Merrick'); climb out of forest. Follow path to gate in fence and dyke beyond.
2 Follow dyke N to Benyellary summit (cairn), then descend to Nieve of the Spit.
3 Take prominent path to The Merrick. In misty conditions proceed no further; retrace route to start. Variant finish: Descend E ridge to Loch Enoch.
4 Follow fence/dyke S, then SW to gate in forestry fence.
5 Follow fire break to Gloon Burn (ford).
6 Continue on forest path to Culsharg. Retrace outward route to start.

SHALLOCH ON MINNOCH

Shalloch on Minnoch is the most westerly Corbett, and Donald, in southern Scotland, lying southwest of Lochs Riecawr and Macaterick; it is regarded as the little finger of the Awful Hand range and may be climbed easily from the top of the Straiton and Bargrennan road. This approach involves tackling a northerly top first before reaching Shalloch on Minnoch. The walk described here starts rather nearer to Glen Trool village, and combines the ascent of Shalloch on Minnoch with that of Tarfessock to the south, which also features in Walk 3, when it is linked with Kirriereoch Hill. Virtually all the lower, westerly slopes of these hills are cloaked in forest, and any start involves dealing with woodland first. Easterly approaches, too, have their share of forest, but tend to be steeper and more abrupt. Wilderness, bog, granite, heather and, sometimes, more water than a body can stand, make these far hills of Galloway the province of the experienced hill-goer, well equipped in body and mind, a testing ground for anyone.

The walk begins from a convenient car park at Rowantree Junction, where David Bell, a local writer and cyclist is commemorated.

Rowantree Junction is a lonely spot, where once stood an inn and toll-house. Close by was the 'Murder Hole', a place where a pedlar's body was dumped. The two men responsible were later hanged for murder, and the event used by Samuel Rutherford Crockett (see reference in Walk 14) in his novel *The Raiders*, though at a different location, near the more wild-looking Loch Neldricken.

From the car park head up the road for a short distance until you can take the track down to Laglanny, then on a rough forest road following a burn to Shalloch on Minnoch Farm **(1)**. Continue past the farm, through a sheepfold and over a stile.

Stay with the Shalloch Burn, past the point where Knochlach Burn joins it, and cross the Shalloch Burn on a bridge of girders. It is worth noting at this point the force of water flowing down Knochlach Burn: towards the end of the walk you will need to cross it, and some idea of how difficult that might be can be gleaned from a moment's assessment now.

Remain with the Shalloch Burn until a tributary burn, Shiel Rig Burn (not named on the OS map) descends from the right through a fire break.

Follow the fire break upwards **(2)**, a wet affair as a rule, and eventually you break free of the forest, with the grassy west ridge of Shalloch on Minnoch before you, and posing no real difficulty to prevent you ultimately reaching the trig pillar on the summit **(3)**, with two cairns close by. The view from such an extreme and elevated vantage point takes in the Mourne Mountains, the fells of Lakeland, the Isle of Man, the Mull of Kintyre, the islands of Jura, Arran and Ailsa Craig in the Firth of Clyde: breathtaking, uplifting and immensely satisfying.

A return can be made by the outward route, of course, but the next stage of the walk described here parallels the top edge of the steep eastern slopes of Shalloch on Minnoch, southeast and south to reach a narrow col, the Nick of Carclach **(4)**. A fairly easy ascent of Tarfessock follows, its slopes rough and stony, dotted with granite outcrops and littered with light grey erratics. A prominent cairn of white quartzite boulders stands at the northern edge of Tarfessock's summit **(5)**, though the highest ground lies at the southern end.

This is all magnificent walking country, rough, untamed, much as God must have left it, and with an exhilarating feeling that makes the effort and trouble of reaching this far-flung corner of southern Scotland well worthwhile.

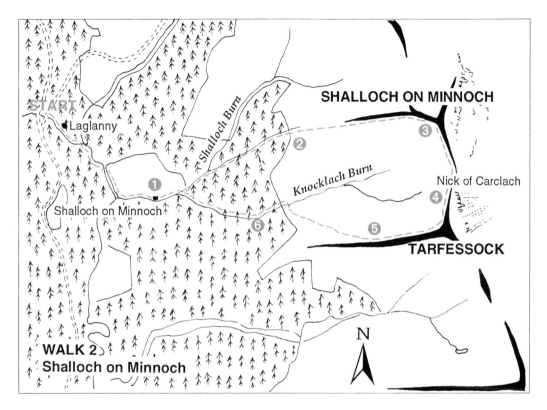

START

Laglanny

Shalloch Burn

SHALLOCH ON MINNOCH

①

②

③

Knocklach Burn

Nick of Carclach

④

Shalloch on Minnoch

⑥

⑤

TARFESSOCK

N

WALK 2
Shalloch on Minnoch

FACT FILE

Map OS Landranger 1:50 000 Series Sheet 77: Dalmellington to New Galloway
Harveys Walker's Map: Galloway Hills
Start/Finish Bell Memorial car park GR 353907
Length 13.5 km (8.5 miles)
Walking time 4–5 hours
Difficulty Fairly rough walking, typical of the Galloway Hills: not for inexperienced walkers

The Route in Brief

Start GR 353907. Follow road, then track, SE to Laglanny, then forest road by burn to Shalloch on Minnoch Farm.

1 Go through sheepfold and over stile. Follow Shalloch Burn NE, past Knochlach Burn junction. Cross on girder bridge. Follow burn to fire break where Shiel Rig Burn descends from R. Follow fire break upwards.

2 Once out of forest, head for Shalloch on Minnoch trig pillar.

3 Head SE and S to Nick of Carclach.

4 Ascend Tarfessock.

5 Head W, then NW to cross Knochlach Burn (cross higher if in spate).

6 Descend to Shalloch Burn girder bridge and retrace outward route to start.

The return from Tarfessock involves crossing the Knochlach Burn; if the burn is in spate, a crossing higher rather than lower in its course is advised. Either way, set off down the western slopes of Tarfessock, aiming north of west, for the upper edge of the forest, and crossing the burn wherever you feel you can do so comfortably, preferably without getting wet.

Once across the burn (6) descend to its confluence with Shalloch Burn, there moving up the Shalloch Burn to cross it by the girder bridge encountered earlier. Continue down to Shalloch on Minnoch Farm, taking the access road out to the starting point.

TARFESSOCK AND KIRRIEREOCH

Tarfessock and Kirriereoch Hill are the middle fingers of the Awful Hand range, and contribute enormously to the strong flavour of wilderness that characterises this limb of the Galloway Hills. Although Tarfessock was used as a line of descent from Shalloch on Minnoch, it combines equally well with Kirriereoch, using it in ascent this time, to give yet another satisfying, if energetic, circuit of these westerly heights. Both summits lie north of The Merrick, and overlook a tormented landscape of rocky hummocks, bog, extreme moorland and forest. They can be joined with Shalloch on Minnoch to give a long and demanding day, and one that will require two cars, if three miles of road walking at its end is to be avoided.

A picnic place just off the Bargrennan to Straiton road, near the Water of Minnoch, makes a convenient starting point. From it, follow a forest trail east to Kirriereoch Loch, and then north towards the farm, Kirriereoch. Before reaching the farm, go east once more, and continue to the point where the track crosses Pillow Burn **(1)**,

On the long ridge ascending to Tarfessock

ignoring both the track to Kirriemore (on the right) and that to Tarfessock (on the left). Over the Pillow Burn, cross a stile (fence) and pursue the track **(2)** as it climbs to its end about 200 metres/yards north of the Cross Burn bothy. There is a path down to the bothy, but ignore this for the time being; it will be used on the return leg.

Turn instead, northeast, through a fire break, climbing until well clear of the tress **(3)**, and from this point head straight up the slopes of Tarfessock's west ridge, passing a sizeable cairn (a useful marker) en route, before pulling on to its rough and stony summit.

This whole region is a fascinating place of study for geologists, who often find the underlying granite forcing upwards, contrasting with the quartz boulders, light grey erratics, and the darker sedimentary and metamorphic rocks of Tarfessock.

Kirriereoch lies imposingly to the south, and is reached by descending in a southeasterly direction **(4)**, to the broad and confusing ridge of Carmaddie Brae **(5)**, a gathering of outcrops and depressions, many filled with small lochans, some of which have acquired names, though none is of great size. It is here that geologists will be most in their element.

Ahead the steep slopes of Balminnoch Brae above Balminnoch Loch look rough and intimidating.

Continue down to a fence, crossed by a stile, and move slightly left to avoid the worst clutches of those Balminnoch screes by ascending grassy slopes to the summit.

The summit, near a large cairn, lies a couple of minutes walking south of a dyke in various stages of dilapidation. Nevertheless, it marks the regional boundary between Strathclyde to the north, and Dumfries and Galloway, and is a useful guide for the return stage of the walk. While the views from the top of Kirriereoch are not dissimilar to those from Tarfessock or Shalloch on Minnoch – wide, and far-ranging – it is the profile of The Merrick that will command most attention, displaying its rugged charms, and its best side, across the splendid corrie of Black Gairy.

To return, set off down the dyke **(6)** on Kirriereoch's grassy west ridge, until it changes direction, there leaving the dyke and continuing ahead to a prominent erratic, the Carnirock Stone. Here turn northwest and follow a line of iron fence posts **(7)** that lead to a stile across a fence, beyond which you can soon reach the Cross Burn bothy. From the bothy, you tackle Cross Burn by a nearby log bridge, climbing through forest to re-gain the outward route at the fire break used on the ascent of Tarfessock. Now retrace your steps to the Water of Minnoch picnic site.

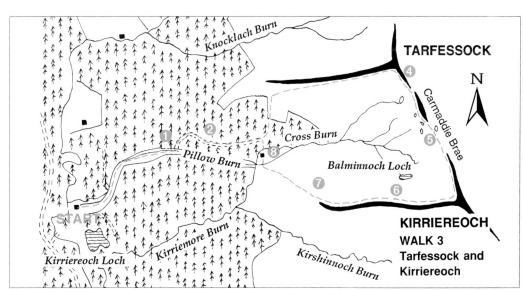

WALK 3
Tarfessock and Kirriereoch

FACT FILE

Map OS Landranger 1:50 000 Series Sheet 77: Dalmellington to New Galloway
Harveys Walker's Map: Galloway Hills
Start/Finish Car park and picnic place, Water of Minnoch. GR 359867
Length 16 km (10 miles)
Walking time 4½–5 hours
Difficulty Rough walking, not for inexperienced walkers, or less than clear conditions

The Route in Brief

Start GR 359867. Take forest trail E to Kirriereoch Loch, then go N. Before reaching farm turn E.
1 Continue on track, ignoring tracks to R and L. Cross Pillow Burn and stile, into forest.
2 Follow track to Cross Burn bothy path junction. Head NE following fenceline until it veers L.
3 Leave fenceline, heading R to Tarfessock (cairn en route).
4 Descend SE to Carmaddie Brae ridge.
5 Continue to stile, then move slightly L to avoid scree when climbing Kirriereoch.
6 Descend W ridge, following dyke until it changes direction. Head to prominent erratic (Carnirock Stone).
7 Turn NW following fence posts via stile to Cross Burn bothy.
8 Climb N, past Cross Burn bothy, to main path and retrace outward route to start.

MULLWHARCHAR BY GAIRLAND BURN

Centrally placed in a bleak wilderness where the awesome power of Nature is keenly felt, Mullwharchar is one of the most inaccessible of the Galloway Hills, and the ways that do lead to it are fraught with difficulty of the most tiring kind. The modest height of the summit (692m 2,270ft) is more than made up for in its rugged composition, and means, among other things, that Donald collectors must go where Corbett baggers need not tread. But anyone who feels that only the Highlands offer a challenge of note, should have a thrash at Mullwharchar.

The approach by the Gairland Burn begins in Glen Trool, and the first main objective the remote Loch Enoch. Gairland Burn proves to be a hanging valley, much like its neighbour, Buchan Burn, on the other side of Buchan Hill. First you must descend, past Bruce's Stone, to

Looking back to Loch Trool, from the start of Gairland Burn

cross Buchan Burn by the Earl of Galloway's bridge, along the rough trail that leads to Glenhead Farm. As you approach a small woodland of sessile oak, look for a sign pointing out a stile by means of which you follow a path (1) across the face of Buchan Hill to the Gairland Burn and Loch Valley. With a suddenness that can seem alarming the loveliness of Glen Trool is lost behind; ahead lies a wilderness that is testimony to the work of the massive ice sheets that once centred on the very spot for which you are heading.

Follow the path until it reaches the banks of the burn. At this point there is a ford, but ignore this and continue along its west bank to reach Loch Valley (2), and, a short way further on, a sheepfold alongside Mid Burn.

An intermittent path now runs on to Loch Neldricken, beside which is a spot known as the Murder Hole. The name derives from Crockett's novel *The Raiders*, though he transported the true Murder Hole, where a pedlar was murdered and his body dumped, from near Rowantree Junction on the Bargrennan to Straiton road, to this lonely spot – all perfectly acceptable literary licence.

As you approach Loch Neldricken a double row of stepping stones invites you to cross Mid Burn. Resist the temptation, and head for the northwestern edge of Loch Neldricken, and there cross a dyke before climbing the slight rise of Ewe

Rig. From the reed-lined banks of Loch Neldricken there is a daunting view of The Merrick, rising above an undulating landscape of tussock-covered moraine.

Continue to the left of diminutive Loch Arron (3) to another rise, Craig Neldricken. It is scarcely a mile from the Murder Hole to Craig Neldricken, but it seems considerably more.

Ahead now you see Loch Enoch, fringed with sandy bays and dotted with islands, its serrated northern shore forming the regional boundary between Strathclyde, to the north, and Dumfries and Galloway. A path, of sorts, works a way through thick tussock grass and the knolls of bare granite that comprise Craig Neldricken, to find a way around the eastern edge of Loch Enoch (4). Follow this, but leave it at the northeastern corner of the loch to head straight up the rough slopes of Mullwharchar to the summit cairn (5).

From such a central position, the view is especially fine both of The Merrick and its Awful Hand companions to the west, and of Corserine and Carlin's Cairn, to the east, beyond the boglands of the Silver Flowe. The great long loch stretching away to the north is Loch Doon, immortalised by Robert Burns in *Ye Banks and Braes o' Bonny Doon*.

If you have enjoyed the tussle this far, then turn round and head back. Alternatively, you could aim for the Little Spear **(6)**, just north of The Merrick, crossing Eglin Lane, and a short way further on a fence (by a stile). Follow the west bank of Loch Enoch **(7)** to a dyke and fence at the southwest corner, and continue along to the forest edge, due east of the summit of Benyellary. A few hundred metres/yards from Loch Enoch is a group of rocks called the 'Grey Man of Merrick'.

As you approach the forest **(8)** head for a gate a couple of hundred metres/yards away from the Loch Enoch fenceline, and beyond it gain access to a fire break by means of which you reach a ford across Gloon Burn. Press on, still in the forest, to a forest track **(9)** that leads to a waymarked track 'The Merrick Climb' leading down to Culsharg **(10)**, an old shieling. From here

follow the obvious path out, through woodland, and down to Buchan Burn with its delightful cascades, finally reaching civilisation back at the Glen Trool car park.

The Grey Man of Merrick gazes out to the domed summit of Benyellary

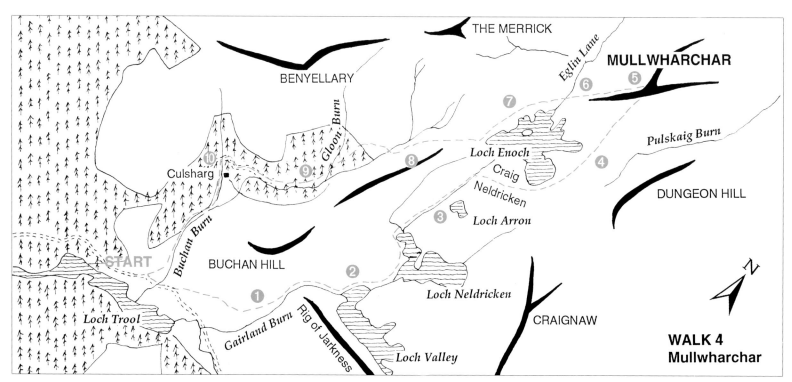

THE MERRICK

MULLWHARCHAR

BENYELLARY

Eglin Lane

Gloon Burn

Pulskaig Burn

Loch Enoch

Craig Neldricken

Culsharg

DUNGEON HILL

Loch Arron

Buchan Burn

BUCHAN HILL

Loch Neldricken

START

CRAIGNAW

Loch Trool

Gairland Burn

Rig of Jarkness

Loch Valley

**WALK 4
Mullwharchar**

Map OS Landranger 1:50 000 Series Sheet 77:
Dalmellington to New Galloway
Harveys Walker's Map: Galloway Hills
Start/Finish Glen Trool GR 415805
Length 18 km (11.25 miles)
Walking time 6–7 hours
Difficulty A tough, demanding and strenuous walk,
across remote, wild and rugged terrain that is invariably
wet. Burn crossing will be necessary

The Route in Brief

Start GR 415805. Descend past Bruce's Stone and
cross Buchan Burn. Take farm trail. At oak wood, look for
stile sign.
1 Over stile, follow path along W bank of burn to Loch
Valley.
2 Through sheepfold, then follow intermittent path to NW
edge of Loch Neldricken. Cross dyke and climb Ewe Rig.
3 Go past Loch Arron to Craig Neldricken. A vague path
leads to the E edge of Loch Enoch.
4 Leave path at NE corner of loch and ascend
Mullwharchar.
5 Head SW from summit.
6 Aim for Little Spear, crossing Eglin Lane and stile.
7 Follow W bank of Loch Enoch to dyke and fence at SW
corner.
8 Continue to forest edge. Take gate 200m from
fenceline, then follow fire break SW.
9 Reach forest track, then waymarked track ('The
Merrick Climb') down to Culsharg.
10 Follow clear path S back to start.

CRAIGLEE AND THE RIG OF JARKNESS

How could anyone resist walking on a mountain ridge with a name like the Rig of Jarkness? Despite its mysterious name the ridge is little more than a fine, if strenuous approach to a relatively minor summit, Craiglee. Together they provide a short excursion to a superb viewpoint set amidst the turmoil of moorland and granite islands that lies at the heart of the Galloway Hills. There is a straightforward approach from Craigencallie, taking a forestry road to Loch Dee, beyond White Laggan, and tackling Craiglee's southern ridge from there, the route of our descent. From Glen Trool, however, the ascent of Craiglee is frequently thwarted by the state of Gairland Burn, which can often be an insurmountable obstacle to progress. But what the southern approach lacks in finesse, the circuit described here makes up for in quality, especially if you enjoy a modicum of effort in your day.

From the Glen Trool car park, set off down the rough track beyond that leads over the Buchan Burn, and then take a signposted path across the flank of Buchan Hill, heading for Gairland Burn and Loch Valley. As you go, so you leave behind the sylvan loveliness of Glen Trool and exchange it for the savage grandeur of mountain wilderness at its rugged best. As the path approaches Gairland Burn **(1)**, a stretch of bright green grass marks the location of a ford across the burn. The burn, however, is often in spate, and if you are unable to cross, you should contemplate modifying your plans and tackling Walk 4 instead.

· Once across the burn the steep western end of the Rig of Jarkness rises above, a rugged

Craiglee: across Loch Dee, with Craignaw and Dungeon Hill beyond

concoction of grass and granite. Climb this and start along the many undulations of the ridge **(2)**, with views left of Loch Valley, and right of the seldom-seen Long Loch of Glenhead and Round Loch of Glenhead. Higher up the ridge, the ground becomes predominantly rocky, with granite slabs and outcrops littering the landscape.

This approach from the northwest is protected by a collection of small lochans and boggy ground, where there is little vestige of a path, and by the impressive rocky face of the Clints of the Buss (not named on the OS map). The summit of Craiglee, visually in a most commanding position, is marked by a trig pillar.

The land that you see around Craiglee inspired the novelist John Buchan, who used his vision of it in his classic thriller *The Thirty Nine Steps*.

The simplest line of return is to move off in a southerly direction **(3)**, losing a little height before swinging down the southwest ridge, aiming to meet the Southern Upland Way at a dyke **(4)** across the col near the head of Glenhead Burn. The col has clear traces of being sculpted by the immense glaciers that covered the whole of this region 10,000 years ago.

Once the Way is reached, follow it west on a good path heading into woodland on a broad forest trail. Before long turn right down a path **(5)**, boggy in places, following Shiel Burn, a tributary of Glenhead Burn, and later keep along the south bank of the burn to a dyke, beyond which you cross the burn by a bridge **(6)**, and turn left, following the track back to the Glen Trool car park.

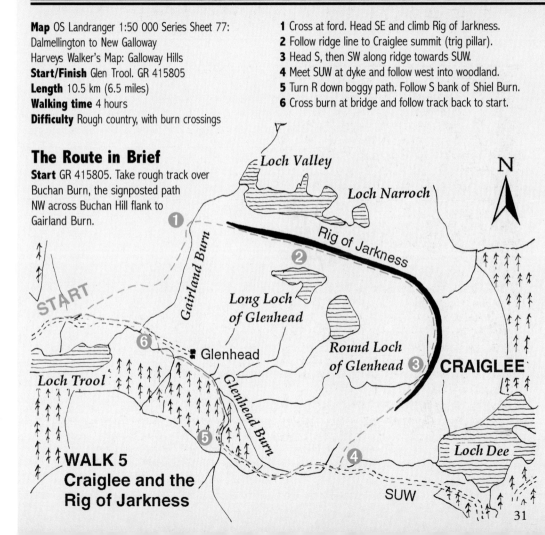

FACT FILE

Map OS Landranger 1:50 000 Series Sheet 77: Dalmellington to New Galloway
Harveys Walker's Map: Galloway Hills
Start/Finish Glen Trool. GR 415805
Length 10.5 km (6.5 miles)
Walking time 4 hours
Difficulty Rough country, with burn crossings

1 Cross at ford. Head SE and climb Rig of Jarkness.
2 Follow ridge line to Craiglee summit (trig pillar).
3 Head S, then SW along ridge towards SUW.
4 Meet SUW at dyke and follow west into woodland.
5 Turn R down boggy path. Follow S bank of Shiel Burn.
6 Cross burn at bridge and follow track back to start.

The Route in Brief

Start GR 415805. Take rough track over Buchan Burn, the signposted path NW across Buchan Hill flank to Gairland Burn.

Loch Valley

Loch Narroch

Rig of Jarkness

Gairland Burn

START

Long Loch of Glenhead

Round Loch of Glenhead

CRAIGLEE

Glenhead

Loch Trool

Glenhead Burn

Loch Dee

WALK 5 Craiglee and the Rig of Jarkness

SUW

N

MEIKLE MILLYEA, LITTLE MILLYEA AND DARROU

Meikle Millyea is the most southerly of the Donalds in the long undulating ridge of the Rhinns of Kells, and provides a good view northwards to Corserine, the highest summit of this linear range. The summit is often combined with Corserine in a fine circuit from Forrest Lodge, but is given here with two lesser hills, that share a distinctive profile viewed across Clatteringshaws Loch.

The walk sets off from a parking space a short distance beyond Craigencallie, reached by an attractive minor road that starts just by the Clatteringshaws dam, signposted: 'Craignell'. Near the northern end of the loch the road enters the forest, and passes beneath an electricity power line before swinging north just after crossing Craigencallie Lane. As Craigencallie Lane is approached, there is a fine view directly ahead of Millfore. On reaching the entrance to Craigencallie, leave the metalled road for a rough side track on the right leading down to the parking space.

Begin by crossing the stile to the right of a gate, and follow a broad forest trail that plods along sedately for just under a mile, with the bulk of Darrou first ahead, then on your right across the River Dee (Black Water of Dee). At a junction of trails, turn right (1), and descend to cross the Dee. Directly up river the distant view is of rugged Craiglee.

Continue beyond the bridge, and bear left, having shared the route with the Southern Upland Way for 250 metres/yards. The route presses on pleasantly, passing McWhanns Stone, a split boulder on the left, close by Curnelloch Burn. A short way further on, the more pronounced of two forest trails branches left, while we pursue an equally broad, but less well-used trail, to the right (2). This branch continues deeper into the forest for another 2 km (1.25 miles), before grinding boggily to an end. Some

Meikle Millyea, viewed across Clatteringshaws Loch

33

Rough ground between Meikle Millyea and Little Millyea

way before its end, however, leave the trail at a prominent fire break, that splits the forest left and right. This occurs not long after the wide clearing occupied by a side stream flowing down the southern flank of Straverron Hill, though it is not immediately obvious. But it is the only significant fire break, rather less obvious on the right, and with a large boulder in the middle of the break down to the left of the track. The arrow-straight directness of the break at this point, with the craggy rise of Craigeazle as a natural target, confirms you have the right place.

Once satisfied that you are where you should be, leave the forest trail, and after a few boggy strides, climb the fire break on the right (3), through which a vague and wet path ascends. The forest trail was the end of the easy going. What remains is quite demanding, and characteristic of these wild hills of Galloway. Go no further unless you are well equipped, in all senses, for wild country walking.

The climb through the fire break is short, and once at the top, with a low wall of rocks on the left, press on ahead, climbing over trackless ground in a series of ledges, each providing improving views to the west of Mullwharchar and Craignaw, with the Merrick Hills (the Awful Hand) beyond. Press on uphill quite energetically to cross unmarked Straverron Hill, a stretch with little to aid you other than a good sense of direction, or a northeasterly heading.

As the gradient eases, Meikle Millyea creeps into view across a vast bowl of heather and tussock grass, where golden plover taunt you, and grouse explode from beneath your feet.

Avoid the dip that lies on a direct line for the summit by moving a little to the left, generally keeping to the highest ground (4). Cross an intervening fence, and continue ascending towards Meikle Millyea, below which a rash of small boulders appears, with a large cairn above. The cairn, a short distance west of a dilapidated wall, marks the highest ground, though the trig pillar and cairn lies to the northeast, along the wall. The summit trig is a restful place, high above Loch Dungeon, and with a fine view of the continuing ridge, over Milldown and Millfire to Corserine.

Unless in search of solitude and hard work, retreat the same way. Otherwise, return along the wall, passing the high point, and follow the wall southwards (5) along the boundary of the Galloway Forest Park. Some slight detours may be necessary to avoid wet ground, but as a rule stay close to the wall, until, directly below Little Millyea, it turns southeast to head for the Garrary Burn. From this point head for Little Millyea, climbing across more rough ground, with compensating views opening up of Clatteringshaws Loch. Any belief, between leaving the wall and ultimately reaching the Southern Upland Way again below Darrou, that you might be following a path is a triumph of optimism over reality!

The summit of Little Millyea is marked by a large cairn, just off the high point, and is a welcome resting point. Southeast, across the loch, rises another tough hill, Cairnsmore of Dee (Walk 14), while to the southwest Lamachan Hill and Curleywee are prominent attendants of Loch Dee.

Leave Little Millyea in a southwesterly direction, heading for Darrou, with another swathe of rough terrain in between with which to contend. The slopes of Darrou, unlike those you have left behind, are littered with small erratic boulders, remnants of the last Ice Age.

Something of a path, a wet one, continues southwest from Darrou to a vague col (6), near which it is necessary to move half left, heading for an unseen quarry near the Dee bridge. By aiming for the visible forest trail beyond, you will set yourself off in the right direction, sufficiently to adjust easily once the Dee bridge comes into view. A grassy, heathery forest ride leads down to the quarry, maintaining the demand for effort until the very end. Once the forest trail is reached, turn right (7) and then left to the Dee bridge, and a welcome, and by comparison, gentle stroll back to Craigencallie.

WALK 6
Meikle Millyea,
Little Millyea
and Darrou

FACT FILE

Map OS Landranger 1:50 000 Series Sheet 77: Dalmellington to New Galloway
Harveys Walker's Map: Galloway Hills
Start/Finish Car park near Craigencallie GR 503782
Length 13 km (8 miles)
Walking time 4½–5 hours
Difficulty Easy forest walks to start, followed by stiff uphill section, and very tiring descent over moorland to the two lower summits

The route in brief

Start GR 503782. Cross stile to R of a gate. Follow forest trail to junction.
1 Turn R and descend to cross Dee. Bear L beyond bridge.
2 At fork take R branch. Follow trail until fire break crosses it.
3 Climb R. Continue over trackless ground across Straverron Hill.
4 Head E for Meikle Millyea summit, keeping to higher ground and crossing intervening fence.
5 Follow wall S from summit. Keep to wall until it heads SE below Little Millyea. Climb Little Millyea (cairn), then head SW to Darrou.
6 Head SW to vague col. Aim for forest trail (half L), then down to Dee bridge (quarry).
7 Turn R on forest trail and return to start.

CORSERINE AND THE RHINNS OF KELLS

Anyone who has hitherto been plundering the summits to the west of the Rhinns of Kells, battling with bog, rugged moorland, rocky summits and gushing mountain streams, will find immense relief among the Rhinns of Kells. And though not entirely devoid of rough going, this outstanding ridge walk unfolds, once you get on it, along a splendid, undulating grassy promenade.

Corserine, the highest of the range, is also the second highest hill in Galloway, and lies midway between Loch Doon and Loch Dee. Most of the lower slopes of the hill are cloaked in forest, concealing quite a broad ridge, almost five miles from the floating bog country of the Silver Flowe to the Polharrow Burn. Only the highest ground, however, pokes above the forest, and offers the walker a superb walk with few obstacles to striding progress.

A very long approach can be made from Craigencallie, west of Clatteringshaws Loch, by using the ascent of Meikle Millyea, described in Walk 6, and continuing along the ridge, northeastwards from there, passing over Milldown, and Millfire before finally pulling on to Corserine. The walk described here is from the east, along the Polharrow Glen, and begins from a car park at the end of the public road just south of Forrest Lodge, where a bridge crosses the Polharrow Burn.

Take the road on the south side of Polharrow Burn running west to Fore Bush **(1)**, and through plantations, keeping left at a junction to the southern shore of Loch Harrow, which was once popular with curlers. From near the end of the loch, follow the route westwards through a fire break **(2)**, and climb beyond the forest on to the rocky slopes of North Gairy Top (681m) **(3)**. Once North Gairy Top is reached, a good proportion of the hard work is over, as you follow a long, gently rising ridge to the smooth grassy dome of Corserine. The summit is marked by a trig pillar and cairn.

Corserine means the 'crossing of the ridges', and if you look at the map you'll see why, with branching arms reaching north to Carlin's Cairn, northeast along Polmaddy Gairy and Craigrine, southeast (the line of ascent), south along the main ridge, and west to Meikle Craigtarson. With only The Merrick achieving greater height, the view from the top of Corserine is of breathtaking ruggedness, bright-eyed lochs, and rolling forests.

Strong walkers, or those planning on returning by the outward route, should consider taking in the next summit to the north, Carlin's Cairn, in many ways the most distinctive and shapely of the Kells Range. An easy ridge descends northwards to a 97m (300ft ascent). Corserine, of course is both a Corbett and a Donald, but poor Carlin's Cairn has somehow come off badly in the claim for Donald's attention, being classed as no more than a top of Corserine, while the lower Milldown, with virtually the same amount of re-ascent makes the list because it is further away!

Carlin's Cairn's claim to fame, however, devolves upon its massive summit cairn, which legend attributes to a miller's wife, who aided Robert the Bruce during his fugitive time among the Galloway Hills, for which she received a grant of land in the Polmaddy Glen.

South from Corserine, the ridge runs on to the shaly tops of Millfire and Milldown. Just below the top of Corserine, the March Burn, flowing westwards, is the highest point of the River Dee. Stay along the ridge, heading south-southeast **(4)**, an uncomplicated expedition, that encounters a dyke on Milldown **(5)**, which you should follow up the easy slopes **(6)** of Meikle Millyea.

At the lowest point of the ridge (628m) there is a cairn that marks the crossing point of an old

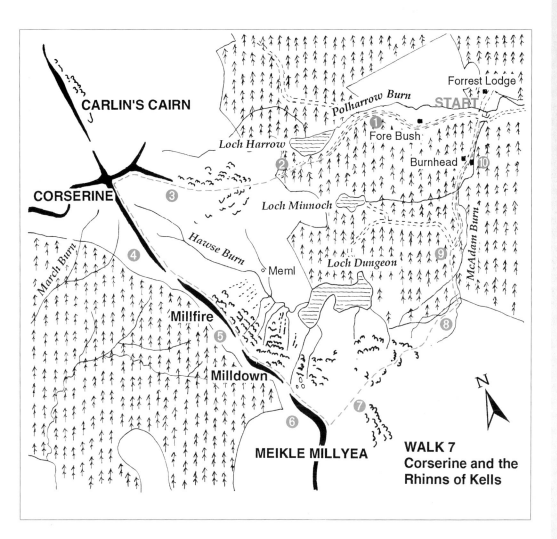

CARLIN'S CAIRN

CORSERINE

Polharrow Burn

Forrest Lodge

START

① Fore Bush

Loch Harrow

② Burnhead ⑩

③

Loch Minnoch

Hawse Burn

March Burn

④

• Meml

McAdam Burn

Loch Dungeon

Millfire

⑤

⑨

Milldown

⑧

⑦

⑥

MEIKLE MILLYEA

N

**WALK 7
Corserine and the
Rhinns of Kells**

Map OS Landranger 1:50 000 Series Sheet 77:
Dalmellington to New Galloway
Harveys Walker's Map: Galloway Hills (part)
Start/Finish Forrest Lodge, along Polharrow Burn
GR 552863
Length 15.5 km (9.5 miles)
Walking time 5 hours
Difficulty Easy, but exposed, along the main ridge; a
steep descent and forest fire breaks at the end

The route in brief

Start GR 552863. Follow road W to Fore Bush.
1 Go through plantation, keeping left at path junction,
to S shore of Loch Harrow.
2 Beyond loch follow fire break W.
3 Climb North Gairy Top, then follow gentle ridge to
Corserine (trig pillar). Possibly visit Carlin's Cairn to N.
4 Head SSE along ridge.
5 Cross Millfire to meet dyke on Milldown.
6 Follow dyke SSE up Meikle Millyea.
7 From N end of summit follow NE dyke towards Meikle
Lump.
8 Continue along dyke to McAdam's Burn.
9 Follow fire break N into forest to forest trail, then go
R to Burnhead.
10 Return to start via forest trail.

and now indistinct track linking the Back Hill of Bush and Fore Bush, a route that was the only means of escape for the shepherd and his family at Back Hill. When his wife died, the funeral party conveying her across the hills was caught by a blizzard, and was forced to leave the body high on the hill for three days before being able to continue the journey.

Some way below to the east, a memorial at the foot of the Hawse Burn, enclosed within a circular dyke, commemorates the death of a shepherd.

Near a dyke junction, at the northern end of Meikle Millyea, there is a large cairn and trig pillar, but the highest ground lies further south, and is marked by a cairn of similar proportions a short distance west of the dyke. From it, return to the northern end of the summit, and follow a dyke **(7)** northeastwards towards Meikle Lump, with the spread of Loch Dungeon before you. Keep following the dyke to the forest boundary at the head of McAdam's Burn **(8)**. A fire break **(9)** then leads you down into the forest, keeping within the burn glen to reach a forest trail **(10)**, which you should follow, right, to Burnhead, beyond which lies the car park near Forrest Lodge.

Cairnsgarroch (R) and the Rhinns of Kells

CORAN OF PORTMARK, MEAUL AND CAIRNSGARROCH

The Kells range is the name usually given to two linear groups of hills which to the south of Corserine are known as the Rhinns of Kells, and to the north, the Rhinns of Carsphairn. In this latter group, the most northerly summit of note is Coran of Portmark overlooking Loch Doon. To the south of Coran of Portmark, an excellent grassy ridge occasionally punctuated by low rocks leads on over a minor top, Bow, and then to Meaul and Carlin's Cairn, before reaching Corserine. This walk, however, leaves the north–south ridge at Meaul, and swings round to visit Cairngarroch before heading back to the Garryhorn Burn.

The walk begins from a spot known as the Green Well of Scotland, where the A713 crosses the Water of Deugh, not far northwest of Carsphairn. Just beyond the bridge a side road

The ruins of mine workings lead up to the grassy heights of Coran of Portmark and Bow

leads to Garryhorn Farm, but there is no room to park or manoeuvre along this road, so park alongside the A713. The road in crosses Carsphairn Lane before reaching Garryhorn, and continues ultimately to the former mining site at Woodhead, which served as the base for lead and silver mining, principally between 1838 and 1873. It is a scene of desolation now, but once engaged more than 300 souls in the arduous business of working galena ore.

Just beyond Garryhorn Farm keep right along the main track **(1)**, heading for an old chimney where the greatest extent of mine remains, most reduced to their foundations, can still be seen. Keep going to the topmost mine building **(2)**, and head for a gate through a dyke about 100 metres/ yards to the left. Beyond the dyke, cross a rough pasture to a gate in a fenceline on the right, and then follow indistinct vehicle tracks in the grassy flanks of Knockower Hill, keeping well below the summit (unless you want to go there), but unavoidably meeting a stretch of marshy ground.

As you ascend Coran of Portmark **(3)**, the vehicle track becomes more pronounced, but near the summit darts away to the left. When it does, leave it and head for the summit cairn. Away to the west, afforested slopes spill down to Loch

Doon, beyond which new plantations flow on to Carrick Lane and Eglin Lane. To the south, Carlin's Cairn rises beyond Meaul, itself a forerunner of the highest of the range, Corserine.

Close by the summit on Coran of Portmark there is a fence, and a good path along the top of the broad ridge **(4)**. Both will lead you on to the next top, Bow, which in spite of its modest height, has three distinct tops squabbling for supremacy, the north (the winner) and south each having their own cairn. The going underfoot is short turf, and in winter, on a clear, crisp day makes for speedy progress.

From Bow, stay close by the fence, perhaps crossing it first to touch the shapely summit cairn. Gradually the ground drops to a shallow col with a small lochan, rising gently, as a dyke approaches the fence from the left, up the gathering grounds of Garryhorn Burn. To the west of the fence a standing stone commemorates John Dempster, a Covenanter, who was shot here. As you approach the top of the hill, the fence bends to the east. If you stay with it you will meet a dyke **(5)**, which can be followed southwest to the summit. Alternatively, on a clear day, simply head for the top.

Meaul has a grassy north ridge, rising to a

41

Meaul and Bow, at the head of Garryhorn Burn

bouldery summit surmounted by a trig pillar, but more impressive is the full length view it holds of Loch Doon to the north.

The return journey from Meaul leaves the north–south ridge. Follow the dyke descending the eastern slopes of the hill **(6)** to meet once more the fence from Bow, and continue alongside it to the col below Cairnsgarroch. On the way down you may notice three chair-shaped stones near the top of Garryhorn Burn, at a spot known as the King's Well; traditionally it is here that Robert the Bruce paused to quench his thirst. Not far away are the Lumps of Garryhorn, fine examples of glacial moraine. From the col climb easily **(7)** to the small cairn, south of the dyke, that marks the summit of Cairnsgarroch.

From Cairnsgarroch, go to a tall cairn, northeast of the highest point, and press on down the northeastern slopes **(8)**, guided by a couple of prominent cairns, but to all intents and purposes without the benefit of a path. Lower down you encounter an electric fence that you can cross by a gate. From the gate another electric fence runs out to a distinctive sheepfold, which, as you descend from Cairnsgarroch, will help with the navigation, but be sure to use the gate to cross the electric fence, which carries high voltages.

Once through the gate, ignore the fence heading for the sheepfold, and turn left on to a grassy vehicle track, passing to the north of Craighit Hill, then swinging round to a gate through another fence **(9)**. Beyond the gate, leave the track and head for a dyke on the left. Pass through this dyke, also by a gate, and on to a bridge spanning Garryhorn Burn, beyond which you can easily reach the outward track, there turning right to walk out, past Garryhorn Farm **(10)**, to the A713.

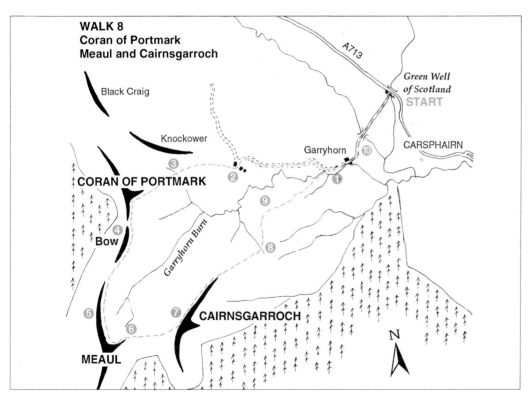

WALK 8
Coran of Portmark
Meaul and Cairnsgarroch

Black Craig

Knockower

③

CORAN OF PORTMARK

②

④

Bow

⑤

⑥

⑦

MEAUL

CAIRNSGARROCH

Garryhorn Burn

⑨

⑧

A713

Green Well of Scotland
START

Garryhorn

⑩

①

CARSPHAIRN

N

FACT FILE

Map OS Landranger 1:50 000 Series Sheet 77: Dalmellington to New Galloway
Harveys Walker's Map: Galloway Hills (part)
Start/Finish A713, Green Well of Scotland; room to park off road near bridge GR 556945
Length 16 km (10 miles)
Walking time 5½–6 hours
Difficulty Very undulating and tiring, but generally easy walking

The route in brief

Start GR 556945. Take side road SW to Garryhorn Farm.
1 Keep R along main track towards chimney and mine ruins.
2 From top building head for gate in dyke 100m to L. Cross pasture to gate in fence, then follow vehicle track to Knockower Hill slopes.
3 Ascend Coran of Portmark, heading for summit cairn.
4 From summit follow fence and good ridge-path S to Bow.
5 Stay with fence, then dyke, to Meaul summit.
6 Descend E, following dyke to fence. Follow fence to col below Cairnsgarroch.
7 Head NE and ascend Cairnsgarroch.
8 From cairn NE of summit, descend NE towards cairns. Cross high-voltage electric fence by gate. Ignore fence heading towards sheepfold and turn L on to grassy vehicle track passing N of Craighit Hill.
9 Track swings round NE to gate in fence. Beyond gate leave track and head for dyke on L. Pass through dyke gate and cross Garryhorn Burn bridge.
10 Retrace outward route to start.

43

LOCH DEE, WHITE LAGGAN AND CURLEYWEE

On those fine days when summer and winter behave as they should, the sight of Loch Dee as you round the northern end of Cairngarroch, set against the hunky bulk of Craiglee, is breathtaking, and sure to rouse anyone's spirit to joy.

How far you go with this walk is for you to decide. As far as Loch Dee, you follow a straightforward forest trail, and can leave it at that. To reach Curleywee, you take on a steep and rugged ascent, in the arena of effort much rewarded.

From the Craigencallie car park used at the start of Walk 6, cross the nearby stile and take the forest trail that heads for the prominent rise of Darrou. Later it swings round to parallel the as yet unseen River Dee. At a junction of trails **(1)**, keep left, and walk on steadily, with little effort, until Loch Dee eases into view **(2)**. As you go, Meikle Millyea and then Corserine fill the retrospective view, with yet more rugged heights, Mullwharchar, Dungeon Hill and Craignaw, set

ready for combat against them across the vast bogland known as the Silver Flowe. This is undoubtedly one of the most rugged landscapes in southern Scotland, and geologically significant as an important centre of ice accumulation. The effect on the land form is especially noticeable along the Silver Flowe and north of Curleywee, where shallow hollows were gouged from the underlying granite to form ragged-edged, half-finished lochans in profusion.

At an admirable vantage point overlooking Loch Dee the family of R. D. Borthwick (1915–1989), a Dumfries doctor for 34 years, have placed a bench to his memory, which on a warm and sunny day proves to be a very real obstacle to further progress. Walkers not bound for Curleywee's craggy top, may elect to call a halt at this point, and, when suitably refreshed by the outstanding scenery of loch, mountain and moorland, set off back to Craigencallie.

Those heading for Curleywee should continue along the forest trail, leaving it at the southern end of a loop, immediately on crossing the White Laggan Burn **(3)**. Go left alongside the burn on a

wet path that soon moves away from the burn and rises easily to White Laggan bothy. Press on southwards along an old cart track, following the line of White Laggan Burn, until a deviation, right, at the col, the Loup of Laggan **(4)**, allows you to climb the steep slopes to the col between Bennan Hill and Curleywee. Suddenly, ahead, across the Penkiln Burn the twin peaks of Larg Hill and Lamachan Hill spring into view above intervening forest, continuing the pronounced ruggedness that typifies these hills.

Northwards the way to Curleywee, without a doubt one of the finest peaks in southern Scotland, lies along a broad ridge **(5)**, and is protected by stretches of boggy ground, a wall, a collection of tiny lochans, a ring of black scree, and an array of rock outcrops that set the summit apart from the grassy slopes around it. The view, when the summit is finally reached, is breathtaking, embracing the Kells and Dungeon ranges, The Merrick, all the Cairnsmore hills – Dee, Fleet and Carsphairn – and many more. Ample reward for the stiff pull up from White Laggan.

Walkers wanting a more direct approach can follow the Well Burn, keeping to its northern side, straight up the hillside from close by White Laggan bothy, a demanding option that also serves as an alternative way down. The going, not surprisingly, is steep and rough, in either direction. Less effort might be expended by ·retracing your steps.

Snow-capped Curleywee from the Southern Upland Way

FACT FILE

Map OS Landranger: 1:50 000 Series Sheet 77: Dalmellington to New Galloway
Harveys Walker's Map: Galloway Hills
Start/Finish Car park near Craigencallie
GR 503782
Length 17 km (10.5 miles)
Walking time Loch Dee: 2 hours:
Curleywee: 4½–5 hours
Difficulty Easy as far as White Laggan, rough uphill to Curleywee

The route in brief

Start GR 503782. Cross stile and take forest trail N towards Darrou.

1 Keep L at junction; approach Loch Dee.
2 Follow forest trail SW to S end of loop. Leave trail immediately after crossing White Laggan Burn.
3 Go L alongside burn. Path rises to White Laggan bothy. Head S on cart track.
(**Alternative route** Climb to Curleywee summit direct from White Laggan bothy.)
4 At Loup of Laggan climb R to col between Bennan Hill and Curleywee.
5 Head N along broad ridge to Curleywee summit.
6 Retrace route to start.

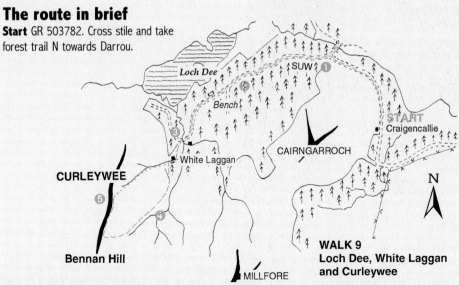

WALK 9
Loch Dee, White Laggan and Curleywee

45

MILLFORE AND CAIRNGARROCH

Strong walkers could combine Millfore at least, with Curleywee, Lamachan Hill and Largs Hill, linking them by the col at the Loup of Laggan, but it is more usual to tackle Millfore by itself, or, as here, with its northern companion, Cairngarroch, in a less demanding day.

The walk begins from Craigencallie, reached along the minor road leaving the Queen's Way (A712) near the dam of Clatteringshaws Loch (signposted 'Craignell'). Approaching Craigencallie leave the metalled road for a pot-holed track on the right leading down to a car park at the start of the forest trail to Loch Dee. Just before reaching the car park, look for a rickety wooden gate on the left of the track, through which the walk begins.

Go through the gate, crossing a small enclosure to a collapsed wall, and then bearing right to reach and pass through another wall. Go left along this second wall beneath the broken crags of Craigencallie for a short distance, until directly behind Craigencallie House and here start ascending the broken ground leading steeply to Cairngarroch.

There is a tradition that Robert the Bruce, while hiding from the English, was sheltered by a widow and her three sons somewhere among the wild hills around Glen Trool, and rewarded her with a grant of land. Whether this was at Craigencallie (*the old wife's crag*), is not clear, but it closely ties in with a tradition that three sons, Murdoch, McKie and McClurg, all by different fathers, and living with their widowed mother, wanted to join Bruce's forces, so he set them an archery test, requiring each to shoot one of three ravens on the wing. Murdoch was successful, McClurg not so, missing his bird, while McKie brought down the remaining two birds with one arrow.

Cairngarroch **(1)** is a stony mound, ringed in its lower reaches with bracken and heather through which sheep traces have evidently been used by walkers to find a way to the top. As a vantage point, Cairngarroch is particularly fine, especially northwards across the floating bog of the Silver Flowe into the lands known as the Dungeon of Buchan.

From the summit descend in a southwesterly direction to a shallow col, the Nick of Rushes, and start aiming for the distant crags of Millfore, crossing a fence en route, and keeping east of Cairnbaber and a couple of small lochans **(2)**. The terrain is knobbly and frequently wet, but most of the worst stretches can be avoided. Another fence in a poor state of repair is encountered just below Millfore's summit, beyond which untidy slopes lead to the summit trig pillar, and proof that Millfore is very much a loner, standing rather detached from the other Galloway Hills, but with outstanding views of Lamachan, Cairnsmore of Fleet, the Dungeon and Kells ranges, and northwest to The Merrick.

Leave the summit, heading southeast down the ridge, Kirkloch **(3)**, and aiming for a wide gap in the forest below. The going continues rough and undulating, and direction is aided by the presence of two large cairns. Press on into the gap to reach a forest track immediately below Poultrybuie Hill, which should be followed left **(4)** (generally northwards) to rejoin the Craigencallie road about half a mile south of the car park.

An alternative descent from Millfore, extending the whole walk to about nine miles and the walking time closer to five hours, heads for the White Lochan of Drigmorn, clearly seen to the west. The best approach is to keep to the high ground as much as possible, setting off southwest

Millfore, from Bennan Hill

to a small cairn above the crags of Red Gairy (shown but not named on the 1:50 000 map), and from there circling north and west to pass to the south of the lochan.

The remains of a stone building on the lochan's northern shore date from a time when curling was in fashion as a winter sport. Those curlers would have reached the White Lochan of Drigmorn not by the route given here, but by the old cart track running up White Laggan Burn to the Loup of Laggan. The scene, no doubt the very same that found its way on to countless Christmas greetings cards, must have been memorable, and the games, at such a chilly elevation, enlivened by the judicious partaking of a fine malted whisky.

The continuing descent runs on westwards, first passing north of a smaller lochan, the Black Loch, before reaching the Loup of Laggan **(5)**. Here turn right, northwards, and set off down to the White Laggan bothy **(6)**, beyond which Loch Dee, Craiglee and the distant slopes of Corserine make a splendid backdrop.

On reaching the main forest trail **(7)**, here used by the Southern Upland Way, turn right, for a relaxed return to the car park at Craigencallie.

Millfore (R) and the rugged slopes of Cairngarroch, viewed from Curleywee

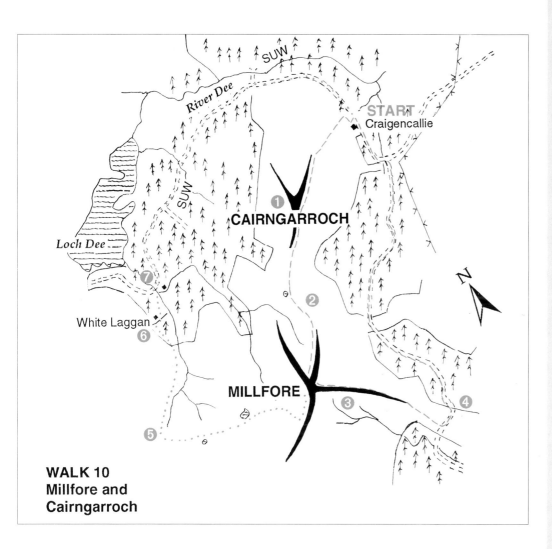

**WALK 10
Millfore and
Cairngarroch**

Map OS Landranger 1:50 000 Series Sheet 77:
Dalmellington to New Galloway
Harveys Walker's Map: Galloway Hills
Start/Finish Car park near Craigencallie. GR 503782
Length 10.5 km (6.5 miles)
Walking time 3½–4 hours
Difficulty A moderate walk over characteristically
rough terrain

The route in brief

Start GR 503782. Take wooden gate on L just before
car park. Cross enclosure to wall, bear R through
another wall then L to rear of Craigencallie House.
Ascend Cairngarroch.
1 Descend SW to Nick of the Rushes.
2 Aim SW for Millfore; cross fence and keep E of
Cairnbaber and lochans. Cross another fence just
below summit of Millfore. From summit head SE down
Kirkloch ridge.
3 Aim for gap in forest via two large cairns. Meet forest
track below Poultrybuie Hill.
4 Head L, following track through forest back to start.
(**Alternative route** From Millfore head W towards
White Lochan of Drigmorn, keeping to high ground via
cairn to SW, to reach Loup of Laggan.
5 Turn R. Head N to White Laggan bothy.
6 Continue to main forest trail (SUW).
7 Follow SUW to start.

LARG HILL AND LAMACHAN HILL

These two summits rise above Glen Trool, from where they may be conveniently ascended, and are the two westernmost summits of the Minnigaff Hills. Combining the two in one outing makes an excellent circuit of good-quality walking, though a fair measure of it, once beyond the confines of Caldons Burn, is across untracked upland. Grass and rock outcrops dominate the going, posing no problems for fit walkers.

Above: Curleywee (L), Lamachan Hill and Mulldonach seen from the Buchan Burn

Right: Lamachan Hill from the Glen Trool forest

The most convenient starting point is the Forestry Commission camp site at Caldons, reached from Bargrennan on the A714, via Glentrool village. There is a large car park conveniently close by.

Leave the car park and turn left to cross the Water of Trool bridge, and just before the next bridge keep to the right of a play area, then taking to the true left (south) bank of the Caldons Burn, passing through woodland to reach a lateral forest trail. Cross the trail, and a subsequent wall, and stay with the burn beyond a lateral fire break,

FACT FILE

Map OS Landranger 1:50 000 Series Sheet 77: Dalmellington to New Gallowa Harveys Walker's Map: Galloway Hills
Start/Finish Caldons Camp Site, Glen Trool. GR 397792
Length 11.5 km (7 miles)
Walking time 4–5 hours
Difficulty Rough, and trackless terrain; splendid scenery

The route in brief

Start GR 397792. Cross water of Trool bridge. Keep R of play area, following S bank of Cauldons Burn via woodland to forest trail. Cross trail and wall, following burn past fire break to gorge.
1 Continue S to Mulmein Burn. Ford it and take goat track to fence at forest edge.
2 Aim S for Larg Hill. Re-cross Mulmein Burn and dyke. Climb the N'most Larg Hill summit (cairn W of dyke).
3 Continue NE following dyke, then iron fence posts to Lamachan Hill summit.
4 Descend W following dyke to Cauldons Burn.
5 Follow path until it meets Mulmein Burn and retrace outward route to start.

passing through a fine gorge before continuing up to a second burn, Mulmein **(1)**.

Ford Mulmein Burn and climb on a path trodden out by feral goats that inhabit these hills to a fence at the upper limit of the forest **(2)**, from where you can start aiming south for the broad slopes of Larg Hill, climbing steeply over untracked ground, re-crossing Mulmein Burn and a dilapidated but fairly substantial dyke, before reaching the northernmost of Larg Hill's two summits **(3)**. A small cairn to the west of the dyke marks the highest point. During a storm in 1917 a small airship came to grief on Larg Hill, though all the crew survived.

The continuation northeast to Lamachan Hill, the highest of the Minnigaff group of summits, follows the dyke down gentle slopes to a narrow col, the Nick of Brushy (Brishie). Here the dyke changes direction, running off to the west, but its duties and responsibilities as a guide are taken over by a line of old iron fence posts that lead to the top of Lamachan Hill from the col.

From both Larg Hill and Lamachan Hill the panoramic view is outstanding, embracing virtually the whole of the Galloway Hills, and further afield (on a clear day) to the Lowther and Moffat Hills.

From Lamachan Hill descend with a dyke **(4)**, westwards, to meet the Caldons Burn near a water gate, and return down the burnside **(5)** by the outward route.

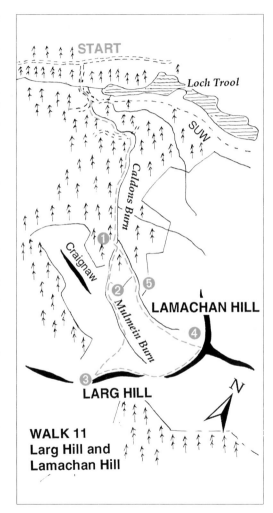

LOCH TROOL TO CLATTERINGSHAWS

At each end of this walk are two stones commemorating the achievements of Robert the Bruce, (from 25 March 1306, King Robert I of Scotland). One, already encountered in Walk 1, concerns the Battle of the Steps o' Trool in 1307, very much a watershed in Bruce's campaign for an independent Scotland, following two defeats in 1306, at Perth and Dalry. The second stone, located not far from the Deer Museum on the shores of Clatteringshaws Loch, celebrates the Battle of Raploch Moss in the same year. Linking the two stones makes a pleasant and fairly easy, if long, walk through some of the grandest scenery the Galloway Hills have to offer. The greater part of it lies along trails used by the Southern Upland Way, but suffers little on that account, and is unlikely to pose any problem more demanding than arranging transport to each end of the walk.

Bruce's Stone, Glen Trool

The first stage of the walk, between Loch Trool and Loch Dee is the expansive setting for the chase in John Buchan's classic spy thriller *The Thirty-Nine Steps*. To reach it, begin from the car park near Bruce's Stone **(1)** at the motorable limit of Glen Trool, and descend to the stone with its superb view over the loch. The loch and the steep-sided valley walls are the product of over-deepening by glacial action, and is as fitting a start to a walk as any.

Go beyond Bruce's Stone and follow a descending path that ultimately leads to Glenhead Farm. Before reaching Glenhead, however, leave the trail for a path heading for Glenhead Burn, which is crossed by a bridge **(2)**. A few strides further on the Southern Upland Way is met, and remains a companion until near the end of the walk. Follow the southern bank of Glenhead Burn, keeping right at a dyke, following a plantation of conifers on the right, and shortly pursuing a small side stream, the Shiel Burn, into the plantation. Climb with the ensuing path, boggy in places, until a broad forest trail is reached, and here turn left **(3)**. Still climbing, the forest is soon left behind, as progress improves, and reaches a col cut by ancient glaciers; beyond stretches moorland.

Now a fine striding route unwinds, heading down to Loch Dee, stocked with brown trout and popular with fishermen, its shores highlighted by small beaches of white granitic sand. Craiglee, a modest summit, stands to the left of the loch, while in the distance, looking over the loch, rise the summits of the Rhinns of Kells, Meikle Millyea and Corserine being especially prominent. The trail loops south to cross the White Laggan Burn, and shortly passes the ruins of Black Laggan **(4)**, a shepherd's cottage set in a maze of dykes, before climbing easily to an angler's hut near a bench overlooking Loch Dee, erected to the memory of a Dumfries doctor.

Continue along the trail **(5)**, ignoring a branching track on the right, but at a later junction descending left to cross the River Dee **(6)**.

Romano-British settlement, along Clatteringshaws Loch

Anyone seeking to shorten the walk should keep ahead instead of descending to the Dee, and follow the trail round to Craigencallie, a good four miles from the Queen's Way at the dam of Clatteringshaws Loch: transport would definitely be needed.

The River Dee, also known as Black Water of Dee, flows from Loch Dee, through Clatteringshaws Loch and Loch Ken before reaching the Solway Firth at Kirkcudbright.

Once across the Dee, turn right beneath the boulder-strewn slopes of Darrou, and follow the trail, an almost straight track, with younger plantations giving way to more mature sitka spruce and lodgepole pine, as far as Clatteringshaws Loch. On the way you pass beneath National Grid power lines linked to Kendoon Power Station **(7)**. Clatteringshaws Loch is not natural, and forms part of the Galloway Hydroelectric Scheme opened in 1936.

After skirting the shore of Clatteringshaws Loch for a while, the trail moves away, heading north to a gate on the boundary of the Galloway Forest

Park, and a short distance on arriving at a T-junction **(8)**. Here, the Southern Upland Way goes left. To finish this walk, we turn right, taking the track out in a straight line, past Upper Craigenbay, to the A712 **(9)**. Turn right along the A712, and in about half a mile, leave it, branching right on a signposted track **(10)** leading into plantations, and by another pleasant lochside path to the second of Bruce's Stones set in a clearing and under the care of the National Trust for Scotland; it is, however, rather less imposing than its companion in Glen Trool.

Return from the stone, and follow the lochside path to the Deer Museum, passing en route a reconstruction of a Romano-British hut, as it would have been around AD 250. The car park just beyond the Deer Museum marks the end of the walk.

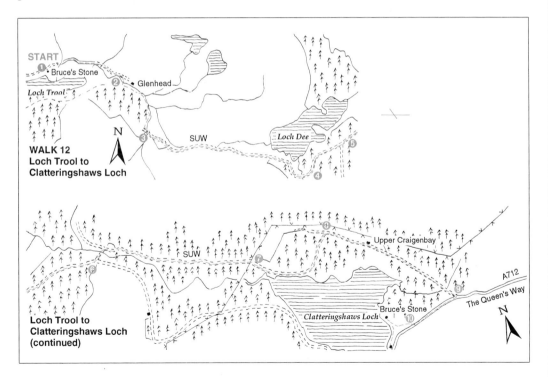

WALK 12
Loch Trool to
Clatteringshaws Loch

Loch Trool to
Clatteringshaws Loch
(continued)

FACT FILE

Map OS Landranger 1:50 000 Series Sheet 77: Dalmellington to New Galloway
Harveys Walker's Map: Galloway Hills (part)
Start Glen Trool GR 415805
Finish Clatteringshaws Loch, Galloway Deer Museum GR 551763
Length 21.5 km (13.5 miles)
Walking time 5½–6 hours
Difficulty Generally easy walking on broad forest trails and good paths

The route in brief

Start GR 415805. Leave car park near Bruce's Stone.
1 Descend to Stone, then follow downward trail E. Leave trail for path to Glenhead Burn bridge.
2 Cross burn and meet SUW. Follow S bank of burn, then side stream (Shiel Burn) into plantation. Climb path to forest trail.
3 Turn L to col and moorland. Trail loops S to cross White Laggan Burn.
4 Pass ruined cottage and climb to angler's hut.
5 Continue on trail. Ignore branch on R.
6 Fork L to cross Dee, soon turning R and follow SUW to power lines.
(**Alternative route** At **6** keep straight and follow trail to Craigencallie, 4 miles from start.)
7 Keep on SUW to T-junction.
8 Turn R to A712.
9 Turn R and in half a mile branch R on signposted track.
10 Follow track through plantation to second Bruce's Stone, then take lochside path to Deer Museum.

CAIRNSMORE OF FLEET

One viciously cold November day, with the wind tearing at the trees, snow and ice covering the upper slopes of the mountain, and a thick blanket of mist that reduced visibility to a mere 30 yards, I scurried to the top of Cairnsmore of Fleet in just under one and a half hours, took a quick look at nothing, and made a hurried 50-minute descent. Fleet of foot was definitely the order of the day, a day that contrasted so starkly with other more leisurely ascents set against a dome of blue and a landscape of rippling purple hills that fought with the burnished bronze of autumn bracken for one's attention.

That I could find the summit in such poor visibility says much for the footpath that marks the way, though the potential for error on Cairnsmore of Fleet's broad summit plateau is enormous, and the consequences of getting it wrong are serious. It is not without good reason that the summit bears a memorial to the crews of eight aircraft, British, American and German, that came to grief on Fleet between 1940 and 1979. A bright clear day is recommended for this one.

Cairnsmore of Fleet is the most southerly of the Donalds, and forms a complex arrangement of granite bedrock overlaid with forestry plantations and coarse grass, neatly divided into two unequal parts. The upper section of the mountain is completely bare, and provides little shelter against winds whipping in from the Irish Sea.

The walk begins from the grounds of the Cairnsmore Estate, accessed from the A75, a few miles southeast of Newton Stewart. A minor road leads in from the A75, at Muirfad, though neither Muirfad nor Cairnsmore are identified from the main road. Ignoring a branching road to Cuil, the minor road winds round to a low-arched viaduct, part of an old railway line. Keep ahead, passing beneath the viaduct to enter Cairnsmore Estate.

A rough road leads on through pleasant woodland alongside Graddoch Burn, and arrives at the entrance to Cairnsmore House. Ignore this, turning sharp right and continuing to reach a large complex of buildings, turning left on arrival, and following the track around them. A short way beyond the buildings, go left at a T-junction to a small parking space among ancient trees, alongside which picnic tables have been provided.

Cairnsmore of Fleet, viewed from 'The Queen's Way'

Map OS Landranger 1:50 000 Series Sheet 83: Newton Stewart and Kirkcudbright area
Start/Finish Cairnsmore GR 472641
Length 9 km (5.5 miles)
Walking time 2½–3 hours
Difficulty A long, but moderate ascent through woodland and across open mountainside

The route in brief

Start GR 472641. Go through nearby gate and head NE across pasture to iron gate. Take short wooded path to steep stile.
1 Enter forest and ascend path, crossing lateral forest trail.
2 Path later bears L, then exits forest.
3 Cross fence and zigzag NE over moor towards Cairnsmore summit.
4 At summit plateau, path veers N to summit. Retrace route to start.

From the parking space head for the nearby gate, and cross the pasture beyond in a northeasterly direction (half right) to an iron gate in the top corner of the field, giving on to a short, wooded path leading to a step stile at the entrance to denser forest **(1)**. Ascend through the forest on a distinct path, keeping ahead through a wall gap and across a lateral forest trail. The gradient, which is nowhere demanding, relaxes in the upper section of the forest, and changes direction **(2)**,

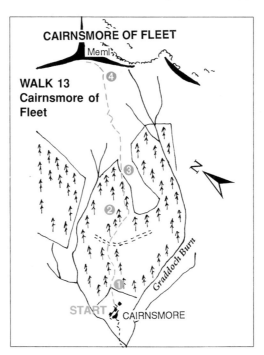

heading directly for the summit. A short level stretch preludes a gentle rise to the forest boundary (fence, ladder stile and gate,) **(3)**, and the wastes of Bardrochwood Moor beyond. The path zig-zags spasmodically in a desultory attempt to ease a gradient that barely needs it, but eventually settles for a direct northeasterly direction, changing to north on the edge of the summit plateau **(4)**.

A short way before the summit trig and shelter-cairn stands the aircrew memorial. If you stroll on in a northwesterly direction you will find yourself gazing down on an adjacent but lesser summit, Meikle Mulltaggart, and the distant monument to Professor Alexander Murray (1775–1813) on the Fell of Talnotry. Murray was a Scottish philologist, born in Minnigaff parish, the son of a shepherd. While himself a shepherd he acquired a mastery of the classics, the principal European languages and Hebrew, and in 1812 became professor of oriental languages at Edinburgh. The panoramic view also embraces most of the Galloway Hills, and the distant form of the Lakeland fells.

A descent by the outward route, taking in the distant views of Wigtown Bay and the Solway Firth, is all that is needed to return to the Cairnsmore Estate. On a clear day, you can head southeast from the summit, when a fence will be encountered leading to a col and a wall running across the ridge of the mountain. A slight rise then takes you to a satellite summit, the Knee of Cairnsmore, from where you can make a direct, trackless descent due west to the stile at the upper edge of the forest.

CAIRNSMORE OF DEE AND BENNIGUINEA

From the western shore of Clatteringshaws Loch, the smooth domes of Cairnsmore of Dee and its minor acolyte Benniguinea form a shapely backdrop, fine grassy summits surrounded by great dark green swathes of forestry plantations. Approaching along the Queen's Way from New Galloway, much the same impression is given: not a lot to worry about there.

Reality, of course, has a nasty habit of poking first impressions in the eye, and what might appear to be a straightforward and brief outing on consulting the map pales when you meet the rough vegetation that grapples with a granite foundation for supremacy. Cairnsmore of Dee is not a Sunday afternoon stroll, it requires strong legs and copious quantities of determination. Another 110 metres of height and it would rank as a Donald, but it falls far short of that, and yet bears all the hallmarks of rugged quality that give many lower mountains great appeal. Alas, there is scant evidence that many walkers share my view, and between the forest trails that start and finish the walk any discernible path is as evanescent as the proverbial Scotch mist. It follows that this walk, which on the highest ground is devoid of anything that aids navigation, should not be contemplated in poor visibility.

Although there is room to park a few cars just off the A712 (Queen's Way), at the start of a forest trail and old drove road known as The Raiders' Road, a purpose-built car park will be found a short distance down the road, on the right. The notoriety of the road derives from a novel, *The Raiders*, by Samuel Rutherford Crockett (1859–1914), a popular Scottish novelist, born in Little Duchrae, Kirkcudbright, of tenant-farming stock, and who paid his way by journalism and travelling tutorships.

Set off along the forest trail **(1)**, and follow it pleasantly, if uneventfully, to an isolated farm, Laggan o' Dee. In the valley to the right flows the River Dee, issuing from Clatteringshaws Loch, while beyond rise the wooded slopes of Fell of Fleet, where a series of experiments were once carried out to combat the effects of acid rain. The woodland on both sides of the road is host to a wide variety of forest birds, that in spring brighten the early stages of the walk with their song.

Shortly after Laggan o' Dee keep right on the forest drive, to start an unwelcome descent that must later be regained. As the gradient levels, and not far from the Dee, look for a small cairn on a boulder to the left of the trail **(2)**, directly below a fire break. Leave the forest drive here, and climb through the fire break on an indistinct path that issues a mediocre challenge to its former status as a drainage channel.

The climb is short and at the upper limit of the forest reaches a line of boulders and a collapsed wall. This is the moment for a rest: beyond lies hard work.

The initial direction onwards is east of north, to gain a broad ridge, the Rig of Craig Gilbert **(3)**, composed of deep, unrelenting heather, bracken and tussock grass, stretches of it wet. It is this combination of vegetation that makes life difficult, but once the centre of the ridge is gained, nunataks of granite pattern the landscape, and these are the key to some easing of progress.

Your objective is the obvious bulk of Cairnsmore of Dee ahead, and skilful linking of the granite islands will minimise the effort required to get there. The final pull to the summit is short and sharp, and the mountain top is marked by a trig pillar, an assortment of cairns

and a small lochan. The view is extensive, over the undulating lands of Galloway, and the summit, after all the effort, a relaxing place to be.

Leave the summit heading west of north between two adjacent cairns (4), and then swing down, northwest, across more tiring terrain, finally to gain a broad col below Benniguinea. Start climbing once more, without the aid of

granite islands this time, but eventually you will reach a graded track (5) servicing the radio mast and fire tower on the summit, by means of which the summit, an untidy, cluttered place, may be reached.

By heading back down the serpentine access track (6), you begin a long return (7) to the Queen's Way, near the Deer Museum on the banks of Clatteringshaws Loch (8), from where less than a mile of roadside walking, with the loch and distant views of Meikle Millyea and the hills beyond on hand, brings you back to the start of The Raiders' Road.

Rugged Benniguinea seen across Clatteringshaws Loch

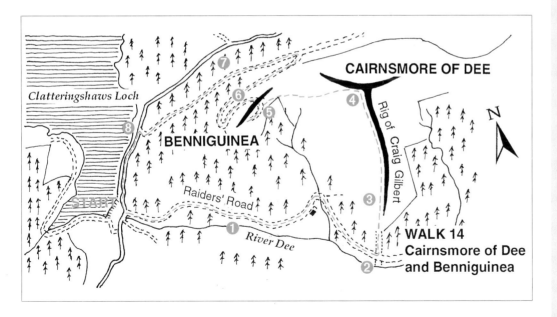

Map OS Landranger 1:50 000 Series Sheet 77: Dalmellington to New Galloway
Start/Finish Start of forest drive (The Raiders' Road), near Clatteringshaw dam GR 546752
Length 14 km (8.75 miles)
Walking time 5 hours
Difficulty A demanding walk once the forest trail is left

The route in brief

Start GR 546752. Follow Raiders' Road ESE alongside Dee.
1 Continue to Laggan o' Dee Farm. Shortly after keep R on the forest drive. Descend.
2 At small cairn on boulder to L of trail, climb L through fire break to boulders and collapsed wall.
3 Continue NNE to Rig of Craig Gilbert. Follow ridge to Cairnsmore of Dee summit (trig pillar).
4 Head W between cairns, then NW to col below Benniguinea.
5 Climb to graded track which leads to Benniguinea summit.
6 Take access track down opposite face.
7 Follow broad trail to Queen's Way.
8 Return to start via road.

61

CRIFFEL

Standing so proudly above the Solway and the Nith estuary, a prominent and distinguished landmark, the great granite bulk of Criffel assumes greater height than it possesses, but its ascent has enough about it to set heart and lungs racing.

The key to the ascent is the village of New Abbey, renowned for its Sweetheart Abbey, a great red Cistercian ruin, founded by Devorgilla, wife of John de Balliol, and both rich and powerful people. When Balliol died in 1269, Devorgilla had his body embalmed and his heart placed in a silver casket, which she carried with her until her death some 21 years later. Both she and her husband's heart were buried beneath the high altar of New Abbey, which she had occasioned to be built following John's death. She also converted the student's hostel at Oxford University into Balliol College, though other records suggest John founded the College in 1263. Their son subsequently became king of Scotland, but by all accounts not a good one.

At the start of the ascent of Criffel

The walk begins from close by Ardwall Farm, reached along an access track from the A710, about 3 km (2 miles) south of New Abbey. Just before the entrance to the farm there is room to park a few cars, considerately, beside the track. To the north lies blue-eyed Loch Kindar, dotted with a few small islands, one of which was built as a *crannog* (a floating settlement).

Start by taking the path running south beyond a nearby gate, and shortly turn right, at another gate, on a track that leads to one more gate at the edge of woodland. Here the farm track goes left, so leave it and climb the fire break directly ahead, continuing upwards after crossing another forest trail. The surrounding forest is mainly conifer and pine, but the fire break, with its cascading watercourse, Craigrockall Burn (not named on the 1:50 000 map), is well-endowed with rowan trees.

At the top of the break, the slopes of Criffel loom to the left, and those of Knockendoch to the right. Cross a step stile, and set off up the wet and peaty slopes of Criffel **(1)** on a distinct path that leads to the trig pillar, large cairn and dilapidated wall on the summit. This is Douglas's Cairn, and thought to date from the Bronze Age, though its name derives from the Middle Ages, when Criffel would certainly have been used as a lookout post to defend the northern territories against the marauding English. There is some suggestion, too, that the cairn is named after Black Douglas, member of one of the Border Clans inhabiting the Scottish West March, who was reputedly killed when his horse fell on Criffel.

With nothing to stand in the way, the view from Criffel, the southernmost hill of any size in southwest Scotland, is outstanding. The nearby Galloway Hills fill the northern horizon, while further east rise the Lowther, Moffat and Ettrick Hills. Across the Firth to the south the fells of Cumbria rise as a distant blue frieze, leading the eye to the grey prow of the Isle of Man. On a clear day, Goat Fell on the Isle of Arran is also visible, but it is the view of the Solway and the Nith estuary that will command most attention, especially if the hasty tide is advancing. The sands of the Firth are a notable wintering ground for wildfowl, particularly barnacle geese, and a large stretch of the foreshore forms part of the Caerlaverock National Nature Reserve.

The return to Ardall can be made by simply retracing your steps, but it would be remiss of you to omit Criffel's northerly companion, Knockendoch, when it can be reached by a convenient linking path. Set off back along the line of ascent for a short distance, but keep your eyes open for a descending path going off left in a northwesterly direction **(2)**. This leads down the connecting ridge, and brings you neatly to the cairn on Knockendoch's summit.

The final descent is not so easy, taking a simple line southeast **(3)** to the step stile at the forest edge used on the ascent. The intervening ground, however, is untracked, and a mix of deep heather and bilberry across which care is needed. Once the forest edge is reached simply return the way you came, with grand views ahead of the Nith estuary, especially beautiful in late afternoon sunlight.

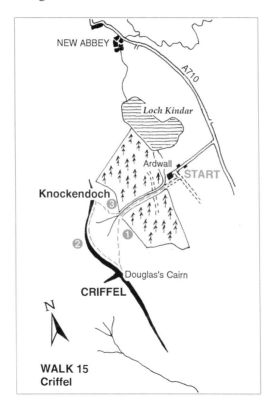

**WALK 15
Criffel**

FACT FILE

Map OS Landranger 1:50 000 Series Sheet 84: Dumfries and Castle Douglas
Start/Finish Ardwall, New Abbey GR 971635
Length 5.75 km (3.5 miles)
Walking time 2½ hours
Difficulty A stiff pull to Criffel, ending with untracked descent through deep heather.

The route in brief
Start GR 971635. Take path S beyond nearby gate, then R at another gate to third gate. Leave track and climb fire break directly ahead W, crossing forest trail, to a stile at the top of the break.
1 Cross stile and ascend path SSW to Criffel summit (trig pillar).
2 Retrace steps briefly, then go L (NNW) on descending path to Knockendoch via ridge.
3 Head SE over difficult ground to stile at **1** above. Retrace outward route to start.

The dark shape of Criffel, viewed from Knockendoch

CAIRNSMORE OF CARSPHAIRN AND BENNINER

An old couplet runs:

There's Cairnsmore of Fleet,
And Cairnsmore of Dee;
But Cairnsmore of Carsphairn
Is the highest of the three.

Whether this supremacy was ever in doubt is not known, but Cairnsmore of Carsphairn is a good 86 metres (282 feet), higher than its nearest rival, Fleet, and more than 300 metres (almost 1,000 feet) higher than the diminutive, but rough summit of Dee overlooking Clatteringshaws Loch. Some of the stronger mortals who take to the

hills have been known to tackle all three Cairnsmores in one outing, but you may prefer to deal with each separately.

Cairnsmore of Carsphairn ranks as a Corbett, among a fine cluster of Donalds, and is the highest hill of the entire range, a superb wedge of hills flanked east and west by forestry plantations, but accessible from most directions. The hill displays contrasting sides, those to the west and south being mainly grassy and smooth in profile, while on the north and east the slopes reveal the mountain's rocky foundations, and have a more rugged countenance, with planed granite slabs and sizeable erratics to denote the passage of some powerful Ice Age glacier.

The walk begins from the bridge at the Green Well of Scotland, on the A713. The Green Well is a neat and attractive rocky gorge flanked by ash and beech, beyond which Cairnsmore forms a shapely backdrop: its waters

Cairnsmore of Carsphairn and Benniner

were once used to treat scurvy. Green Well is said to be quite deep, and, if you believe the tale in the 1972 edition of the SMC's *Guide to the Southern Uplands*, it contains the master dies of a counterfeiter, a Mr Dodds, who made a fair living making coins from local ore, and disposed of the incriminating evidence in the well when excise officers appeared on the horizon.

Set off along a vehicle track, on the east side of the Water of Deugh, passing cattle sheds and soon crossing the Benloch Burn by a footbridge. Continue to a cattle grid **(1)** and keep on to a gate. Press on along the track, and through two more gates at fences. About half a mile further on there is a small cairn perched on a rock on the right, about 50 metres/yards away from the vehicle track **(2)**. You need to leave the track at about this point, and head for the cairn, but first you must find a convenient point to do so; the track has been cut across the hillside, and as a result its sides are quite steep. A small quarry proves a suitable spot.

Above and to the right is the minor top, Dunool, and beyond that Black Shoulder marks a change from grassy going to stony. Aim for the low point between the two tops, and you will meet a dyke that leads you steeply up to Black Shoulder **(3)**. From Black Shoulder, where the dyke ends, the way lies northwards, an easy pull on granite-punctuated turf to the trig pillar and cairns on the summit of Cairnsmore **(4)**. As you explore the granite summit, so the view changes, across the remaining summits of the Cairnsmore range to the Lowther Hills and their clutter of radar paraphernalia, and the hazy Moffat Hills beyond. Westwards rises the mass of the main Galloway

Hills, with The Merrick standing high above the Kells summits in the foreground.

The walk continues down Cairnsmore's southeastern slopes to Benniner **(5)**. There is a cairn halfway along the connecting ridge, which Hamish Brown in *Climbing the Corbetts* puts at 600 paces, followed by a little more descent before the easy pull on to Benniner. The smooth summit is topped by a modest cairn.

Turn south from Benniner, descending to reach a line of fence posts, leading down to a fence in a dip, at the top of Polshagg Burn **(6)**. A gate gives access to another fence, and you should follow this, keeping west of the top of Knockwhirn, to reach a dyke, then followed to a gate in a high voltage electric fence **(7)**. Keep ahead, through the gate, following the continuing dyke. As it ends, the fence runs on and meets another dyke. Stay with this for a short distance, until you encounter a line of old fence posts. Close by there is a low, double line of electric fence wires, quite often obscured by the grass. Once found, follow them down, through a meadow, and on to an access road **(8)**, leading left to Knockgray Farm. At a T-junction, facing a barn, go right, to reach the B729, and the A713 near the War Memorial **(9)**. Now all that remains is about a mile's walk along the A713 to the Green Well of Scotland.

Walkers with two cars at their disposal could leave one near Liggat, on the small loop road behind the War Memorial.

The Green Well of Scotland marks the start of the ascent of Cairnsmore of Carsphairn

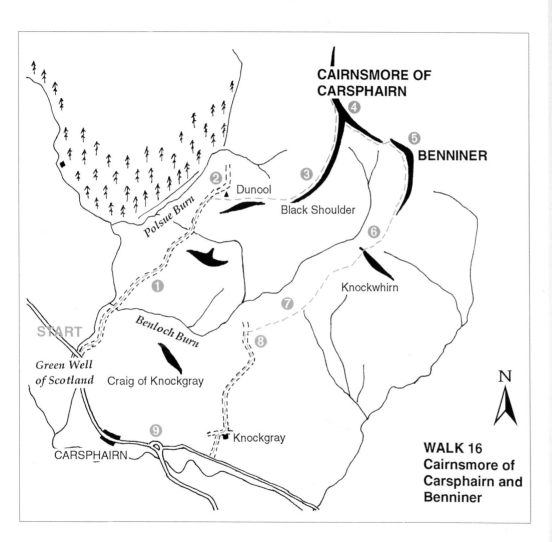

WALK 16
Cairnsmore of Carsphairn and Benniner

FACT FILE

Map OS Landranger 1:50 000 Series Sheet 77: Dalmellington to New Galloway
Start/Finish A713, Green Well of Scotland; room to park off road on north side of bridge GR 556945
Length 16 km (10 miles)
Walking time 5 hours
Difficulty Moderate; beware of electric fences

The route in brief

Start GR 556945. Take vehicle track E of Water of Deugh NE to Benloch Burn bridge.
1 Continue past cattle grid and three gates. In another half-mile notice small cairn on rock 50m to R.
2 Head E for cairn via small quarry. Aim between Dunool and Black Shoulder to meet dyke.
3 Follow dyke up Black Shoulder, then go N to Cairnsmore summit.
4 Head SE to Benniner.
5 Head S to fence posts. Follow posts to fence above Polshagg Burn.
6 Pass through fence-gate. Follow fence SW to dyke, then gate in high-voltage fence.
7 Follow dyke, then fence, then another dyke SW to fence posts. Follow nearby double electric fence wires down through meadow.
8 On meeting access road go L to Knockgray Farm, then R at T-junction and L on to B729. Turn R to A713.
9 From the War Memorial follow road through Carsphairn village to start.

2

THE LOWTHER HILLS
HEATHER'D HEIGHTS

*Occupying a large wedge of land to the north of the Forest of Ae, and roughly
sandwiched between Nithsdale and the upper Clyde valley, the Lowther Hills are simple,
rounded, exposed summits that make for easy walking and ferocious weather.
In late summer, carpeted with iridescent heather, there is no more relaxing excursion than
around the main Lowther Hills, while a winter blanketing of snow makes them irresistible
skiing country. Nevertheless, the whole area, in terms of land use, is regarded by Brussels
as 'Severely Disadvantaged', because of its poor quality, acidity and poor drainage.*

The Lowthers, named after Lothus, King of the Picts, are broken by two notable passes, the Dalveen and the Mennock. The Dalveen Pass links Carronbridge on the Nith with Elvanfoot on the Clyde; the Mennock Pass, where the Nith and Mennock Water meet, links Carronbridge with Wanlockhead and Leadhills. On an off day, walkers with time to spare will find the drive around the high Lowther Hills, linking the two passes, a splendid day, especially if time is taken to explore the towns and villages en route.

Leadhills has been the scene of mining activity for centuries, the hillsides yielding up significant quantities of gold, silver, lead and other valuable

The meandering Daer river (source of the Clyde) and the Lowther Hills

minerals. It was even suggested at one time that chickens could not survive in the area because of the risk of lead poisoning, but there has been little to sustain that claim. Nearby Wanlockhead has also seen its share of mining, and gold from the area was used in the Crown of Scotland. Much of the mining was carried out during the nineteenth century by the Duke of Buccleuch, and is all the more remarkable since Wanlockhead is Scotland's highest village, at 425 metres (1,394 feet) above sea level. It is probably the finest point from which to explore the full range of the Lowther Hills, a range rather wider than the present work allows, and a town of great interest to those for whom industrial archaeology holds the fascination it rightly deserves.

Mining, of one form or another, went on around Wanlockhead from 1675 until the 1950s, though

the village has since become popular as a place of residence for the sake of its surrounding beauty, its mining antiquity, and its history. It is a reasonable supposition that mining goes back even to Roman times, since there is a Roman road in the next valley, linking a small fort at Durisdeer and a larger, main fort at Crawford.

Wanlockhead is notable too for having a library for its miners as long ago as 1756, though nearby Leadhills had one fifteen years earlier, making it the oldest public library in Britain, in spite of a similar claim by Strathpeffer in Fife. This library was founded by a local poet, Allan Ramsey (1686–1758). Leadhills is renowned also for one of the occupants of its cemetery, John Taylor, who his tombstone proclaims 'died in this place at the remarkable age of 137 years'. It is said that he laboured as a miner for almost a hundred of his years.

There is a reasonable and sustainable claim that the Lowther Hills, at least those to the east, around what is now the Daer Reservoir, are the source of the Clyde. This is potentially a controversial issue, since tradition has long held that the Clyde rises on Beattock summit, at Little Clyde Burn. As might be expected, much depends on interpretation. In an account of Crawford parish, given in 1792 by the Reverend James Maconochie, it is firmly stated that 'the three principal rivers in the south of Scotland, viz. the Clyde, the Tweed and the Annan, have their sources in the hills which divide us from Tweedsmuir'. Any proposal counter to the notion that all three rivers rise on the same mountain, falls foul of the romantics, but scientific geographers claim, of any river, that its source is that of its longest tributary. For the Clyde, that means Daer Water, in the Lowther Hills. The arguments are well rehearsed in Jack House's book *Portrait of the Clyde,* but it suits our purpose to have the Clyde rising on Thick Cleuch Moss, making Walk 18 even more interesting.

The two walks that follow concentrate on the main Lowther Hills, a place of heather'd heights and tranquil beauty, and the Daer gathering grounds, grassy, open hills, where the views are far and wide. Anyone wanting to explore the hills further can telephone the Buccleuch Countryside Service for a range of leaflets covering riverside and woodland walks (Tel: 01848 331555).

Heather-burdened Riccart Cleuch, Lowther Hills

Lowther Hills: rich green valleys, purpled hills

LOWTHER HILL AND GREEN LOWTHER

Walkers undertaking that fine trans-Scotland trek, the Southern Upland Way, pass two milestones on the Lowther Hills; one is the halfway stage in their journey, the other its highest point.

There is, too, a better than average prospect of encountering some of the worst weather of the crossing, for the high ground of the main Lowther Hills and beyond, around Daer Water, is often mist-embraced, and potentially dangerous. Wind speeds of over 160 kph (100 mph) have been recorded on these mountains, more than enough to buckle the massive steel masts that adorn the Lowther summits. But set against that daunting message, the caresses of a cerulean sky, the spark of sunlight on rippling waters, the ever-changing hue of heather in full bloom, and the hills repay manifold the effort of their conquest.

Sunlight and shadows bathe the Lowther Hills

The walk described here is a splendid circuit of the main hills, following for part of its length the Southern Upland Way, but thereafter, once Green Lowther is left behind, rambling freely across wide heather-clad hills and glens, a perfect panacea to workaday ills. We begin from the point where the Way meets the A702, at Overfingland, just north of the Dalveen Pass. There is a small parking spot here, close by a Southern Upland Way signpost, and from it a narrow path leads to a stile across a nearby fence. At about this point we cross the line of a Roman road which came north from Nithsdale, passing southeast of the Dalveen Pass, rejoining the route of the present road near Overfingland, and following it to Elvanfoot.

Beyond the stile, a wet path ascends easily beside a small, walled plantation, and later, at a dyke corner, changes direction **(1)**, still following a dyke, heading for Laght Hill. At a junction of dykes we arrive at the boundary between the regional authorities of Strathclyde, and Dumfries and Galloway. The continuing dyke leads to a steep drop to a narrow col, beyond which an even longer pull takes us on to Comb Head and Cold Moss **(2)**. The top of this elongated minor summit affords a good view of the Dalveen Pass and across to East Mount Lowther beyond Enterkin Burn. The intervening gullies of Dinabid Linn,

Enterkin Burn, Wether Hill and Steygal here take on a fascinating folded formation, far more so than the map suggests. These were fashioned towards the very end of the last Ice Age, about 10,000 years ago, by glaciers that filled these broad ravines to a quite low altitude, and so, on a geological timescale, must represent the very last touches to one of Nature's masterpieces of sculpting.

Another drop, and another long steady climb finally brings the domes of Lowther Hill into view. A fence leads towards the summit buildings, closely followed by our path, but at a stile, we branch left, below the buildings, to cross the shoulder of the hill above Enterkin Pass, finally gaining the access road to the buildings by another stile **(3)**.

It was on this hill above the Enterkin Pass that in 1684 the Covenanters scored one of their notable successes, ambushing a party of dragoons and releasing their six Covenanter prisoners. A dejected Bonnie Prince Charlie also came this way after his retreat from Derby, little knowing that he was moving ever nearer to the slaughter at Culloden.

On a macabre note, Lowther Hill was used in the past as the final resting place for anyone who committed suicide. Until well into the nineteenth century suicide occasioned great shame, and the

Radar domes mark the summit of distant Lowther Hill

bodies of local suicides were carried to these windswept and isolated hillsides to be buried without ceremony. The carts and horse harnesses used on the journey, cursed by their duty, were left to rot.

The onward route now takes its leave of the Southern Upland Way, and curves round on the western side of the summit buildings to reach the access road, following this to the gates of the compound. This is probably as near as anyone can get to the summit of Lowther Hill, without prior arrangement. Far below, the undisciplined houses of Wanlockhead dot the landscape, their white walls gleaming brightly against the sombre hillsides, their arrangement the product of necessity rather than planning law, from which they were, in any event, well isolated.

The access road passes through the compound and exits a short distance away, heading directly along the ridge for the BT masts on Green Lowther. Since we are not permitted to enter the compound we need to follow the perimeter fence to begin the easiest linking of two mountains imaginable (4). With such easy going underfoot, there is time aplenty to appreciate the panorama which takes in the Pentland Hills, near Edinburgh, the Grampian Mountains, notably Ben Vorlich and its companion Stuc a'Chroin, Ben Lomond, the Isle of Arran, the Galloway Hills, Criffel, the Lakeland summits and the Ettrick Hills.

As we leave the summit of Lowther Hill behind, so we venture into unguided territory, for few books explore the region beyond Green Lowther. Here lies a fascinating landscape of sculpted hills and valleys, of rolling hillsides that will uplift even the most downcast walker, and reward hours of exploration with secret ravines, heathery braes, meandering streams and all the solitude you can handle.

Beyond the buildings on Green Lowther a gap in a chestnut paling fence leads to a post-and-wire fence running northeast across the col at the head of Riccart Cleuch to Peden Head (5), and, as it starts to descend, meets another fence heading down the length of Riccart Law Rig. These fences are a good guide in misty conditions, but on a clear day a faint vehicle track from the col can be used, keeping to the southern flank of Riccart Law Rig, which improves as we descend. The ridge fence meets a wall on Stowgill Dod (6), and if necessary the wall will guide you down towards the Potrenick Burn. But it is easier to reach and cross the burn by following a partially concealed gully that starts near GR 921114. The gully is filled with heather and inhabited by rabbits that have a tendency, if caught by surprise, to 'explode' from beneath your feet with startling effect. The gully is friable in a few places, and tracks come and go, but the easiest way is to remain faithful to it, only moving away from its side to ease a short passage or two. As we descend, so a prominent vehicle track across the burn comes more fully into view, and this we need in order to make our escape from these hills. It can be gained at the end of Riccart Cleuch, a beautiful, heather-filled valley, and a most peaceful spot to linger for a while.

A few damp moments lead across the burn and on to the track which should then be followed out to the farm buildings at Overfingland, a delightful prospect that at one point recrosses the burn at a shallow ford (7). As Overfingland is reached, the track leads past the farm buildings and cottages, usually to the cacophony of kennelled dogs, and down to meet the A702 only a short distance north of the starting point.

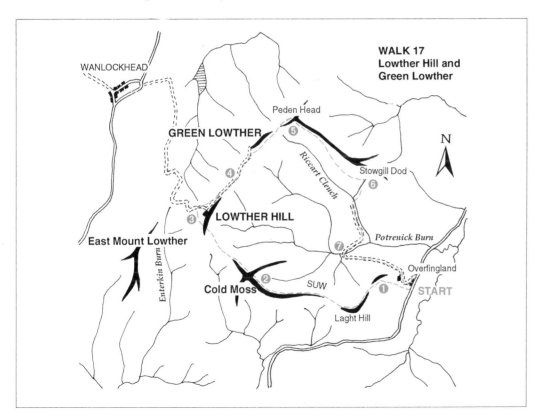

WALK 17
Lowther Hill and
Green Lowther

FACT FILE

Map OS Landranger 1:50 000 Series Sheet 78: Nithsdale and Annandale area
Harveys Walker's Map: Lowther Hills
Start/Finish Parking space, near Overfingland GR 929094
Length 13 km (8 miles)
Walking time: 4½–5 hours
Difficulty Tiring, undulating ascent to the summit ridge, followed by easy walking

The route in brief

Start GR 929094. Take narrow path WNW to stile. Cross, then ascend path past plantation to dyke.
1 Follow dyke L (SW) to Laght Hill. Drop to col and then ascend Cold Moss following SUW.
2 Descend NW, then cross Lowther Hill's shoulder above Enterkin Pass.
3 Gain access road via stile, and leave SUW. Climb to compound, and follow perimeter fence to regain access road.
4 Follow road to Green Lowther. Beyond buildings pass through gap in wooden fence to post-and-wire fence. Follow this NE to Peden Head.
5 Head SE at fence junction, following fence down Riccart Law Rig towards wall on Stowgill Dod.
6 Turn R (SW) at GR 921114 and descend gully to Potrenick Burn. Cross burn and follow track to ford.
7 Re-cross burn and continue via farm at Overfingland to start.

RODGER LAW, BALLENCLEUCH LAW AND WEDDER LAW

The hills that lie to the south and west of Daer Reservoir (pronounced: 'Dahr') are wide, grassy, largely untrodden and bathed in solitude. These heights quietly feed the reflective waters of the reservoir, which in turn feeds the thirsts of what used to be Lanarkshire. These eastern summits of the Lowther Hills are a delight to walk, and form the birthplace of the Clyde, one of Scotland's most important rivers, (although traditionalists might not agree – see page 70).

This walk follows much of the Daer watershed, and returns down the length of Daer Water. Walkers wanting to extend their day will find little difficulty in continuing to Gana Hill and Earncraig Hill, before descending a long and fine ridge northwards to Crookburn.

Crossing Thick Cleuch Moss, a possible source of the River Clyde

We begin from the lonely farmstead of Kirkhope, reached from the A702 by a minor road from Watermeetings to Daerside, and leaving this access road at a Southern Upland Way signpost well before the reservoir buildings and its houses are reached. The road continues through woodland, emerging alongside the reservoir, and continuing to Kirkhope, where, with care and consideration, a few cars may be parked off-road.

We begin along a grassy farm track on the north side of the burn descending from Rodger Law, soon crossing it by a plank bridge and following a fence to a gate giving access to the open hillside beyond. The track meanders a little, but leads onwards and ever upwards to within striking distance of Rodger Law. As the highest part of the track is reached **(1)**, we leave it, and move left to the trig on the summit.

With height comes a commanding view of the distant paraphernalia of the main Lowther Hills, and the first real sense of openness and freedom. Looking backwards we can see how well Daer Reservoir, inaugurated by Queen Elizabeth in 1956, blends in with the surrounding hills, though only at the cost of community spirit, for now the names of long-drowned hamlets and farms – Hitteril, Hapturnell, Nether and Upper Sweetshaw – are preserved nowhere but in memories and guidebooks.

A faint grassy trod leads us on from Rodger Law to Ballencleuch Law **(2)**, the highest summit of this circuit, to which we are guided by a fence that joins the ascent from the direction of Hirstane Rig. The foothills and farmlands of the Dalveen Pass lie to the west, and provide an attractive patchwork contrast to the grassy terrain beneath our feet.

The fenceline presses on to the regional boundary at the northern end of Scaw'd Law, where it meets a dyke, beside which a conveniently placed sleeper offers a comfortable seat for a short break **(3)**. We are here at the head of Carsehope Burn, one of the feeders of Daer Water, and by following the dyke we reach and follow a fence running down the hillside to a new, bulldozed track ascending from Durisdeer **(4)**. The track crosses the top of Glenleith Burn, a steep-sided narrow ravine, and quite unexpected among so many rolling hillsides.

A short pull, using the track as far as it goes, and then making for a couple of posts that guide us to another fenceline on the regional boundary, takes us on to Wedder Law, a bald summit with a fine view **(5)**.

Anyone wanting to abridge the walk could head down the broad ridge running northeast from Wedder Law, over Shiel Dod and Ewe Gair to reach Daer Water not far from Kirkhope. Otherwise, we follow the fence, having crossed it by a gate on the summit of Wedder Law. The fence guides us steeply down to the wide, boggy col of Thick Cleuch Moss, across which the map shows a right of way linking Kirkhope and Nithsdale, but there is no trace of it on the ground. Ahead the slopes of Gana Hill and Earncraig Hill invite those who want a longer walk.

The narrowing of Thick Cleuch, however, discernible to the northeast, beckons the rest of us, reached by a tiring, trying romp across heathery, tussocky, boggy terrain – good fun, but potentially ankle-twisting – that finally leads to the broad track **(6)** up Daer Water valley, which has been extended to circle round on to Shiel Dod. As we go we can speculate as to which trickle of water is the infant Clyde.

Once the track is reached, only a simple walk out to Kirkhope remains, passing en route the isolated farmstead of Daerhead **(7)**, a lonely, shepherd's cottage in a remote and idyllic spot.

Approaching Kirkhope and Daer Reservoir

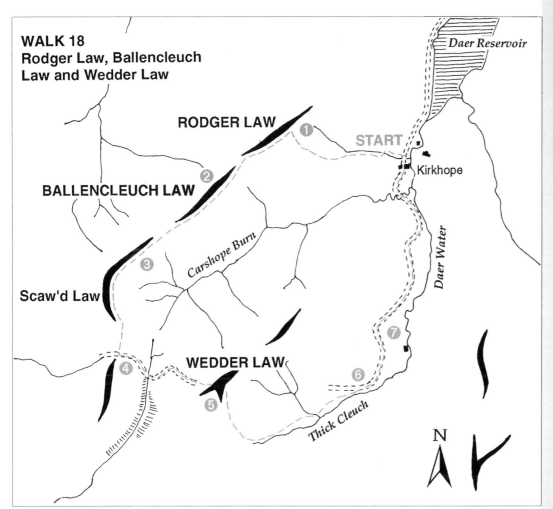

WALK 18
Rodger Law, Ballencleuch
Law and Wedder Law

RODGER LAW ①

START

Kirkhope

BALLENCLEUCH LAW ②

③

Carshope Burn

Scaw'd Law

④

WEDDER LAW ⑤ ⑥ ⑦

Thick Cleuch

Daer Reservoir

Daer Water

N

FACT FILE

Map OS Landranger 1:50 000 Series Sheet 78:
Nithsdale and Annandale area
Harveys Walker's Map: Lowther Hills
Start/Finish Kirkhope GR 963055
Length 14 km (8.75 miles)
Walking time 5 hours
Difficulty Easy walking on broad grassy ridges and
access tracks, with only the barren, boggy ground of
Thick Cleuch Moss to interrupt progress

The route in brief

Start GR 963055. Take farm track WNW on N side of
burn, then cross by plank bridge. Follow fence W to
gate on to hillside. Follow track to highest point.
1 Leave track L (SW) to Rodger Law trig. Follow grassy
trod SW to Ballencleuch Law via fenceline.
2 Follow fenceline to Scaw'd Law.
3 Follow dyke S, then fence down bulldozed track E.
4 Cross Glenleith Burn. When track ends head for
fence posts, then fenceline to Wedder Law summit.
(**Abridged route** Return NE over Shiel Dod and Ewe
Gair to Daer Water and Kirkhope.)
5 Cross fence via gate, then follow it down SE, E then
NE to Thick Cleuch Moss and Thick Cleuch.
(**Extended route** Gana Hill and Earncraig Hill lie ahead.)
6 Meet broad track leading N up Daer Water valley to
Daerhead.
7 Follow track to start.

3

THE PENTLAND HILLS, MOORFOOT HILLS AND THE BROUGHTON HEIGHTS AT THE CITY GATES

There can be no greater satisfaction in a weekend walker's life than having a splendid range of mountains within a few minutes' drive of home among which to let off steam, restore one's sanity or put one's problems in perspective. In that respect, the people of Edinburgh are fortunate. Not only do they have the ancient volcano of Arthur's Seat and Salisbury Crags in their midst, but just beyond the city gates lie the graceful Pentland Hills, the wild moorland expanses of the Moorfoot Hills and the grassy ridges of the Broughton Heights.

The Pentland Hills

Technically, the Pentland Hills lie within the area of the Central Lowlands, on the 'wrong' side of the Southern Upland Fault. The hardcore of the outdoor fraternity may feel the Pentlands lack a thousand feet or so, but it would be a mistake to ignore these summits for this reason alone. Long, high treks share the hills with easy rambles along quiet lanes and ancient pathways that have inspired many down the years. Scott wrote, after a sunset drive near Edinburgh: 'I think I never saw anything more beautiful than the ridge of

Castelaw Hill and Glencorse Reservoir, at the heart of the Pentland Hills

Carnethy against a clear frosty sky, with its peaks and varied slopes. The hills glowed like purple amethyst; the sky glowed like topaz and vermilion colours. I never saw a finer series than Pentlands considering that it is neither rocky nor highly elevated.'

The Pentlands provide an idyllic habitat, for flora and fauna, reflecting a rich diversity commensurate with the hills' equally varied land form and usage: from rough, heather moorland to tidy managed grassland where sheep farming is the mainstay, from coniferous and deciduous woodland to large expanses of open water. Not surprisingly, there is a wealth of birdlife, with over 100 species recorded around the hills. Threipmuir Reservoir on the northern flank of the hills, enjoys

Class I status among Britain's Sites of Special Scientific Interest, where more than 70 species of plants have been found. They are, of course, well-protected by the ranger service of the Pentland Hills Regional Park Authority.

Access to the hills is limited in places. Most of the land is privately owned and actively farmed and the Ministry of Defence uses parts of Castlelaw Hill quite frequently for military exercises. On the whole, however, the considerate walker will experience no difficulty in finding walks of all lengths to suit his or her taste.

The Moorfoot Hills

The Moorfoots lie slightly east of south from Edinburgh, and slot neatly between the Pentland

Hills and the Lammermuir Hills. Unlike the Pentlands, the highest summits do not always stand proud of the surrounding terrain, and are more of a plateau-like formation than a series of hills. It is this that prevents water from escaping to the valleys, leaving large tracts of the upland reaches waterlogged and making walking conditions difficult.

The highest summit of the group .is Windlestraw Law, standing apart from the rest of the hills, which form a distorted H-shape at the head of the valley of the River South Esk. The South Esk flows northwards through Gladhouse Reservoir, which, together with the reservoirs of the Pentland Hills, provides an essential wintering area for geese. To the south, the hills are bounded by the Tweed, linking the town of Peebles with Innerleithen, a short distance to the east. Much of this southern part of the hills is given to forestry, and the Glentress Forest has the distinction of being the oldest forest in southern Scotland planted by the Forestry Commission. The land to the north of the range is more traditionally farmed, with sheep-rearing predominant.

Broughton Heights

Broughton Heights is the name of both a small and compact group of low hills northeast of the village of Broughton, and the highest point of

(Left) The soft green landscape of the southern Moorfoot Hills

the group. With the Pentland Hills not far away, the Moorfoots knocking on their door, and the Culter and Manor Hills only a short drive further south, it is easy to overlook the Broughton Heights, as many do. But they have many of the qualities walkers seek, and offer days of good wandering, despite their modest proportions.

The northern end of the range is largely afforested, while the south is given to farming, woodland and fine heathery moors. Enough pathways enter the range to provide more than a day's exploration, although those with strong legs and lungs could conceivably tackle all the summits in one day.

Gladhouse Reservoir and the hills of the South Esk Watershed

THE PENTLAND RIDGE

Lying only a short drive from the heart of Edinburgh, the Pentland Hills receive considerable attention from walkers of all standards. Their modest elevation is deceptive, as anyone who follows this exhilarating walk will realise, and the main ridge is as exposed to the prevailing winds as any in southern Scotland. The whole range has been included in the Pentland Hills Regional Park, with two smaller country parks, at Bonaly and Hillend, at its northern end. There are, alas, no Munros, Corbetts or Donalds to collect, but despite this an exploration of the Pentland range will be time well spent.

A fair sampling of these popular hills and their natural history begins from the Flotterstone Visitor Centre, along a minor road from the A702, where there is a small car park. Pass the centre and take a nearby path through light woodland, and shortly join the road that runs alongside. A short distance beyond the end of

the path, as the road bends to the right, go left through a gate (ignoring the nearby bridge), and follow a path for a few yards, then cross the Glencorse Burn on your left by a footbridge.

It was close by here that on 28 November 1666, the Battle of Rullion Green was fought, when a force of Covenanters retreating from a march on Edinburgh, were overtaken and slaughtered for their 'defence of the covenanting work of Reformation', by General Thomas Dalziel (Tam Dalyell).

Across the bridge, turn right and climb to gain the end of an obvious ridge that leads up to the

first summit on the main ridge, Turnhouse Hill **(1)**, passing through an attractive stand of larch and Scots pine on the way. Directly below lies Glencorse Reservoir, and beyond that Castlelaw Hill, an active firing range, around which flags are flown when it is in use.

After Turnhouse Hill the ridge flows on, undulating and rhythmical, each peak quite distinct from the rest, as far as West Kip. A steady descent to a neat col, crossing an intermediate fence by a stile, preludes a climb on to Carnethy Hill **(2)**, surmounted by a much-disturbed Bronze Age cairn. From this vantage point there is an

Heading for Carnethy Hill along the main Pentland ridge

excellent view over the region of Fife, the adjoining Moorfoot Hills, and to Bass Rock in the Firth of Forth.

Follow the ridge as once more it descends to a col, this time one much used as a trans-ridge link between Penicuik and Balerno. Ahead lies Scald Law, by three metres the highest summit in the Pentland range **(3)**. Its configuration has greater potential for confusion in poor visibility than the other peaks, with short misleading ridges running out from the highest point. Its summit is bare of any feature other than the OS trig pillar, and it is claimed that on a clear day you can see as far as Ben Nevis.

A western spur of Scald Law continues the route to West Kip **(4)**, gaining first the steep-sided grassy bump of East Kip by a brief pull, before another short ascent reaches the exceedingly narrow, ridged summit of West Kip. On the col before East Kip a large erratic boulder betrays the sometime presence of glaciers that were largely responsible for fashioning these shapely hills.

Continue across West Kip to turn northwest and then north, heading for Hare Hill. At the foot of the hill **(5)**, near a gate, turn northeast and climb to its summit, from where there is a fine view of the walk thus far. On leaving the summit **(6)**, aim for Carnethy Hill, descending through heather to a footpath leading to Green Cleuch Glen (the gap between Hare Hill and Black Hill, not named on the OS map). The way lies down to the Loganlea Reservoir **(7)**, with road walking thereafter along the Logan Burn **(8)** and around Glencorse Reservoir **(9)**, back to the visitor centre.

FACT FILE

Map OS Landranger 1:50 000 Series Sheet 66: Edinburgh and Midlothian area
Start/Finish Flotterstone Visitor Centre GR 232631
Length 16.5 km (10.25 miles)
Walking time 4–5 hours
Difficulty Generally easy, but with many undulations along the ridge

The route in brief

Start GR 232631. Pass Flotterstone centre and take path through woodland to road. As road bears R, go L through gate. Follow path for a few metres, then cross Glencorse Burn footbridge on L. Turn R and climb to ridge, then ascend Turnhouse Hill.

1 Follow ridge SW. Cross fence via stile and climb Carnethy Hill (cairn).
2 Still following ridge, descend to col, then climb Scald Law.
3 Head W to West Kip via East Kip.
4 Go NW, then N to cross burn.
5 At foot of Hare Hill turn NE near gate and climb to summit. Leave summit heading E.
6 Descend E through heather to footpath to Green Cleuch Glen (between Hare Hill and Black Hill). Bear NE to Loganlea Reservoir.
7 Follow road along Logan Burn.
8 Head NE to Glencorse Reservoir.
9 Follow N bank of reservoir, heading SE to start.

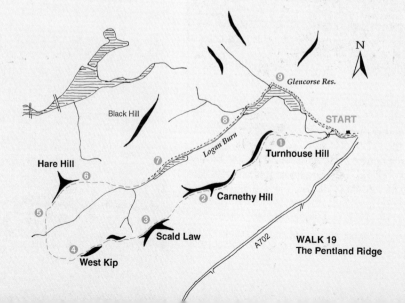

WALK 19
The Pentland Ridge

SOUTH ESK WATERSHED

Lying at the northernmost limit of Borders Region, this walk around the water-gathering grounds of the River South Esk, moves constantly to and fro between that region, and Lothian to the north, and centres on the course of the South Esk. There is clear evidence too, in the steeply falling northwestern slopes of the hills and the distinctive flat ground to the north, that they lie to the south of the Southern Upland Fault, a feature they share with the Lammermuir Hills to the east.

The walk may be followed in either direction, and begins from Moorfoot, immediately south of the broad expanse of Gladhouse Reservoir, a favoured haunt of wintering wildfowl. Seekers of Donalds, will find three of them on this circuit.

Follow the track south from Moorfoot until Gladhouse Cottage is passed. Nearby a bridge spans the South Esk, and gives access to the ruined tower house, shown on the map as Hirendean Castle. Disregard the bridge, and continue along the west, true left, bank of the river, crossing the streams flowing down from Jeffries Corse **(1)**, and then ascending the shapely ridge directly ahead, climbing quickly above the river. As the gradient eases, so grass gives way to heather, and you soon reach the regional boundary, with a large cairn nearby. In *Munros Tables*, which also lists the Donalds of southern Scotland, the highest point of this part of the ridge, shown on the maps as Dundreich, shares the name Jeffries Corse **(2)**. Dundreich, however, lies some 800 metres/yards to the southwest.

To continue the round you must set off from Dundreich in an easterly direction in order to avoid a pointless deviation of the regional boundary into a small gully that contains the source of Leithen Water. Keep as much as possible to the highest ground, and in due course, turn southeast, and later south, across rough terrain to meet a fence on the minor top (582m) **(3)**. The fence can now be followed to a shallow col, before a short, sharp pull on to Bowbeat Hill.

The view northwards from this point is quite splendid, and worth a moment's pause, with Gladhouse Reservoir providing a stop to the V-shaped trench of the South Esk valley; the outskirts of Edinburgh lie beyond.

Continue with the fence **(4)**, northeast to Emly Bank, dropping to a col **(5)** below Blackhope Scar, before climbing again, still with the fence, to meet another fence just south of the summit. A short walk northwards leads to the summit trig.

There is a sharp contrast hereabouts between the obvious, steep slopes falling to the South Esk, and the almost plateau-like moorland to the south and southeast. It would be most unwise to wander off in that direction, even with a fence to guide you.

Instead, set off along the fence heading down the northwest ridge of Blackhope Scar **(6)**. Stay with the fence, which later heads north, and just before it moves off in a northeasterly direction leave it to cross The Kipps **(7)**, and descend the

clear ridge to Hirendean **(8)**, aiming directly for Gladhouse Reservoir. Alternatively, you can use the corrie to the south of The Kipps, joining the valley track further south, but with a little less rough ground to contend with.

A simple retracing of the outward route is all that remains to reach Moorfoot.

Jeffries Corse and Dundreich start the walk around the South Esk watershed

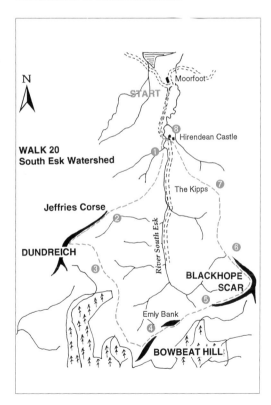

WALK 20
South Esk Watershed

FACT FILE

Map OS Landranger 1:50 000 Series Sheet 73: Peebles, Galashiels and surrounding area
Start/Finish Moorfoot, near Gladhouse Reservoir GR 297523
Length 14 km (8.75 miles)
Walking time 4½–5hours
Difficulty Mainly easy walking on grassy or heathery ridges

The route in brief

Start GR 297523. Follow track S past Gladhouse Cottage. Keep to W of river, crossing stream flowing in from R.
1 Ascend ridge straight ahead SW to Jeffries Corse.
2 Follow ridge to Dundreich. Go E on highest ground, then SE and S to fence at 582m.
3 Follow fence via col to Bowbeat Hill.
4 Follow fence NE via Emly Bank to col below Blackhope Scar.
5 Climb with fence to meet another just S of summit. Follow this along NW ridge of Blackhope Scar.
6 Fence heads N, then NE where it is left behind.
7 Head NW across the Kipps. Descend ridge to Hirendean Castle and retrace outward route to start.

WINDLESTRAW LAW

Windlestraw Law is by 8 metres (26 feet) the highest point of the Moorfoot Hills, though its separation from the rest by the courses of Glentress Water and Dewar Burn at one stage prevented its inclusion in the Moorfoots. Nor could it rank as one of the Lammermuir Hills, from which it is even more distant. Since then common sense, or practicality, has prevailed, and Windlestraw Law is now seen as the culminating point of a vast phalanx of hills north of the Tweed and south of the Southern Upland Fault.

The hill lies on the local district boundary, and if all you want to do is bag its summit the most direct way of doing so is from near the top of the B709, from where you can climb on to Eastside Heights, and follow the district fenceline to the summit. The going is decidedly wet, bedevilled by peat hags, and follows a fence, the district boundary, all the way. (Walkers with a predilection for hard walking might like to consider following the regional and district boundaries from Middleton Moor to the Tweed Valley, a rough and tough journey of about 20 miles.)

Our route begins from Walkerburn, taking the east bank of Walker Burn, heading north, to the ruined house of Priesthope. You can make life easier by asking permission at the farm to pass through their yard to a forest road following the west bank. This approach to the hills twists and turns with alluring fascination, leaving civilisation behind as you venture deeper into the folds between Cairn and Priesthope Hills **(1)**.

When the burn divides, take a path up the hillside ahead **(2)**. The ascent is steep, eases a little halfway up, and then climbs again before reaching a fence northeast of Glebe Knowe **(3)**, that takes you across the southwest summit of Windlestraw Law (654m), on which there is a

The highest point of the Moorfoot Hills, Windlestraw Law

small cairn **(4)**. With all the hard work now over, continue across a slight depression to the summit itself, marked by a trig at the meeting of three fences.

The long ridge leading gently up to the summit provides splendid views of the Tweed valley and of the numerous ridges radiating from Windlestraw Law, many of them boggy and peat-ridden, but all of them rarely visited. They carry fascinating names of long lost origin – Bareback Knowe, Wallet Knowe, Deaf Heights, Pringles Green and Scawd Law. Indeed, we can return by Scawd Law, with the prospect of visiting a chambered cairn.

Return to the southwest summit of Windlestraw Law, but instead of turning down the broad ridge used on the ascent, head almost due south from the cairn to begin with **(5)**, and then south-southeast to gain a fine, narrow ridge sandwiched between Walker Burn and Gatehopeknowe Burn **(6)**. The ridge is densely heathered, but carries a vehicle track that eases progress considerably.

Further south lies Cairn Hill, almost encircled by forestry. Press on to its top, where there is a cairn, and then keep going southwards through a fire break, to reach a second, chambered cairn, beyond which the ridge trends towards the southwest **(7)**. As you descend there is a particularly fine view of the northern Manor Hills, and the town of Innerleithen in the Tweed valley below. When you come to the lower limit of the forest, pass the high wall you meet by turning it on the right, and so reach the A72 a short distance east of your starting point.

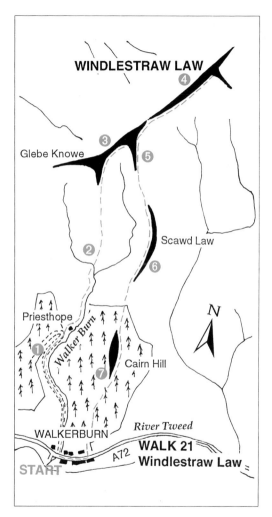

FACT FILE

Map OS Landranger 1:50 000 Series Sheet 73: Peebles, Galashiels and surrounding area
Start/Finish Walkerburn GR 360372
Length 13 km (8 miles)
Walking time 5 hours
Difficulty 6 km (4 miles) of continuous ascent, with some boggy going on the tops, but not unduly difficult

The route in brief

Start GR 360372. Either follow E bank of Walker Burn to Priesthope, or pass through farm (permission required) to forest road on W bank of burn.
1 Follow to where burn divides.
2 Ascend hillside via steep path NNW to fence NE of Glebe Knowe.
3 Follow fence NNE across SW summit of Windlestraw Law (cairn).
4 Follow ridge to main summit; retrace steps to cairn. Head S, then SE.
5 Gain ridge between two burns and follow it S.
6 Continue S to Cairn Hill and beyond where ridge trends SW.
7 Descend through forest. Turn high wall on R and regain A72 just E of start.

BROUGHTON HEIGHTS AND TRAHENNA HILL

Rarely visited because they lack height, the compact group of the Broughton Heights offer superb hill-walking, and one of the finest viewpoints in southern Scotland. And they are easily accessible. You could spend days wandering about their grassy folds, or even tackle all of them in one tour. The walk given here covers as many as is reasonably possible.

Start from the village of Broughton on the A701, where the River Tweed starts its eastward journey. There is room to park at a few spots, and a large car park close by the main hotel. Walk north along the A701, to about 200 metres/yards beyond the junction with the B7016. Here turn right on a tree-lined access road to Broughton Place Farm, beyond which a green track, sometimes indistinct, leads into the glen of Hollows Burn **(1)**, circling the double-topped Clover Law **(2)**, to the Hammer Head Pass.

In order not to omit Broughton Heights itself from this tour you must climb north from Hammer Head Pass, following a fence that joins

another on Broomy Side, leading easily on to Green Law **(3)** and onward to Broughton Heights.

This highest point of the group has extensive views of the Central Lowlands, the Pentland Hills, the Manor Hills, the Culter Hills and Tinto beyond the Clyde valley. The demarcation between the great mass of summits south of the Southern Upland Fault and those to the north, with the Pentland Hills and Tinto rising neatly from a distinctly more level base, is at its most obvious when seen from this vantage point.

Return from Broughton Heights, back over Green Law and down to Hammer Head Pass. There follow a dyke and fence on to the ridge **(4)** running to Trahenna Hill. Starting in a south-easterly direction, the ridge later turns southwest, directly above a branching arm to Hog Knowe. Follow the dyke along the ridge, and then leave it to pursue a fence out to Trahenna Hill, the top of which is marked by a few stones and a post.

Return down Trahenna Hill's south ridge **(5)**, staying beside a series of fences and dykes that bring you to the Dreva road, just north of a prominent hill fort **(6)**. A short diversion to the hill fort is well worthwhile for its fine view over the Tweed Valley, the Manor Hills and the Culter Hills. All that remains is for you to follow the minor road northwest back to Broughton, a simple stroll with only light traffic to worry about.

Trahenna Hill from the hill fort above Dreva road

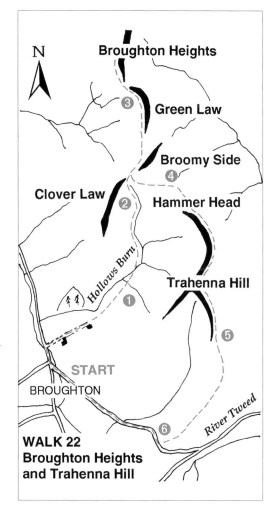

**WALK 22
Broughton Heights
and Trahenna Hill**

FACT FILE

Map OS Landranger 1:50 000 Series Sheet 72: Upper Clyde Valley
Start/Finish Broughton car park GR 113366
Length 14.5 km (9 miles)
Walking time 5 hours
Difficulty Generally easy walking, but undulating. Some quiet road walking to finish

The route in brief

Start GR 113366. Walk N to 200m beyond B7016/A701 junction. Turn R on to farm access road, then green track to Hollows Burn.
1 Cross two streams, following burn to Clover Law.
2 Continue N to Hammer Head Pass. Follow fence to Broomy Side, then another to Green Law.
3 Trend NW to Broughton Heights summit. Retrace steps over Green Law to Hammer Head Pass.
4 Follow ridge SE, then SW. Follow dyke, then fence to Trahenna Hill summit.
5 Descend S alongside fences and dykes to Dreva road (hill fort to S).
6 Regain minor road and follow NW to start.

4

THE CULTER HILLS AND TINTO BASTIONS OF THE CLYDE

At Lamington, not far north of Abington, the River Clyde finds its way through a flat gap between the Tinto Hills to the northwest and a large and compact group of summits, the Culter Hills, to the east. It is very much as though the two groups of mountains form a gateway protecting the Clyde, comparatively infant although much grown in stature from its birthplace among the East Lowther Hills, and through which it must pass before becoming the mighty river around which Glasgow and its suburbs are built.

The Tinto Hills are a small, attractive arrangement of hills on the north side of the Southern Upland Fault, formed from red felsite, a rock that gives the group a distinctive pinkish hue. The main summits lie to the north of Garf Water, a minor tributary of the Clyde, and are circled by the A73 trunk road. To the south, Dungavel Hill stands in splendid isolation, overlooking a crook in the Clyde containing the Bower of Wandell, once the hunting seat of King James V of Scotland.

By comparison, the Culter Hills sprawl across a sizeable area bounded on the west by the Clyde and on the east by the Tweed. Since the Tweed flows ultimately into the North Sea, and the Clyde into the Irish Sea, the Culter Hills must lie

on the watershed of Britain, their highest summit precisely so. Most of Culter's summits are low, rounded hills, but quite a few exceed 2,000 feet, culminating in Culter Fell itself (748m/2,454ft), almost centrally placed among the group. There are no Munros or Corbetts among the Culter and Tinto Hills, but in the former there are five Donalds, and four of these form a semicircle around Culter Waterhead Reservoir, with the fifth, Chapelgill Hill lying northeast of the main summit.

Access to the Culter Hills is possible at a number of points, though the walks that follow start from the village of Coulter (pronounced: 'Cooter') on the A702, about 4 km (2.5 miles) southwest of Biggar. Linking Coulter and Broughton, a minor road running south of Goseland Hill gives access from Kilbucho, with both Holms Water and Kingledoors Burn thrusting southwest into the hills from

Tweeddale. At the southern end of the range the village of Crawford provides a means of accessing Camps Reservoir, and from there along Grains Burn to reach the low summits of Backwater Rig, Whitelaw Brae and Ewe Hill. In spite of that, the whole area is a gathering ground for the supply of water to Strathclyde, and this means that access to reservoir areas is not encouraged. The hills are also tended for grouse-rearing purposes, and walkers visiting the region need to be at their most thoughtful and considerate in the way they interpret the general freedom to roam.

Tradition has it that Culter Fell and Tinto are on a par in terms of altitude, an old rhyme suggesting that 'Between Tintock Top and Coulter Fell / But scarce three handbreadths and an ell', but in fact Culter Fell exceeds Tinto by 41 metres. In terms of setting and panorama, however, there is nothing to chose between them.

Birthwood (in trees) and the greenery of the Culter Water valley

CULTER FELL AND CHAPELGILL HILL

Both Culter Fell and Chapelgill Hill are listed among the numerous Donalds of southern Scotland, and this walk combines the two in an uncomplicated circuit best tackled at a leisurely pace if the surrounding beauty of the Culter Hills is to be fully appreciated. There are fine views of the neighbouring Manor Hills, across the Tweed valley, and of Tinto, across the Clyde, for the Culter Hills are flanked by these two mighty rivers.

Leaving the A702 at Coulter, a minor road leads along Culter Water, past Culter Allers Farm, to Birthwood, and though it continues to Culter Waterhead Reservoir, Birthwood is as far as private cars may go. Just as the entrance to Birthwood is reached, the road bends sharply left, and here it is possible to park a few cars, off-road.

Set off south along the road, soon crossing a cattle grid, and, just after a small plantation on the left, much-favoured by pheasants, we reach King's Beck. Across the stream a broad track

leaves the road and starts to ascend the hillside. Take this, but only for a short while. When a distinct path appears, ascending the steep hillside ahead, Fell Shin, leave the track and take to the path **(1)**. Any temptation to follow the track along King's Beck as a means of reaching Culter Fell will terminate in a seriously steep climb.

As we follow the path up Fell Shin, the gradient steepens, and we encounter a line of shooting butts, each becoming an occasion of respite. Progress is demanding for a while, relieved by retrospective views of Tinto and the minor summits across Culter Water, Ward Law and Woodycleuch Dod, but the slope succumbs to a

steady plod, passing en route a couple of wooden posts that guide us to a large cairn. This is not the summit, though it does give the first fine view of Chapelgill Hill.

Beyond the cairn, now on a less distinct path, lies a dry tarn and a passage of boggy ground, before finally the summit trig pillar, positioned on a small mound, is hauled into view. The view from the top of Culter Fell, free of intermediate obstruction, is wide ranging, while a short diversion southwest will bring Culter Waterhead Reservoir into view, backed by the dome of another Donald, Hudderstone.

A fence crosses the summit ridge in a north–

Chapelgill Hill from the col at the head of King's Beck

south direction, and this serves to guide both to the head of Culter Water, at Holm Nick, and northwards, our continuing direction, to reach Chapelgill Hill. It also serves as the boundary between Strathclyde and Borders regions.

To reach Chapelgill Hill, we need to descend northwards (2), following the fenceline to a broad, tussocky col at the top of King's Beck (3). Mountain hares, as well as numerous grouse, buzzards and golden plover frequent these slopes, and quiet progress may reward you with the sight of one.

From the col the route makes an out-and-back trip to Chapelgill Hill, initially following the fence on to King Bank Head, and later swinging round, leaving the boundary fence, to reach the easterly end of what proves to be a semicircular hill, with Chapelgill Hill at the eastern end, and a slightly lower summit, Cardon Hill at the northern tip. This east-facing corrie basin is not obvious from our direction of approach, but is quite distinctive

viewed from the Tweed valley. The view from Chapelgill Hill (4) reaches out across the Tweed and Biggar Water to the rounded domes of the Broughton Heights.

Having visited Chapelgill Hill, and so secured another Donald, we must return to the col below Culter Fell. To the northwest the distant shape of Tinto is a good target on a clear day, and leads to the rim of the steep drop to King's Beck. Moving a little more to the northwest, keeping away from the steep slopes, a broad green track (5) runs down Tippet Knowe accompanied by a fence. This will ultimately lead to Culters Allers Farm, but as the 'pheasant' plantation met with on the outward journey comes into view below, leave the track, and descend through banks of heather (6), later following the boundary of the plantation down to rejoin the service road to the reservoir, not far from King's Beck, from where only a short distance remains to Birthwood.

FACT FILE

Map OS Landranger 1:50 000 Series Sheet 72: Upper Clyde Valley
Start/Finish Parking space near Birthwood GR 031310
Length 10.5 km (6.5 miles)
Walking time 4–5 hours
Difficulty A steep pull leads to Culter Fell, followed by tussocky terrain of only moderate difficulty.

The route in brief

Start GR 031310. Head S along road, across cattle grid and past plantation to King's Beck. Cross stream and take to broad track. Soon leave track for path SE up Fell Shin.
1 Follow line of shooting butts and two wooden posts to large cairn. Continue on less-distinct path past dry tarn and bog to E Culter Fell summit trig pillar.
2 Follow fence N, descending to col above King's Beck.
3 Follow fence NE to King Bank Head, then SE to Chapelgill Hill summit.
4 Retrace steps to col below Culter Fell.
5 Move NW to broad green track and fence descending Tippet Knowe until the plantation near start is visible.
6 Descend W, first through heather then following plantation boundary, to reach service road. Retrace outward route to start.

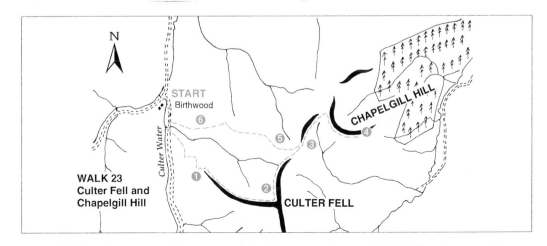

WALK 23
Culter Fell and Chapelgill Hill

CULTER WATERSHED

The round of the Donalds that circle Culter Waterhead Reservoir should only be contemplated by strong and experienced walkers. As usual, the reward is proportional to the energy expended, and the circuit provides good, if occasionally arduous, walking high above the glens and silvery watercourses. The walk has the added distinction of following the British watershed. The waters to the east all flow into the Tweed, which finds its way into the North Sea near Berwick, while streams to the west flow ultimately into the Clyde, on its westward journey.

The route described here embraces the watershed fully, and so takes in Culter Fell (Walk 23), but this principal summit, if previously ascended, can be omitted, by heading directly up Culter Water, past the reservoir, and on by a good track to Holm Nick, at the base of Glenwhappen Rig. There will be little saving in distance, but the ascent will be reduced by about 300 metres (985 feet). Much of the ground covered is used for the rearing of grouse, and walkers should show consideration at all times.

We begin from a small parking space near Birthwood, and follow Walk 23 **(1)** as far as Culter Fell summit **(2)**. From the top of Culter Fell, we turn south, following a fenceline marking the boundary between Strathclyde and the Borders regional councils steeply down to a shallow col below Moss Law, then making a modest ascent over Moss Law **(3)** before descending once more to Holm Nick, where we cross a road/track rising from Culter Water, but not shown on the map (this would prove an efficient and speedy escape route, if needed).

A moment's pause will prove beneficial at Holm Nick before getting to grips with the long and tiring ascent of Glenwhappen Rig **(4)**. Once the Rig has been dealt with, Gathersnow Hill lies only

a short distance away, and holds an impressive position above Kingledoors Burn to the south, and the feeders of Culter Waterhead Reservoir to the north.

The regional boundary continues beyond Gathersnow Hill to the next Donald, Hillshaw Head, a summit that is a little out on a limb. The linking ridge is straightforward and grassy, with the continuing fence for guidance, and we need to retreat to the col between the two **(5)** before we can pursue the rest of the walk. Once Hillshaw Head is reached, you may want to take in the top of Coomb Dod. It does not rank as a Donald, being too close to Hillshaw Head for that, but although serious peak-baggers will find it impossible to resist, they may rue the decision

when faced with a return over Hillshaw Head: the re-ascent is not significant, but it can be trying at this stage in the walk.

The next, and final summit of note is Hudderstone, called Heatherstane Law on some maps. Between it and Hillshaw Head lies some very demanding territory that should only be tackled in clear and settled weather **(6)**. It is largely a question of keeping as much as possible to the highest ground, and good navigation will be needed if we are to pick our way successfully across this stretch of upland **(7)**. Far-ranging views do much to lighten the toil, while the impressive V-shaped notch of Windgate, west of our objective, and the scree of the Deil's Barn Door beyond Whitelaw Brae also help visually to offset the effort.

Once Hudderstone is reached **(8)**, the quickest way of returning to base is probably east, over Snowgill Hill to the dam of the Culter Waterhead Reservoir, and out along the road. But our route continues in a northwesterly direction, descending steadily to intersect a vehicle track high above Cowgill Upper Reservoir **(9)**, which we then follow, roughly northwards, along Cowgill Rig, for a fine and fairly easy finish. The track reaches the Cowgill road less than a mile from Birthwood **(10)**.

Anyone with strength enough to face a few more undulations, might consider heading directly for Birthwood along the fine grassy ridge of Woodycleuch Dod and Ward Law.

On the summit of Culter Fell

FACT FILE

Map OS Landranger 1:50 000 Series Sheet 72: Upper Clyde Valley
Start/Finish Parking space near Birthwood GR 031310
Length 17.5 km (11 miles)
Walking time Very variable: allow 6 hours
Difficulty A long and strenuous walk which on some stretches crosses difficult, untracked grouse moors

The route in brief

Start GR 031310. Head S along road, across cattle grid and past plantation to King's Beck. Cross stream and take to broad track. Soon leave track for path SE up Fell Shin.
1 Follow line of shooting butts and two wooden posts to large cairn. Continue on less-distinct path past dry tarn and bog E to Culter Fell summit trig pillar.
2 Follow fenceline S to col below Moss Law. Ascend Moss Law.
3 Descend to Holm Nick. Cross road/track and climb Glenwhappen Rig.
4 Ascend Gathersnow Hill and follow ridge SW to Hillshaw Head.
(**Extended route** Continue to Coomb Dod and back.)
5 Retrace steps to col.
6 Head W, then NW towards Hudderstone, keeping to highest ground.

7 Ascend Hudderstone.
(**Abridged route** Head E over Snowgill Hill to Culter Waterhead Reservoir dam and road.)
8 Descend steadily NW to vehicle track above Cowgill Upper Reservoir.
(**Alternative route** Head NE to Birthwood via Woodycleuch Dod and Ward Law.)
9 Follow track N along Cowgill Rig to regain road.
10 Follow road NE to start.

START
Birthwood
Culter Water
CULTER FELL
Moss Law
Ward Law
Woodycleuch Dod
Culter Waterhead Res.
GATHERSNOW HILL
HUDDERSTONE
HILLSHAW HEAD
N
Coomb Dod

**WALK 24
Culter Watershed**

97

TINTO AND SCAUT HILL

Almost entirely encircled by the Clyde and its tributaries, the Tinto Hills, lying to the north of the Southern Upland Fault, hold a sentinel position in the upper part of the Clyde valley. Composed of red felsite rocks, the hills have a distinctive pink colouring, while the cairn on the highest summit is one of the largest in southern Scotland.

Although part of the Midland Valley of Scotland, the Tinto Hills are generally regarded as the extreme northwestern edge of the Border Hills, and they boast a splendid panorama.

The ascent of Tinto is a popular excursion, and on days of perfect clarity the Grampian mountains are easily caught, while eastwards a keen eye will pick out Bass Rock in the Firth of Forth. To the west Goat Fell on Arran is visible, and southwards the view extends as far as Cumbria and the Mountains of Mourne in Ireland.

Given Tinto's commanding position, it is inevitable that tales and mystery abound. Once described as 'a Sphinx brooding over Clydesdale', it was known to the Druids as 'The Hill of Fire'.

The most popular ascent of Tinto rises from Fallburn, just off the A73, and though the route given here is in the form of a circular walk, there are a number of other possibilities, most of which involve a measure of road walking. Anyone who can arrange secondary transport will find the continuation from Tinto summit to Wiston on the B7055 to the south makes a splendid traverse of the hill.

At Fallburn there is a convenient car park, from which, through a nearby gate, an enclosed track leads on to another gate and a ladder stile. Ahead Totherin Hill, the northern guardian of Tinto, rises steadily, and beyond the ladder stile we continue on a broad and obvious track.

Just to one side of the track stands one of the many fascinating relics of prehistory that dot the southern Scotland landscape, in the shape of a circular hill fort (1). There are about 30 of these Iron Age forts in the former county of Lanarkshire alone, all dating from the first millennium BC. The fort at Fallburn is a particularly fine example (and better viewed later, as we ascend Tinto). It is of almost circular construction with double ramparts and ditches, and two entrances, built first to defend against rapacious neighbours and later against the forces of Rome.

Totherin Hill brings a temporary easing of the gradient as we reach a more level stretch of ground, with Tinto's summit now coming into

The final strides to the top of Tinto

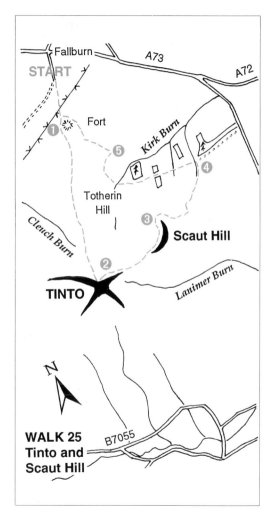

FACT FILE

Map OS Landranger 1:50 000 Series Sheet 72: Upper Clyde Valley
Start/Finish Fallburn car park GR 965374
Length 10 km (6.25 miles)
Walking time 3 hours
Difficulty Straightforward but energetic pull to the summit of Tinto, followed by good walking around Scaut Hill and towards the Clyde valley. Some (almost) trackless walking to finish

The route in brief

Start GR 965374. Pass through nearby gate to enclosed track. Follow SSW to gate and ladder stile, continuing on broad track to hill fort.
1 Continue S to Totherin Hill. Path continues above edge of Maurice's Cleuch to meet fence leading to Tinto's summit.
(**Abridged route** Retrace outward route to start.)
2 Retrace steps a short distance to path on R (E) leading to and around Scaut Hill.
3 Descend to plantation at GR 975352.
4 Turn L (W) on narrow path to gap at GR 970353. Take path, leaving it beyond the last stand of trees for a narrower one through heather by a wall. Cross Kirk Burn and climb N alongside wall/fence to wall corner. Branch half R on broad green trod to fence junction.
5 Head L along fenceline to Fallburn Fort. Retrace outward route to start.

distant view. Most impressive at this point is the retrospective view of Fallburn Fort, and the sweeping profile on the right of Maurice's Cleuch, a steep ravine of shale, scree and heather. As the path nears the edge of the cleuch, a slightly higher path appears on the left, but there is little value in following this.

Keeping above the edge of Maurice's Cleuch the path, more stony underfoot now, presses on to meet a fence which we follow all the way to the summit. A little below the summit there is a path branching left to Scaut Hill, though it may not be immediately obvious. This will be needed for the continuation of the walk, but it can be reached quite easily across heather banks from the top of the mountain.

The summit of Tinto is marked by an enormous pile of stones into which has been fashioned a circular stone shelter, and on top of which there is an orientation table, a little the worse for wear, but adequate to help us identify the distant peaks that dot the horizons: it is a splendid prospect, a most outstanding viewpoint, and worth the walk on that count alone.

For a speedy return to base, there is no quicker way than a direct retreat, but the continuation described here will lead you into a beautiful corner of the hills, not often visited.

From the summit we need to gain that branching path **(2)** running eastwards to Scaut Hill, and this can be done either by retreating a short distance until the path is reached, or by simply heading directly for Scaut Hill for a few heathery, trackless minutes, when the path will

come into view, ahead and to the left, and can then be reached. This leads to and around Scaut Hill **(3)**, atop which there is another, more widely scattered assortment of rocks, boulders and collapsed wall debris that neatly frames a distant view of the Culter Hills.

By following the path around Scaut Hill we eventually descend to a small plantation (GR 975352) **(4)** from where the main path runs out to the A73. To follow this option then involves just over two miles of road walking to reach the Fallburn car park.

But instead of heading for the road we go left (west) on a narrow path (one of a number of sheep traces), heading for a gap in another plantation at GR 970353. Here a more sustained path materialises and continues until, after the last stand of trees, we can leave it to follow a narrow path through heather alongside a wall. This takes us down to a wet corner where, with a little casting about, we can cross Kirk Burn at an attractive and peaceful moment in its journey to the Clyde.

Climb steeply away from the burn, alongside a wall/fence, through bracken and heather, to reach a wall corner. Here branch half right on a broad green trod, and stay on this to a meeting of fences **(5)**, where we head left, along a fence and on a rough and wet path eventually passing Fallburn Fort once more to regain the ladder stile crossed on the outward journey.

King's Burn crossing, Tinto Hills

5

THE TWEEDSMUIR HILLS
A LAND WHERE TIME FLOWS SOFTLY BY

In hazy-blue shades of aerial perspective, the gentle green hills and ridges of Moffat and Manor slip easily into the vagueness of distant horizons, a relaxed, untroubled, unhurried landscape, with a touch of ruggedness here, a smooth, counter-balancing softness there. Elsewhere, the sinuous flow of silver water – the Annan, the Tweed, Manor, Megget, Talla, Moffat and Yarrow – adds a spark of light to ignite in any sensitive visitor the flame of desire to roam at ease in the seductive embrace of a landscape where time flows softly by.

The name 'Tweedsmuir Hills' is often used to refer to the whole of the upland region between the towns of Moffat and Peebles. When John Buchan (1875–1940), Scottish author and statesman was elevated to the peerage in 1935, he became the 1st Baron Tweedsmuir, a title he took for his love of these hills. They are delineated on the north and west by the River Tweed, which has its source among the western Moffat Hills. North and northeast of Moffat, the River Annan and Moffat Water form another natural boundary, while beyond the watershed at Birkhill, the Little Yarrow flows first to the Loch of the Lowes before entering the larger St

Barely seven miles from its source, the Tweed at Tweedsmuir displays a loveliness that characterises its course

Mary's Loch. As it leaves, so the Yarrow is born, meeting Ettrick Water not far from Selkirk, both surrendering to the Tweed on the plain of Philiphaugh, where the Covenanters, under their best general, Leslie, defeated Montrose in 1645. When the Tweed is encountered again, much grown in stature, so the embracing ring of the Tweedsmuir Hills comes full circle.

Within and around this upland mass, an incredible wealth of legend, history, mystery and mayhem abounds, fair game for the curious, and ingredients enough to add to any walker's diet. Today, they provide enjoyment for many, and are also a rich preserve of natural history and geological intrigue. Yet there is precious little evidence to tell of life in prehistoric times, or of early settlement in the region.

The valley of Moffat Water was one of the main connecting routes from southwest Scotland to the

Firth of Forth, though it is more notable for its use in the turbulent period of Border Troubles during the thirteenth to seventeenth centuries. But its history as a thoroughfare is much older than that, as a Royal Commission Inventory for Dumfriesshire in 1920 observes: 'From the succession of fortified sites along both sides we may infer that it was also a well-trodden pre-historic route'. Such assumption is supported by the siting of just such a fort at the base of Tail Burn.

Stray finds fuel yet more speculation that prehistoric and early historic cultivation and cattle raising took place across the Tweedsmuir Hills, though the recent discovery of a mesolithic yew longbow, calibrated at 4040–3640 BC and so the oldest longbow yet found in the United Kingdom, at Rotten Bottom, two miles southwest of Loch Skeen, suggests more tangibly the sometime presence of hunter-gatherer groups.

Apart from these few scant items, the only remaining evidence of early occupation of the hills is the appearance of Anglian, Norman and Cumbrian placenames – farms incorporating the words 'fell', 'beck', and 'gill', as in Blaebeck, Capplegill and Bodesbeck.

There is a good case, too, for supposing that many of the upper reaches of the side valleys that insinuate themselves into the hills became the retreat for successful reivers, notably the Devil's Beef Tub and the upper reaches of the Grey Mare's Tail. Certainly, there is clear evidence that during the time of the Covenanter upheavals in the seventeenth century the government forces looked on the Moffat Hills especially as a Covenanter stronghold. And there is a strong possibility that many of the remains of sheilings, sheep stells, and drystane march dykes date from about the same time.

Beyond the cottage at Birkhill, where four Covenanters were shot by government troops, the valley slips quietly along in the company of the Little Yarrow as far as St Mary's Loch, with the exception of Loch Lomond the most renowned loch in southern Scotland, and described by Wordsworth as bearing a 'pastoral melancholy'.

Many poets and writers have been inspired by St Mary's Loch, and a rare and fine sight it is in the stillness of a clear autumn morning, reflecting the heavens and the hills, as might have been seen by Alexander Anderson when he wrote:

What boon to lie, as I lie now I lie,
And see in silver at my feet
Saint Mary's Lake, as if the sky
Had fallen 'tween those hills so sweet.

But the most noted of the native writers to glean inspiration from these charming hills and valleys were Sir Walter Scott, for 33 years Sheriff of Selkirk, and James Hogg, the 'Ettrick shepherd'. Of St Mary's Loch, Scott wrote a very fine description in *Marmion:*

Oft in my mind such thoughts awake,
By lone Saint Mary's silent lake;
Thou know'st it well, – nor fen, nor sedge,
Pollute the pure lake's crystal edge;
Abrupt and sheer, the mountains sink
At once upon the level brink;
And just a trace of silver sand
Marks where the water meets the land.

Scott and Hogg would meet often at the Tibbie Shiels' Inn on the narrow neck of land between St Mary's Loch and the Loch of the Lowes, along with a coterie of poets and writers hopeful. The inn was for many years run by the redoubtable Isabella (Tibbie) Richardson (maiden name, Shiels), who died in 1878 at the then remarkable age of 95. Even now the bronze statue of Hogg overlooking the two lochs seems to gaze out towards the inn with a yearning for fond memories. For two centuries the inn remained a popular and entertaining resting place for travellers, and by the time H. V. Morton toured

Scotland again in the early 1930s, 'Tibbie's' had become 'slightly sophisticated', but still retained the look of an 'auld clay biggin'. His account of scenes at Tibbie's is deliciously evocative of a time now probably gone forever.

Tibbie Shiel was an Ettrick woman who married a Westmorland mole-catcher named Richardson. When he died she, encumbered by six children, began to let her spare room to lodgers, the first being Robert Chambers. [He was working on his book *The Picture of Scotland*.] So the inn developed that became famous throughout the Scottish Lowlands. Tibbie was a woman of character and managed her difficult literary guests with great skill. Her trout fried in oatmeal, her luscious slices of ham, and her fresh fried eggs brought many a genius, who had been wandering the lochside all day, rushing to her like a starving schoolboy. She was acquainted with all the vagaries of the literary mind. And she had many a good laugh, too! One night when a group, which included Hogg, had talked themselves dry and the bottles were empty, Hogg begged her 'to bring in the loch'. Thankfully, for those of us who gaze today on its beauty, she must have declined. With a wry and prophetic sense of humour, Tibbie Shiels once remarked: 'I dare say when I'm deid and gone this place will still be ca'ed Tibbie Shiels's'.

But, in spite of their fondness of Tibbie Shiels' Inn, it was at a different inn, the Gordon Arms, where the B709 runs north to Traquair and Innerleithen, that Scott and Hogg were to meet for the last time. It was autumn in 1830, and Scott had already suffered a slight stroke, and walked but slowly. Something in his manner distressed his friend, Hogg: 'He often changed the subject very abruptly and never laughed.' Scott lies buried at nearby Dryburgh Abbey.

Selkirk and Melrose, but a short way further, mark the turning point and northeastern boundary of the Tweedsmuir Hills. Both are historic Border towns: Melrose boasts a fine Cistercian abbey, founded in 1136 by King David I. Nearby Abbotsford House was the home of Scott from the time of its completion until his death. Originally, Scott had bought the farm of Cartley (Clarty) Hole, in 1811, adding to it in 1813 and 1817. His first move was to build a cottage on the estate, to which he moved from Ashieteel in May 1812. From 1818, Scott started to enlarge the existing farmhouse, but demolished this in 1822 in favour of a more elaborate construction, completed in 1824. John Ruskin felt it was 'perhaps the most incongruous pile that gentlemanly modernism ever designed'.

Not far away, at Traquair, just south of Innerleithen, stands Traquair House, said to be the oldest continuously inhabited dwelling in Scotland, dating back to the tenth century. Twenty-six Scottish and English kings have resided here since Alexander I in 1107: at that time the house was no more than a simple wooden structure. The magnificent 'Bear' gates to the house were last closed following a visit of Bonnie

Prince Charlie in 1745, the then Earl of Traquair swearing they would never open again until a Stewart ascended the British throne. So, at least, goes Scott's explanation: another view suggests they were closed following the funeral of the Earl's beloved wife, until, he decreed, another, worthy of the title of Countess, was found.

Peebles, a Royal Burgh, received its charter from David II in 1367, though its origins date at

Talla Reservoir: set like a jewel among the Tweedsmuir Hills

least from the twelth century, and its natural attractiveness, perched on the Tweed, has been nurtured and carefully developed over many years. Here the river, confined by tidy banks, progresses forcefully by the town on its hurried way to the North Sea.

The final stage of this Tweedsmuir circumnavigation leads, fittingly, to the source of the Tweed at Tweed's Well, though some would claim that the true source lies much higher, on the flanks of Hart Fell, high above the town of Moffat.

Moffat is the most easily accessible of the border towns. From the 1650s onwards the town was renowned for its sulphurous well, and though the well-house pavilion and Hydropathic Hotel have now gone, the former Bath House, built in 1827, is a reminder of the past popularity of Moffat as a health spa. One contemporary writer pronounced the mineral waters of Moffat as 'bilge water or the scourings of a foul gun', a complaint that seemingly did nothing to hinder the growth of the town as people travelled from far and wide to drink it in the hope of curing rheumatic, gout, skin and stomach disorders. In the town square a statue of a ram was erected in 1875 to commemorate the town's strong links with sheep farming, while the cemetery is the last resting place of John Loudon McAdam (1756–1836), the great road builder, and former surveyor-general of metropolitan roads.

Within this fascinating ring of history, the spirits of the hills speak for themselves. Deep, thrusting valleys – Carrifran, Blackhope, the Grey Mare's Tail, and Dobb's Linn – penetrate the heart of the Moffat Hills, as much as the steep-flanked valleys of Polmood, Stanhope and Manor Water give shape and form to the Manor Hills to the north. Between the two ranges a lonely moorland road winds past the piercing blue of Talla Reservoir, and up across the watershed to slip quietly down to Megget and St Mary's Loch.

The Manor Hills are somewhat less dramatic than those of Moffat, but have the benefits of gentleness of form and firmness underfoot: a sure combination for long striding days. Both groups of hills, but those of Moffat especially, are of immense interest scientifically, archaeologically and botanically, and a sizeable area around the Grey Mare's Tail has been designated a Site of Special Scientific Interest.

The hills remain a delectably wild retreat, where feral goats roam free, and where indeed, borrowing a worthy tribute to James Hogg, the wandering winds are taught to sing.

BROAD LAW, CRAMALT CRAIG AND DOLLAR LAW

The great wedge of the Manor Hills, largely embraced by the River Tweed, seem to be perfectly conceived with peak-bagging in mind, 'the itch, of purpose to be scratch'd' (Samuel Butler). Thrusting outwards from the main central, if convoluted, ridge, a host of supporting ridges flow west to the Tweed or east to Manor Water, tempting the walker into demanding days. Beyond Manor Water yet more of these delectable hills tumble away, losing height, but still numbering five Donalds among their company, to produce a total of 13 for the whole group of hills.

Broad Law, the highest of the range, and indeed second only to The Merrick in the whole of southern Scotland, is both a Corbett and a Donald, and one of the easiest to acquire. In this walk it combines with Cramalt Craig and Dollar Law further along the main ridge to make a long but fairly easy out-and-back walk. Virtually the whole of the walk is on short turf, characteristic of the whole range, with the security of a fence to guide you should mist begin to gather.

Given the overall consistency of height, it is hardly surprising that the hills have magnificent views in all directions. Cramalt Craig and Dollar Law, which can but should not be omitted from the walk, are both Donalds. (Cramalt Craig is a demoted Corbett, although it has lost nothing in stature.)

It is possible to park a few cars near the cattle grid at the Megget Stone on the regional boundary but better to use a convenient parking space near the Talla Water bridge, just under half a mile to the west. One of the beauties of this approach from the Megget Stone is that whether you approach from east or west, your drive is sure to be amid splendid scenery. On the one hand Talla Reservoir is an attractive creation, while Megget Reservoir is no less appealing, and both adorn the landscape better than most reservoirs. Not so long ago, Talla Water flowed through a steep-sided valley. Now just under three miles of reservoir fill its basin, leading to the isolated building at Talla Linnfoots. Behind, the Talla Linn waterfalls make a fine spectacle, though their beauty would have held little interest for the Covenanters who held a secret meeting there in 1682.

From the parking space head east along the road, climbing easily to reach the Megget Stone (1). In spite of its prominence in walking literature, the Megget Stone is no more than a simple boundary stone, less than a metre in height, and, tucked away close by the cattle grid, could easily be overlooked. Leave the Stone behind and set off north, climbing beside a fence to the end of a minor ridge, Fans Law. The fence runs all the way to the summit of Broad Law, and to remain in its company is the only direction needed. However, shortly after leaving Fans Law an intermittent path bears away from the fence, and climbs to a couple of prominent cairns on Cairn Law (2). It is no hardship to divert to these important landmarks and take in the view the other Moffat Hills to the south, notably Nickies Knowe, Lochcraig Head and Molls Cleuch Dod (Walk 31).

Returning to the fence, across springy turf, the

Broad Law (R) and Cramalt Craig viewed from the Culter Hills

Culter Fells rise into view to the northwest, another outstanding collection of hills. Gradually, the top of Broad Law approaches, and with it the radar masts for which the summit is renowned. In the last few strides, a most oddly shaped structure appears, a curious affair serving the purposes of high-flying jets. Turn your back on it and move on along the fence **(3)** to reach a towering radar mast. Your attention now will be on the prominent top of Cramalt Craig, a little over a mile away. A large cairn adorns its summit.

Leave the east summit of Broad Law, sticking closely to the fence for the unseen cliffs of Polmood Craig lie a short distance to the north, and descend to cross a broad boggy patch **(4)** before climbing to Cramalt Craig.

The onward route now lies east of north, along the main ridge **(5)**, a fine and mostly flat affair with a fenceline for guidance. To begin with the way lies across a couple of minor tops, Dun Law and Fifescar Knowe, that need cause no alarm, before you move on to Dollar Law **(6)**.

Dollar Law is the fifth highest summit in the list of Donalds, considerably overtopping such noteworthy, and more distinctive, heights as Hart Fell, Lochcraig Head and Culter Fell. It is usually ascended from Manorhead in the attractive valley of Manor Water to the east, but this linking with two other important hills makes a fine and fairly easy excursion.

To return to base, we simply retrace our steps as far as Cramalt Craig, and on across the boggy depression beneath Broad Law. From the col it is possible to contour across the southern flank of Broad Law to the source of Wylies Burn, from where Porridge Cairn can be reached, but it is simpler to stay with the fenceline, returning to the top of Broad Law. Once there, continue

The green bulk of Broad Law rises above the Talla-Megget road

alongside the fence until the broad ridge leading down to Porridge Cairn appears on your left **(7)**, and then head down this splendid grassy and heathery ridge, keeping to the centre of it, as far as the col just below Wylies Hill **(8)**. Here a path crosses the col, and if you follow it right (southwest) you will enter the top of a narrow gully feeding down to the valley below. Sheep traces flank both sides of the stream, and will take you safely down; that on the east, the true left, bank is a little more substantial, though both have short sections were some landslip has occurred.

Once the valley road is reached, turn right (W) a short stroll back up to the Megget Stone, the cairns of Cairn Law especially prominent now, and then on to the parking space at Talla Water bridge.

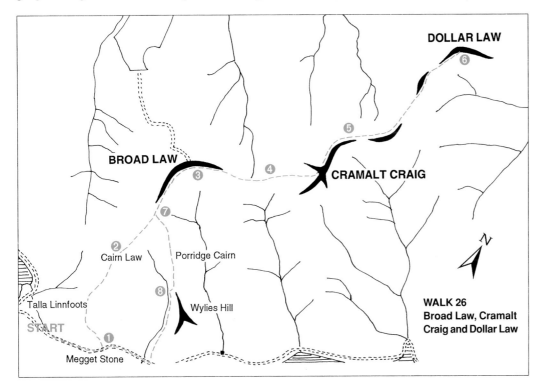

BROAD LAW

DOLLAR LAW

CRAMALT CRAIG

Cairn Law   Porridge Cairn

Talla Linnfoots

START

Wylies Hill

Megget Stone

WALK 26
Broad Law, Cramalt Craig and Dollar Law

FACT FILE

Map OS Landranger 1:50 000 Series Sheet 72: Upper Clyde Valley
Start/Finish Parking area on the Talla-Megget Road, just beyond Talla Water GR 143201
Length 22km (13.75 miles)
Walking time 6 hours
Difficulty A long, but straightforward walk, mostly on close-cropped turf

The route in brief

Start GR 143201. Head E to Megget Stone (near cattle grid).
1 Head N following fence to end of Fans Law ridge. Follow fenceline, diverting to Cairn Law cairns en route.
2 Continue N along fenceline to Broad Law.
3 Head E from summit, following fenceline across boggy patch.
4 Ascend Cramalt Craig.
5 Head E of N following ridge/fenceline via Dun Law and Fifescar Knowe to Dollar Law.
6 Retrace steps to Broad Law and beyond until broad ridge down to Porridge Cairn appears on L.
7 Keeping to centre, descend to col below Wylies Hill where a path crosses.
8 Head R (W) to gully. Descend gully on L (E) bank to valley road. Turn R and return past Megget Stone to start.

HART FELL

Riding high above the wide glen of Annan Water, the grassy dome of Hart Fell, best seen, at a distance, from the A701, throws down a challenge to any red-blooded walker. North of Moffat, a fan of grassy ridges and glaciated valleys buttress the summit, while to the east, the crags above the Black Hope valley seem to offer little prospect of success from that direction.

Given the complexity of the mountain, there are quite a few lines of ascent: our route takes advantage of a splendid, undulating line of minor summits to the west, starting on the watershed, not far from the source of both the River Annan and the River Tweed. This approach pursues, as far as the summit of Hart Fell, the administrative boundary between the Borders Region and Dumfries and Galloway, a distinction that serves also to separate Tweeddale and Annandale and Eskdale districts.

The walk begins from the top of the Edinburgh road at Annanhead. There is parking space close by, and, from a bend in the road, a fine prospect of the Devil's Beef Tub. An earlier name for this vast grassy hollow was Corrie of Annan, and during the Border Troubles, notably during the sixteenth century, it was used by the Johnstone family as a safe haven for stolen cattle, hence the appellation, 'Beef Tub'. Yet more troubles, those of the Covenanters, are commemorated nearby in the form of a stone to the memory of John Hunter, a Covenanter shot at this spot by Douglas's Dragoons in 1685.

The steep, sweeping slopes that flank the Beef Tub, perilous as they seem, were nevertheless used in August 1746 by one of the prisoners from Prince Charlie's army which was being marched this way to Carlisle. With more luck than judgement one of the men made his escape by rolling down the slopes in thick mist. Walter Scott, never one for letting such a good tale go to waste, had seen this man in his youth, and used the adventure for one of the characters in *Redgauntlet*, writing: '... it looks as if four hills were laying their heads together, to shut out daylight from the dark hollow space between them. A d–d, deep, black, blackguard-looking abyss of a hole it is, and goes down straight from the roadside, as perpendicular as it can do, to be a heathery brae. At the bottom, there is a small bit of a brook, that you would think could hardly find its way out from the hills that are so closely jammed round it.'

Putting these real and fictitious reminders of less peaceful times behind us, **(1)** set off west along the road for a short distance to a gate on the right, giving access to a forestry plantation. A broad service track heads towards the first of the trees, but is almost immediately abandoned for a narrow grassy trod ascending between forest and a fence. As the gradient eases, and height is gained above the trees, so the distant hills to the west and north begin to appear, bringing a fresh, invigorating feeling of openness and freedom.

The regional boundary is met at a gate from where the trig pillar on Annanhead Hill **(2)**, the first of many minor summits along the ensuing fine ridge, is easily reached. Very little of the walk between Annanhead Hill and Hart Fell is served by prominent footpaths, nor are any needed. But on the approach to Whitehope Heights and across to Hart Fell good navigational skills would not go amiss in poor visibility.

The administrative boundary across these first few summits is a convoluted affair, dipping this way and that for no apparent reason. A nearby wall and fence, much less erratic, serves as a guide as far as the lower slopes of Whitehope Heights, but for the moment the easy descent to the top

of the Devils' Beef Tub is followed by an equally straightforward pull to the top of Great Hill.

Onward **(3)** the wall/fence guides us up and over Chalk Rig Edge, and across a narrow watershed to start the ascent to Whitehope Heights. On Spout Craig first the wall and then what remains of the fence come completely and mysteriously to an end.

The steady plod on to Whitehope Heights **(4)** is relieved by the inviting view of Hart Fell ahead, and of its minor acolytes to the north, among which Garelet Dod and Strawberry Hill are especially prominent, the latter perched above the waters of unseen Fruid Reservoir. A cairn at spot height 562 lures us into thinking the top is nearer than it is, but eventually that moment does come and Hart Fell looms across the Lochan Burn, awaiting our attention.

A direct assault from Whitehope Heights is ill-advised, involving pointless descent and re-ascent. Easing along the grassy ridge to Whitehope Knowe **(5)** is a far better option, allowing time aplenty to work out the best line of approach to Hart Fell top. While preparing this book I watched a young red deer rocket up the opposite hillside, disappearing from view bound for Black Hope valley in the space of two minutes: the same ascent, puny by comparison, took me 40.

Once across the boggy col at the source of Lochan Burn **(6)**, a zigzagging route, slanting obliquely towards the conspicuous gully of

Rolling green hills: Hart Fell across Annan Water

Strong Cleuch (shown but not named on the 1:50 000 map), will put us in a position to follow it as far as it goes, from there continuing with much less effort to intersect the fence that will now lead us to the summit of Hart Fell.

Hart Fell is the second highest summit in the Moffat Hills, and one of only seven 'Corbetts' in Southern Scotland. Although the summit plateau of Hart Fell is rather flat, there is still a fine view across to the hills of Lowther, cluttered by the man-made metal monstrosities that serve aviation and other needs, but no less satisfying walking country for that.

The fenceline leads on across Hart Fell's summit (7), heading roughly southeast towards the gradually revealed gulf of Black Hope valley. Across the deep trough, carved long ago by glaciers, and deepened since by the scouring agents of erosion, the twin peaks of Saddle Yoke and Under Saddle Yoke command greater attention than the higher dome of distant White Coomb, the highest of the Moffat Hills.

A steepening descent leads to a narrow col bearing the name on some maps, Hass o' the Red Roads (8). Here walls reappear, that leading across the top of Falcon Craig serving as a good guide to Swatte Fell. But between the wall and the crags of Falcon Craig, an exhilarating path leads on across the top of the steep drop to Black Hope. All around now steep-sided hills draw the eye, the peaty, grassy summits of Falcon Craig, Swatte

The Devil's Beef Tub, Annanhead

Fell and Nether Coomb Craig, buttressed, on the east at least, by fragile cliffs and spilling screes.

The top of Swatte Fell **(9)** is a flat expanse of peaty tussocks, through which a path of sorts meanders out to the imposing cliffs of Nether Coomb Craig, the top of which is marked by a small cairn. From it a carefully plotted course southwest will lead to the crest of the steeply descending ridge, Pirnie Rig. At the end of the ridge, as Mossgrain Burn is reached, a new forest track **(10)**, with no accompanying trees of any stature, leads round to join Birnock Water. Now a delightfully simple walk out is all that remains, first to Blaebeck, and joining a metalled road in the vicinity of Moffat Well **(11)**, one of the mineral water sources that brought prosperity and fame to Moffat. Down through Archbank the road leads unerringly back to Moffat town, reaching the Selkirk road only a few hundred metres east of the town centre.

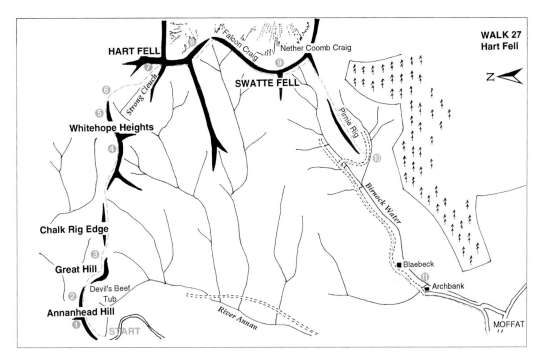

FACT FILE

Map OS Landranger 1:50 000 Series Sheet 78: Nithsdale and Annandale area
Start Annanhead GR 055127
Finish Moffat town centre GR 084052
Length 20 km (12.5 miles) **Time** Allow 5–6 hours
Difficulty Easy grassy hills, sometimes trackless, until Birnock Water is reached, from where a good track leads to the road into Moffat. Transport difficulties will need resolving; a lift or taxi ride to Annanhead would suffice. On Fridays, Saturdays and Sundays, the Edinburgh bus leaves Moffat at 10.35 am, and crosses Annanhead

The route in brief
Start GR 055127. Head W.
1 Soon enter plantation through gate on R. Almost immediately leave service track on to trod ascending N, then E, between forest and fence. Go through gate (regional boundary). Climb to Annanhead Hill trig pillar.
2 Descend to Devil's Beef Tub, then ascend Great Hill.
3 Follow wall/fenceline E to Spout Craig.
4 Ascend Whitehope Heights (cairn at 562m).
5 Take grassy ridge to Whitehope Knowe.
6 Cross boggy col (Lochan Burn source), then zigzag SE towards Strong Cleuch gully. Follow gully to end.
7 Fenceline beyond ascends Hart Fell, then veers SE to Black Hope valley.
8 Descend to col (Hass o' the Red Roads). Follow walls over Falcon Craig SW towards Swatte Fell.
9 Take indistinct path SE to Nether Coomb Craig (summit cairn). Descend SW – Pirnie Rig ridge – to Mossgrain Burn.
10 Take forest track to Birnock Water, then path SW to Blaebeck/Moffat Well.
11 Follow road to Moffat via Archbank.

THE BLACKHOPE BURN ROUND

L ike a rapier thrust that might long ago have pierced the side of many an outlaw hiding in these hills, the deep wound of Black Hope glen cuts to the heart of the mountain massif north of Moffat Dale. It is a dramatic and savage incursion into the hills that for those intent on nothing more sinister than a pleasurable day's walking yields a delightful round. From the outset, however, you are left in no doubt that a good part of the walk is decidedly 'up', indeed most of the hard work comes in the first two hours.

We begin from the cottage at Blackshope, passing through a nearby gate on to a vehicle track that winds its way into the recesses of Black Hope glen. Anyone seeking no more than a simple, straightforward stroll amid extravagantly wild surroundings need only follow this track into the glen until it peters out, continuing then to the very heart of the

On the ascent of Saddle Yoke, at the start of Blackhope Burn Round

mountains beneath Falcon Craig and Saddle Craigs, and returning by the same route.

More energetic souls should keep right on the approach to a large circular sheepfold not long after the start, continuing to a gate. Beyond, the hillside seems to rise for ever, but a succession of sheep tracks and a little ingenuity will tease out a manageable line of ascent as the broad base of the hill narrows to a fine, grassy ridge sandwiched between Blackhope Burn and Spoon Burn. As we reach the ridge so the view widens and, as if reserved for those with the energy to reach this far, a path begins to materialise, pressing forward to the greater height of Saddle Yoke.

To the east, beyond the curving ridge of Peat Hill, the dome of Carrifran Gans eases into view, its western flank plunging abruptly to the glen below. Further back, and much less prominent at this stage, the top of White Coomb, the highest of the Moffat Hills, starts to muscle in on the act. But it is undoubtedly the impressive, fragile cliffs across Blackhope Burn that command most attention, great sweeping spills of scree and boulders, divided by long, carving gullies, some of which provide sport for the winter expert.

A few too many false summits herald our final approach to Saddle Yoke, a gradual rise to a fine point, bearing a small cairn just below the highest point **(1)**. Only now do we see its slightly higher

sibling, Under Saddle Yoke, but thoughts of moving on should be shelved for a while, the more fully to appreciate the steep-sided and wild declivities both east and west. The great gulf of Carrifran Burn is outstandingly impressive, and there is a line of ascent, for the energetic, to White Coomb.

Cross the narrow linking col, a little airy for anyone suffering from vertigo, and climb easily to the top of Under Saddle Yoke. Now before you stretches a vast wilderness of moorland, devoid of signs of human habitation, though it is certain hunter-gatherer groups would have frequented this region in prehistoric times.

The onward route requires careful thought. Hartfell Rig is the next main objective, but this requires a wide sweep across the peaty gathering grounds that feed Blackhope Burn, even to the point of heading for a minor, unnamed summit southeast of Cape Law. A direct line, crossing the top of Whirly Gill, involves needless descent and re-ascent, though a steep descent, roughly following the line of the gill, is a useful escape route for anyone electing to call it a day. From the foot of the gill, a path runs out of the glen, soon reaching the broad vehicle track mentioned earlier. This abridged version, incidentally, is a fine circuit in its own right.

If continuing with the full round, however, this

down-and-up section is something we can avoid by setting off from Under Saddle Yoke on a grassy trod **(2)**, soon forking right, and heading just west of north until the slopes leading up to Hartfell Rig take on a more acceptable profile. Rather more definite is a crossing (north) to the unnamed summit above Raven Craig and southeast of Cape Law, where a fenceline, the boundary between the Borders and Dumfries and Galloway regions, is encountered. Wherever this is intersected it may then be followed as it ascends westwards **(3)** across the mere incidence of Hartfell Rig **(4)**, directly to Hart Fell summit.

We share the next stretch of the route, as far as Nether Coomb Craig, with Walk 27, but unlike that walk, immense satisfaction comes from looking back, across Blackhope Burn, to the twin summits of Saddle Yoke and the long ascending ridge, knowing that we tackled all of that earlier in the day. Follow the fenceline roughly southeast from Hart Fell's summit **(5)** to reach the narrow col between Hartfell Craig and Falcon Craig, from where we can take a clear path along the very rim of the steep crags, though a line closer to the nearby wall should be used in less than perfect visibility, windy or winter conditions, or by anyone suffering from vertigo. Otherwise, follow the onward path, keeping the wall at a distance on the right (west), and gradually moving away from the escarpment to cross the top of Upper Coomb Craig and Swatte Fell **(6)** to reach the cairn on the top of Nether Coomb Craig. If you do keep close by the wall, on Swatte Fell it will need to be abandoned, or a long and unwanted descent to Moffat might ensue.

As we descend from the final point of note, Black Craig, where the path is once more perilously close to the edge, the trail becomes less distinct **(7)**. We need to move away from the crags, heading south to cross Hang Burn (above Hang Gill, but not named on the 1:50 000 map), and aim for a gate in a fence **(8)**. A steep descent ensues by a broad farm track running down to Capplegill, where the valley road is rejoined. The starting point at Blackshope Cottage is only a short distance away.

Whirly Gill provides a useful escape route to the Black Hope Valley

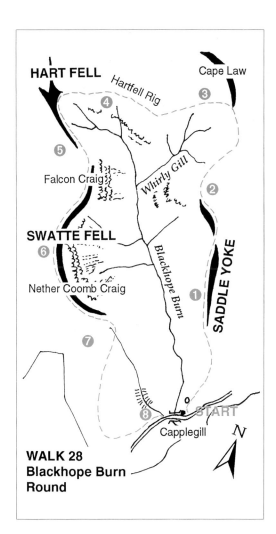

HART FELL

Hartfell Rig

Cape Law

④

③

⑤

Falcon Craig

Whirly Gill

②

SWATTE FELL

⑥

Blackhope Burn

SADDLE YOKE

Nether Coomb Craig

①

⑦

⑧ START

Capplegill

N

**WALK 28
Blackhope Burn
Round**

Map OS Landranger 1:50 000 Series Sheet 78: Nithsdale and Annandale area
Start/Finish Capplegill, adjoining Blackshope cottage GR 147098
Length 14.5 km (9 miles)
Walking Time 5–6 hours
Difficulty Generally grassy walking across trackless terrain, and with a fair amount of ascent overall, making this challenging walk quite strenuous in the early stages. The scenery, however, more than adequately compensates the effort. If necessary, the walk may be shortened by descending along the line of Whirly Gill to Black Hope valley

The route in brief

Start GR 147098. Go through nearby gate and take winding vehicle track N into Black Hope glen. Keep R on approaching circular sheepfold and continue to gate. Ascend to ridge between Blackhope Burn and Spoon Burn.
1 Take path to Saddle Yoke (cairn just below summit). Cross exposed col, then ascend Under Saddle Yoke.
2 Head NW on trod. Cross untracked ground (N), and ascend to fenceline (regional boundary) at unnamed summit SE of Cape Law.

(**Abridged route**   descend via Whirly Gill and return.)
3 Follow fenceline W to Hart Fell Rig.
4 From Hart Fell Rig continue W to Hart Fell.
5 Head SE to col. Follow exposed path (or nearby wall line) across Falcon Craig and Swatte Fell.
6 Leave wall, heading for Nether Coomb Craig (summit cairn), then head E to Black Craig.
7 Descend S, to cross Hang Burn. Aim for gate in fence.
8 Turn E then NE. Make steep descent to farm track, then L for Capplegill and main road.

GREY MARE'S TAIL AND LOCH SKEEN

The spectacular dash of Tail Burn as it plunges into the narrow rocky gorge of the Grey Mare's Tail is a sight no one should miss. The foaming tower of white water is a vivid contrast to the mainly heather-and grass-clad hillsides above, while the immense rock basin that houses Loch Skeen and its hummocky, peat-covered moraines is surrounded by stark, rocky summits.

Apart from the shapely beauty of the Grey Mare's Tail, many walkers with an interest in the landscape will find the walk to Loch Skeen fascinating, for it displays abundant evidence of the erosive power of the ice-sheets that once covered the area. Above the waterfall, and around Loch Skeen the glacial moraine is a particularly fine example, and supports a landscape of bog and heath unique in this part of southern Scotland.

Ascending above the Grey Mare's Tail, en route for Loch Skeen

The falls are set in a narrow ravine, and before setting off for Loch Skeen, it is worth a short diversion to inspect them at close quarters. From the car park on the south side of Tail Burn a gentle path leads into this steep-sided sanctum to near the foot of the falls. Further progress to the falls is barred by a short fence, beyond which the passage is difficult and dangerous. But the view of the falls remains breathtaking.

In the ravine and on the slopes above, a group of feral goats have established a pungent home, and may frequently be seen roaming freely. Descended from domestic flocks, feral goats have inhabited these slopes for more than 150 years, and are now classed as a 'primitive' breed worthy of preservation. Roe deer, too, inhabit the hillsides around the falls and Loch Skeen, but these are much fewer in number, and only rarely seen.

To reach Loch Skeen, however, we must leave the proximity of the Grey Mare's Tail, and cross the Tail Burn to start climbing a steep and energetic flight of steps constructed by the wardens of the National Trust for Scotland, who own the land all around the Tail Burn.

Barely have we set foot on the trail than we encounter a place of some prehistorical significance, for at the foot of Tail Burn, and marked on some maps as a 'Giant's Grave', are to be found the remains of an Iron Age or medieval fort.

Half way up the path a viewing point is reached (1), with a fine view of the Grey Mare's Tail. Before long the gradient eases as the path crosses a landslip section, where accidents, caused mainly by inattention, occur with alarming frequency. The section is not difficult, but the adjacent slopes are steep, and can feel intimidating. Beyond this the path continues above the main falls, and reveals an attractive succession of falls of varying sizes and intensities before the burn eases the pace.

To the west, the great green slopes of White Coomb rise above heath moorland, while, less noticeable, to the east, stands Watch Knowe, thought to have been named after the hill's function as a lookout post during the time of the Covenanter upheavals in the seventeenth century.

The onward path, as it approaches the as yet unseen and unsuspected Loch Skeen, flirts around the many moraines that line the route, always heading from the narrow-shaped summit of Mid Craig. Gradually, a more rounded summit, Lochcraig Head, appears in the distance and within minutes we are bursting upon the edge of the loch with surprising suddenness (2).

A few stepping stones cross the outflow from the loch, and enable us to reach a short heathery promontory, a fine vantage point from which to view the lake and its surrounds.

Described by members of the embryonic

Scottish Mountaineering Club on one of their earliest meets in the spring of 1891, as a 'lovely little loch, lying in a veritable cradle of bare stony slopes topped by precipitous crags', Loch Skeen was formed by a natural plug of moraine debris. It is almost 150 feet deep, and contains numerous brown trout.

Anyone wandering too far from the well-trodden paths is likely to encounter bog, and a complete circuit of the loch, though feasible, involves tackling some most awkward and boggy terrain, and is not advised. The only safe retreat to the car park is back along the Tail Burn, retracing our outward steps.

Back in the valley, a short stroll northeast along the north bank of Moffat Water, will lead to another complex of steep-sided ravines, that of Dob's Linn. It was here that an amateur geologist, Charles Lapworth (1842–1920), while staying at nearby Birkhill Cottage, carried out studies of graptolites, fossilised marine organisms from the Lower Palaeozoic period (about 250–300 million years ago). Lapworth's studies contributed significantly to our understanding of the way landscapes were formed, and graptolites are now widely used in establishing the age of the rocks in which they are contained.

(Far left) Talla Reservoir and (left) The Grey Mare's Tail, Moffatdale

FACT FILE

Map OS Landranger 1:50 000 Series Sheet 79: Hawick and Eskdale area
Start/Finish Grey Mare's Tail car park, Moffatdale GR 186145
Length Total: 4 km (2.5 miles)
Walking time 2 hours
Difficulty A fairly straightforward and short walk on a good path throughout, leading to the superb setting of Loch Skeen. The first part of the ascent, until above the Grey Mare's Tail, is potentially dangerous, and has seen some fatal accidents in recent times. By sticking firmly to the path the risk can be minimised, and the walk should present no difficulties to sensible walkers. Once above the waterfall, the ensuing walk along the Tail Burn is almost level

The route in brief

Start GR 186145. After visiting waterfalls cross Tail Burn and climb steps.
1 Follow path (beware of landslips) to Loch Skeen outflow.
2 Retrace route to start. Visit Dob's Lin NE of start point along N bank of Moffat Water.

WALK 29
Grey Mare's Tail and Loch Skeen

121

MID CRAIG AND WHITE COOMB

There is a delicate balance to be achieved by walkers following this route, between the undoubted pleasure of enjoying outstanding scenery of crags, glacial moraines, lochs and waterfalls, and the need to preserve and maintain the fragile existence of locally rare plants and birds. The vagaries of the climate, terrain and ecology around Loch Skeen have allowed species to gain a tenuous hold where otherwise they might not, for instance the raven, fairly common in Britain's mountainous areas, but rather rare in this part of Scotland. There have been reports, too, of dotterel, but these shy, elusive birds are passage migrants, and as such are present only for a brief period. Please keep to the route, and avoid wandering.

The walk begins from the National Trust for Scotland car park at the base of Tail Burn, serving the Grey Mare's Tail, and remains on National Trust property throughout. The

White Coomb rises far above Tail Burn

ascent to the outflow of Loch Skeen **(1)**, is described in Walk 29 and needs no further explanation here. As you complete the awkward section leading above the Grey Mare's Tail, and begin the pleasant walk to Loch Skeen, so the mound of White Coomb appears on the left. After about half a mile's walking, though it will feel like considerably more, a dilapidated wall will be seen coming down the slopes of White Coomb, literally to the banks of Tail Burn, and it is here that you will need to cross it on the return route. If it is in spate, that could be a problem. Decide now whether the burn can be crossed safely on the descent: the penalty for not doing so could be a rough diversion back to the outflow of Loch Skeen.

As Loch Skeen is reached we must cross the outflow. A set of stepping stones make this a simple matter, and give on to a peaty path through heather that meanders a little to avoid the worst clutches of a short stretch of boggy ground. A few knolls and small promontories provide suitable places to relax by the loch for a while before the ascent of Mid Craig, the sharp profile of which here takes on greater presence than the higher summits of Lochcraig Head or White Coomb.

The climb up Mid Craig follows a path that zigzags up the steepest section and remains fairly

evident until the grassy summit of the mountain is reached. The view from the top is contained by the higher summits and the ridge linking Firthybrig Head and Donald's Cleuch Head, though Broad Law, the highest of the Manor Hills, can be seen through the gap of Talla Nick.

The next short section is trackless, and simply heads for the wall/fence on the Firthybrig ridge **(2)**. There is a suggestion of a grassy trod, but 650 metres/yards in a northwesterly direction will intersect the wall, the regional boundary between the Borders and Dumfries and Galloway, at some point.

Since Firthybrig Head is only a short distance away, a brief extension to its flat, wall-decked summit will tax no one, though it is also included in Walk 31 from the Talla–Megget road.

The next objective is the flat top of Donald's Cleuch Head **(3)**. This modest height is named after the Reverend Donald Cargill, an outspoken minister from Glasgow, who lived during the seventeenth century, and denounced the Restoration. As a result he had to go into hiding from time to time and spent many lonely months among these hills, away from the dragoons of Claverhouse, principal protagonist of the Covenantors.

Firthhope Rig, another bare summit, lies only a short distance south, and is easily reached by

123

following the wall/fence, which suddenly changes direction, heading east-southeast finally to reach the top of White Coomb.

White Coomb, another Corbett, is a wide, spacious summit with a splendid panorama. There is little of dramatic appeal about White Coomb the way we have come, but the descent, steeply down Rough Craigs will make up for that.

The wall we noted as we ascended beside Tail Burn is a tumbledown affair, but it reaches to the summit of White Coomb and so proves a sure guide for the descent. The way down (4), following the wall closely, is steep in places and awkward, calling for complete concentration until the relative safety of the lower slopes above Tail Burn.

As we reach Tail Burn, so we must cross it. In less than spate conditions, there is usually no difficulty or discomfort beyond wet feet. Once across, the path back to Moffatdale is followed, and requires as much care in the descent as it did on the way up.

Crossing the outflow of Loch Skeen, bound for Mid Craig

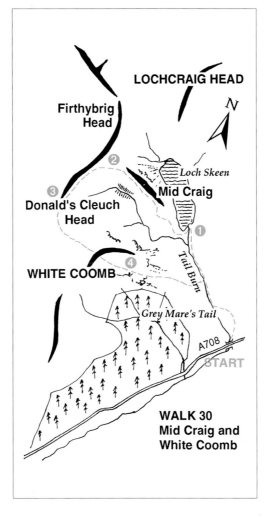

**WALK 30
Mid Craig and
White Coomb**

FACT FILE

Map OS Landranger 1:50 000 Series Sheet 79: Hawick and Eskdale area
Start/Finish Grey Mare's Tail car park, Moffatdale GR 186145
Length 9 km (5.5 miles)
Walking time Allow 4 hours
Difficulty The first part of the ascent, above the Grey Mare's Tail, has a moment or two where care is needed, but leads to a pleasant walk as far as Loch Skeen. The outflow of the loch is crossed on a line of boulders, followed by a straightforward ascent both of Mid Craig and around the main grassy ridge to White Coomb. On the descent from White Coomb care is again needed while passing through Rough Craigs, and when recrossing Tail Burn

The route in brief

Start GR 186145. Follow marked path to Loch Skeen outflow (beware of landslips).
1 Cross outflow and climb Mid Craig via zigzag path W. Head for wall/fence on Firthybrig ridge 650m to NW.
(**Extended route** Ascend Firthybrig Head, then retrace steps to main route.)
2 Head S to Donald's Cleuch Head.
3 Follow wall/fence S to Firthhope Rig and then ESE to White Coomb.
4 Follow wall down to Tail Burn. Cross burn (difficult in spate) and retrace route to start.

125

TALLA WATER AND LOCHCRAIG HEAD

Visiting four of the northerly summits of the Moffat Hills, this walk is understandably popular since it is easily accessed, generally straight-forward to follow, makes no great physical demands and has splendid views throughout of rolling hillsides and distant lakes.

Pride of place is reserved for Lochcraig Head, with its spectacular view of Loch Skeen, reposing in the glen below, surrounded by the countless hummocks of glacial moraine for which this part of the Moffat Hills is renowned. But with a fine supporting cast of lesser hills, there is no fault to find in this excellent circuit.

Begin from a parking area near Talla Water bridge, accessible either from Tweedsmuir by way of Talla Linnfoots, or from St Mary's Loch, by way of Megget Reservoir. Walk down the road to the bridge, noting the fine view of Talla Reservoir from above unseen waterfalls.

Looking back to the Manor Hills from the ascent of Molls Cleuch Dod

Cross the bridge and take the broad track immediately on the left, running along the line of Talla Water, but gradually distancing itself from it. The track, with the final summit of the walk, Nickies Knowe, directly ahead, leads to a corrugated iron barn **(1)**. Here we ascend slightly, to a gate, and continue beyond on a track, which shortly dips to cross the stream gully of Molls Cleuch. At this point the path ascending Molls Cleuch Dod, our first objective, becomes indistinct and can easily be missed, but this is not a problem, simply continue ahead (in a southeasterly direction), rising gradually, soon to intersect a fence which you now follow upwards. Higher up, the path reappears in better condition, and parallels the fence to the beckoning summit ahead. Alas this is not the top of Molls Cleuch Dod, but of Talla Craigs, a small spill of rock outcrop overlooking Talla Water. At least at this point the uphill work ends for a while.

Nearby the fence changes direction, and we need to cross it at a gate and start walking in a southwesterly direction – you can soon pick out the first of a couple of small cairns as a guide. This direction moves gradually away from the fenceline, but unavoidably collides with a dilapidated wall lining the flat top of Molls Cleuch Dod **(2)**. The highest point of this first summit is just before the wall, though the customary cairn

has been built beyond it.

Now follow the wall along an easy stretch of grassy hillside southeast to Firthybrig Head, with more time to take in the following summit, Lochcraig Head. A junction of walls and fences, neither in the best of health in spite of representing the regional boundary, marks the top of Firthybrig Head. One wall/fence heads roughly southwest to Donald's Cleuch Dod, while our route takes the third option, north of east, and descends quite steeply **(3)**, to the boggy col of Talla Nick. If bad weather approaches and you need a quick escape route back to the start, you can go left at Talla Nick, over a wall/fence and down towards Talla Water, but this is untracked and wet, and a safer choice would be to retrace your steps from Firthybrig Head.

Onward, our route lies across the boggy depression of Talla Nick (usually easiest near the wall), and up the shoulder of Lochcraig Head, following the line of a wall. The effort of this ascent is short-lived, and leads to a massive plateau of close-cropped grass, surmounted by a large cairn. By moving right, away from the wall, you approach the steep slope falling to Loch Skeen below. The view is spectacular, flowing beyond the gorge of Tail Burn to the Ettrick Hills in the blue distance. But these top reaches of Lochcraig Head are loose and friable, and you

should resist the temptation to go more than a few steps beyond the rim.

The cairn on Lochcraig Head does not mark the highest point, though it tends to be credited with that distinction, but if from it you walk north, you rejoin the boundary wall near a wall and fence junction. Cross this, and follow a fence north across the true summit of Lochcraig Head (GR 167176), and through a rash of boulders to Lochcraig Head's northerly terminus at Talla East Side, marked by two large cairns. At some point en route you will need to cross the fence.

Just below Talla East Side the fence forks **(4)**, and we follow the left branch, down to a broad col, from which there is a distant view of Megget Reservoir. Ahead, across the Talla–Megget road the Manor Hills rise to their greatest height in Broad Law, distinguishable by the radar masts that pinpoint its summit, while away to the right lies Cramalt Craig, once a Corbett but now demoted.

Stay with the fence, and climb easily to the top of Nickies Knowe, continuing **(5)**, always alongside the fence, until it drops to within 100 metres/yards of Talla Water. Now we simply follow the stream on an improving path, and cross it by a rickety bridge, rejoining the outward route not far from the corrugated iron barn.

On the summit of Molls Cleuch Dod

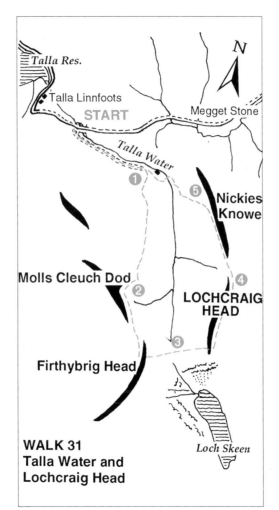

WALK 31
Talla Water and Lochcraig Head

FACT FILE

Map OS Landranger 1:50 000 Series Sheet 79: Hawick and Eskdale area; Sheet 72: Upper Clyde valley
Start/Finish Parking area on the Talla–Megget road, just beyond Talla Water bridge
GR 143201
Length 10km (6.25 miles) **Walking time** 4 hours
Difficulty There is little difficulty about this walk. Most of it follows good paths, walls or fences

The route in brief

Start GR 143201. Walk down road W to bridge. Take track E along S bank of Talla Water to barn. Through gate, follow track for short distance.
1 Either take indistinct Molls Cleuch Dod track on R or continue SE to fence. Head S up Molls Cleuch Dod. At top of first rise fence changes direction. Cross via gate then head SW (cairn markers) to wall atop Molls Cleuch Dod.
2 Follow wall SE to Firthybrig Head summit (wall junction).
3 Follow wall NE down to Talla Nick (possible escape route NW down Talla Water), keeping near wall, and ascend Lochcraig Head. Walk N from summit cairn to boundary wall (near junction). Cross it and follow fence N across true summit (GR 167176). Cross fence where convenient.
4 When fence forks, go L down to col; then follow fenceline up Nickies Knowe.
5 Stay with fence NW to Talla Water, then follow stream W. Cross at bridge and retrace outward route to start.

THE ETTRICK HILLS AWAY FROM IT ALL

That part of the Ettrick Hills with which this chapter is concerned lies immediately south of Moffat Water and the Yarrow, and comprises a large sparsely populated area that seems to flow unendingly southwards. For the walker, the mile after mile of present-day Eskdalemuir Forest is largely inaccessible, but thankfully at the northern extreme of this wooded land, sandwiched between Moffat Water and Ettrick Water, is as fine a collection of hills as any walker could wish to encounter. They have about them an air of remoteness, somewhere to get away from it all, yet they rise less than a half-hour's journey from Selkirk. They possess an indefinable quality that evokes peace and tranquillity, heavy with the mood of relaxation, even in driving rain.

The most convenient area for walkers lies along Ettrick Water, though the hills are accessible too, from Moffat Dale and near St Mary's Loch. Along the northern flank one of the finest ridges in southern Scotland raises its shapely profile above Moffat Water, a linear walk, with all the attendant transport difficulties, but exquisite walking country with good views of the Moffat Hills to the north. But while the Moffat Hills are crowded with walkers, the visitor to Ettrick will find relative solitude among their hills and dales, rolling grasslands, wooded slopes and deep-cleft sinous glens.

St Mary's Loch

Ettrick, though having seen much of Scott, is indisputably Hogg country. James Hogg, a descendant of the Hoggs of Fauldhope, was born in 1770 in a cottage now gone, but near the spot where a monument commemorates the event. He styled himself the 'Ettrick shepherd' since much of his early life revolved around the demands of sheep. He was the son of a poor sheep farmer whose farm failed. At the age of seven James had to go herding, and at 15 went to shepherd at Blackhouse, where he read voraciously, and developed a graphic knowledge of the many border tales and ballads. He worked for a time for the Laidlaws of Yarrow, which is where Scott found him in 1801.

Hogg seems to have been always a rough diamond of a character, and though Scott later introduced him to publishers and the grand society of Edinburgh, to which he could never adjust, James only ever wanted to be a shepherd, a man of the open hillsides. Though much of his work was of a poor standard, he produced many a gem of vision and romance which provided the foundation for enduring fame.

Hogg died in 1835, and lies buried in Ettrick kirkyard, along with Tibbie Shiels and his fairy-speaking grandfather. Overlooking St Mary's Loch there is a monument inscribed with the last line of Hogg's poem 'The Queen's Wake' – 'He taught the wandering winds to sing'. Would that we were all so skilled.

The Ettrick Hills are of modest proportions, and contain neither Munros nor Corbetts, but they have more than a handful of Donalds, seven of

which are featured in the walks that follow. For most of the way navigation is no problem, only rarely do the walks take you away from some semblance of a footpath, or a guiding fence or dyke. The whole of the walks around the head of Ettrickdale, and along the line of summits extending northeast from Bodesbeck Law, follow the southern Scotland and British watershed and the regional boundary, Borders on the one hand, Dumfries and Galloway on the other.

The valley of Ettrick Water is a charming place, narrow and outstandingly beautiful, but the valley road remains a single track affair for much of its length. Along the sides of the valley a few remnant stands of pine, as distinct from the cloak of Forestry Commission plantings, survive from the original Ettrick Forest, a royal hunting ground used by Scottish monarchs when not fighting either each other or the English. Originally, the forest covered most of the former county of Selkirk, and was in existence at the time of David I, certainly by the mid-1130s. It would undoubtedly have formed part of the massive Caledonian pine forest that covered much of Scotland following the last Ice Age, and was highly valued as a hunting reserve and as a hiding place for reivers.

That Ettrick remains firmly in Scotland is in great part due to the determination and well-placed guile of one man, William Wallace, a thirteenth-century outlaw, who effectively thwarted Edward I's endeavours to add Scotland to his English kingdom. While Wallace, and later Bruce, carried the torch against the English king, the borderlands learned what it was to be the scene of so much turmoil, and the scene was set for a lasting state of attrition that would not, could not, end while the two countries remained politically separate. Such at least was the evidence of the past.

Thankfully, little is evident today of those horrendous times. What remains is a feast of fine walking for those who enjoy the feel of the hills beneath their feet. Lending themselves to both summer and winter visits, the Ettrick Hills are indeed far away from it all, and yet so close to home.

Ettrick Water makes its way unhurriedly through the dale

133

BODESBECK LAW

This brief introduction to the Ettrick Hills is a fine and simple walk, yet one that provides outstanding views of the adjoining mountains, of the Ettrick Round (Walk 33), of the main ridge, of which Bodesbeck Law is the southerly terminus (Walk 34), and of the Moffat Hills to the north. Requiring only half a day, you are likely to have this mini-circuit entirely to yourself for a good part of the way, and gain from it enough inspiration to explore further. Navigation is not a great problem, but the stretch from Bught Hill to Bodesbeck Law is to all intents and purposes trackless; even so, miss the summit and you will eventually intersect a dyke that will guide you there.

The walk begins from the road end in the Ettrick valley, near Potburn, where, on the edge of a turning circle, a few cars may be parked. The drive through the valley is one of the most memorable imaginable, with Ettrick Water adding ever-changing moments of bright reflection to a lush and green landscape. A good part of the valley road is used by the Southern Upland Way, so give any heavily laden walkers you encounter a wide berth.

Adjoining the turning circle there are two gates: one leads to Potburn, the other, on the right, to a broad forest trail. Follow this, shortly to pass through another gate. Beyond, the trail climbs and turns steadily. A short distance on, note an indistinct descending track on the left, crossing Longhope Burn into the forest; this is the way we will return, and, for future reference, the start of the Ettrick Round.

Continue following the main trail which, as the upper limit of the forest is reached, swings round to reach a gate giving on to the open hillside. The trail goes on beyond the gate for a while, finally ending near a curious earthwork (1). Here the view reaches out across the Whiteyaud Burn below, to the undulating hills that rise to Andrewhinney Hill, backed by the great bulk of White Coomb.

As the trail ends so an indistinct grassy vehicle track takes over, and leads you on to the slopes of Bodesbeck Law. But first, divert a little, to reach the vantage point of Bught Hill, its top marked by a single, small stone. On a warm summer's day, when the skies are filled with the song of birds, this is a most idyllic spot, so easily achieved.

When you have had enough relaxation on Bught Hill, start heading for the obvious dome of Bodesbeck Law. The grassy track is soon regained and leads below the highest ground, but as you go you will see a prominent cairn above, perched on a small rock outcrop. Make for this, and from it you will see the dyke across the summit, beyond a short stretch of peaty ground. Head towards the highest point, crossing the dyke at a convenient gap and continue to the modest cairn that adorns the summit (2). The summital view is most memorable, and stretches away to the Galloway Hills, the Cheviot Hills and the northern fells of Lakeland.

Bodesbeck Law from Bught Hill

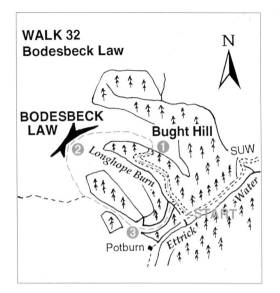

WALK 32
Bodesbeck Law

N

BODESBECK LAW

Bught Hill

SUW

Longhope Burn

Ettrick Water

START

Potburn

The return journey is made by descending in a roughly southerly direction down the regional boundary to meet a broad track that links Ettrickdale with the Moffat valley. The ground just before the track is rather boggy, but not problematical. Once the track is gained, go left to a gate, and continue ahead, shortly re-entering the forest. At a sheepfold (3), ignore the track descending, right, to Pot Burn, but keep ahead to a gate giving on to a forest fire break through which a narrow path now runs. Follow this as it circles through the forest, finally descending to Longhope Burn, just after which the main forest trail along which the walk began is reached.

FACT FILE

Map OS Landranger 1:50 000 Series Sheet 79: Hawick and Eskdale area
Start/Finish Parking space at the end of the valley road, near Potburn GR 189093
Length 6 km (3.75 miles)
Walking time 2–2½ hours
Difficulty Easy walk on forest trails and springy turf

The route in brief

Start GR 189093. Take RH gate on to forest trail. Go through second gate and follow trail NW as it climbs. Pass through gate at forest edge.
1 At earthwork, trail becomes vehicle track. Follow W to Bodesbeck Law slopes (diverting via Bught Hill). Head for cairn, then summit dyke. Cross dyke and reach summit cairn.
2 Descend roughly S to meet track. Go L through gate, then soon re-enter forest.
3 Keep ahead at sheepfold (ignore Pot Burn track to R) and reach fire break. Follow narrow path E and NE through fire break down to Longhope Burn and main forest trail. Retrace outward route to start.

THE ETTRICK ROUND

The circuit of this outstanding horseshoe walk, high above a ring of valley conifers, is aided by the company along the highest ground of either a dyke or a fence. This simple feature relieves the outing of too much map-reading, replacing it with the pleasure of striding confidently across magnificent country. This is a walk for either spring, when the hillsides are at their most verdant and the roadsides embellished by Nature's company of wild flowers, or autumn, when the angled light of approaching winter brings gold and lustre to every tree and stream and at each turn in the trail.

Begin from the turning circle at the road end, and pass through the right hand of two gates, following a forest trail to another gate. A short distance further on an indistinct track drops left to cross Longhope Burn, continuing beyond through a lateral fire break to emerge at a gate, not far from a sheepfold, high above Pot Burn.

Ettrick Pen is the final summit of the Ettrick Round

Ignore the track heading towards Pot Burn, but continue ahead, flanked by conifers, eventually to reach a gate on the regional boundary (1), immediately below the great mound of Bodesbeck Law, which here rises mightily on your right.

At the boundary gate, leave the track to follow a dyke on your left, which works its tortuous way around the gathering streams of Bodesbeck Burn to the first summit of note, White Shank (2). The route undulates first across Smidhope Hill (not named on the 1:50 000 map) before reaching

Capel Fell **(3)**, by which time the dyke has become a fence. From a gate on the summit of Capel Fell descend southeast to reach the peaty col of Ettrick Head where the walk encounters the Southern Upland Way – a means of escape if needed **(4)**.

From the col below Bodesbeck Law to that at Ettrick Head the walk has followed the southern Scotland and British watershed – to the west Selcoth Burn feeds into Moffat Water, which later joins the Annan and flows into the Solway Firth, while the waters from Ettrick valley ultimately join the Tweed on its long journey to the North Sea.

A sign at Ettrick Head welcomes Southern Upland Wayfarers to the Borders Region, but our journey continues across the peat hags of the col and up on to Wind Fell to begin the second stage of the walk.

The next objective is Hopetoun Craig **(5)**, lying to the northeast of Wind Fell, beyond which a clutter of cairns leads to the less well-defined one on the top of Ettrick Pen **(6)**, which marks the highest point of the walk.

To return to the valley, head northwest for about 300 metres/yards and then leave the companionable fence behind, to descend, heading west, down broad grassy slopes, eventually to be captured by the boundaries of plantations **(7)** as well as by Pen Sike and the Entertrona Burn, and funnelled on to a hill track, sandwiched between conifers.

The ensuing grassy track leads down to the Southern Upland Way, met again at the Over Phawhope bothy, and followed across Ettrick Water bridge out to Potburn **(8)**, finishing with a gentle rise to the starting point.

FACT FILE

Map OS Landranger 1:50 000 Series Sheet 79: Hawick and Eskdale area

Start/Finish Parking space at the end of the valley road, near Potburn GR 189093

Length 13.5 km (8.5 miles)

Walking time 6 hours

Difficulty Sustained, undulating high-level walking, aided navigationally by a continuous dyke/fence

5 Follow cairns NE to Ettrick Pen summit.

6 Head NW for 300m along fence, then descend W on grassy slope to plantation.

7 Take path between plantations to rejoin SUW to Potburn.

8 Follow SUW back to start.

The route in brief

Start GR 189093. Take RH gate NW on to forest trail. Shortly after next gate take indistinct track L down to Longhope Burn, then through fire break to gate near a sheepfold. Continue NW (ignore Pot Burn track to L) to gate on regional boundary.

1 Leave track. Follow dyke on L to White Shank summit.

2 Follow dyke, then fence, S across Smidhope Hill to Capel Fell.

3 From gate descend SE to Ettrick Head and SUW (possible escape route).

4 Continue E up Wind Fell, then NE to Hopetoun Craig.

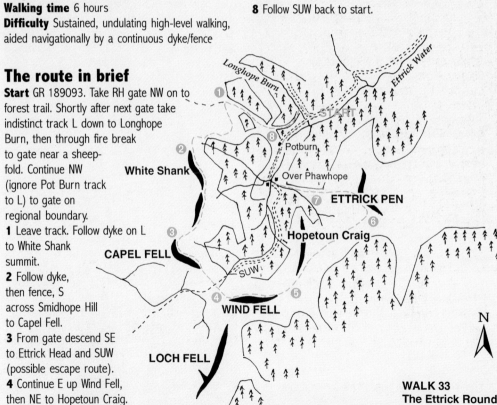

**WALK 33
The Ettrick Round**

THE BODESBECK RIDGE

Rising along the whole of the southeastern flank of Moffat Dale in its upper reaches the splendid grassy ridge that extends from Herman Law, above the lonely cottage of Birkhill, to Bodesbeck Law is, one of the finest outings in southern Scotland. Strong walkers could tackle the walk in both directions from Birkhill, returning once Bodesbeck Law is reached (18km/11.25 miles). Others will need to resolve the transport difficulties.

Directions are minimal since a fence or dyke guides you the whole way, leaving your attention free to wander over the adjoining Moffat Hills, or further afield to the neighbouring Ettrick Round (Walk 33), the Cheviot Hills, and the far, far hazy blue of Lakeland fells, Blencathra and Skiddaw.

There is a small parking space in a forest nook just off the A708, not far northeast of the regional boundary. From there, walk to Birkhill Cottage. Formerly a toll house, Birkhill was where amateur geologist Charles Lapworth stayed between 1872 and 1877, while he studied graptolites in the rock strata of Dob's Linn. Lapworth's studies led to the placing of Silurian and Ordovician periods in their correct geological chronology.

Climb behind Birkhill Cottage, on the true right bank (north) side of Birkie Cleuch (not named on the 1:50 000 map). The initial gradient is steep, easing as height is gained, but quickly brings its rewards in a fine view across the glen to the Moffat Hills. A fence on your left, accompanied by a faint grassy trod, guides you unerringly to the first of these retiring and infrequently visited summits, Herman Law.

Herman Law is the most northerly and easterly of the Ettrick summits, the highest point of which lies close by the meeting of three fences. Southwards the fence (1) leads across a stretch of boggy ground to a minor elevation, Trowgrain Middle, the next objective, marked by an angled cairn of flat stones, though marginally higher ground lies a short way northwest. A little further on, Mid Rig is reached, again marked by a cairn, of neat construction and about 10 metres/yards from a bend in the accompanying fence (2).

Remaining with the fence, press on to Andrewhinney Hill, the highest summit along the ridge and surmounted by a large cairn, approaching which the fence changes direction in order to keep to the high ground. Again, on leaving Andrewhinney Hill the fence changes direction, this time heading southwest, but as it does take the time to go a short way down the slope in a northwesterly direction (3), when you will be rewarded with a most outstanding view of the Grey Mare's Tail and the upland basin around Loch Skeen. Most of the land you see is owned by the National Trust for Scotland, and its dramatic structure challenges those who maintain that anything south of the main Scottish Highlands is flat. The country here compares very favourably with many a Lakeland fell or Snowdonian peak.

Continue towards the next summit, Bell Craig, one of four Donalds along the ridge (Herman Law, Andrewhinney Hill and Bodesbeck Law are the others), crossing a boggy col in the process. Three fences meet on the top of Bell Craig, and it is important here to remain on the watershed,

Looking back along the Bodesbeck Ridge to Andrewhinney Hill

FACT FILE

Map OS Landranger 1:50 000 Series Sheet 79: Hawick and Eskdale area
Start Small roadside parking space, just east of Birkhill Cottage GR 203161.
Finish Blackshope Cottage, Capplegill, Moffat Dale GR 147098
Length 13 km (8 miles) **Walking time** 4–5 hours
Difficulty A fine, grassy ridge, undulating over many tops, with a fence as a guide throughout

The route in brief

Start GR 147098. Climb E behind Birkhill Cottage on N side of Birkie Cleuch. Follow fence on to Herman Law.
1 Follow fence S over Trowgrain Middle (flat stone cairn) to Mid Rig.
2 Follow fence to Andrewhinney Hill. Go NW a short way for views. Return to fence and head SW.
3 Continue to fence junction on Bell Craig summit. Avoid SE ridge, remaining on watershed and crossing fence near junction. Bear half R, regaining main ridge above Salmongill Craig.
4 Cross another Mid Rig (616m), then Nowtrig Head (608m) (both unnamed on OS map). Continue generally SW to dyke/fence junction.
5 Follow dyke/fence up Bodesbeck Law. From summit descend SE to Ettrick Dale/Moffat Dale right of way.
6 Head W down towards Bodesbeck Farm. Cross burn. On entering farm, go L on access road for 200m, then R to Cappelgill Bridge and Blackshope Cottage.

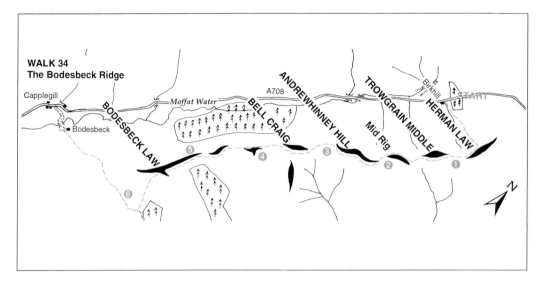

WALK 34
The Bodesbeck Ridge

and not to be drawn into descending the southeast ridge. Cross the fence near its junction and head half right to regain the main ridge above Salmongill Craig **(4)**.

Another Mid Rig (616m), not quite so high as the first, is next, and leads on to another hummock, Nowtrig Head (608m). Neither of these minor summits is named on the 1:50 000 map.

All that remains now is the bulk of Bodesbeck Law, a formidable proposition for weary legs, but nothing like so difficult as it seems. On its northern ridge the fence joins up with a dyke **(5)**, and the two lead you to within a few paces of the summit cairn. From the summit head down in a south-easterly direction to the right of way linking Ettrick Dale with Moffat Dale, and, on reaching it, turn right (west) **(6)**, following it down to Bodesbeck Farm. A trackless descent southwest from the summit will intersect this track at some point, but saves less than a kilometre of walking, and is tough and tussocky going, through which small rocks project at intervals to trip an unwary boot.

Just before Bodesbeck Farm you will need to ford Bodesbeck Burn (not usually a problem), beyond which you reach the curtilage of the farm. Go left at this point on a metalled access track for 200 metres/yards, and then sharp right to follow the access road out to Capplegill Bridge and the nearby Blackshope Cottage.

LOCH OF THE LOWES AND ST MARY'S LOCH

So much of eloquence has been written by poets and others adept with words about St Mary's Loch and its smaller sibling Loch of the Lowes (to rhyme with 'rose'), that it demands inclusion in a book purporting to sample the beauties of southern Scotland. This walk, though linear, and requiring transport at both ends, is sufficiently brief to allow you simply to retrace your steps, or to tackle it from the middle, at the renowned Tibbie Shiels' Inn, doing just as much as you feel able, and perhaps returning another day. The scenery is magnificent whatever the season.

The walk begins on the A708, at Chapelhope, not far from Riskinhope Farm. It is not easy to park here, but a little care and thought will find a place. Alternatively park near Tibbie Shiels, and walk the short distance back along the road to Riskinhope.

Leave the road at Chapelhope and follow the farm road to Riskinhope, from where it is an easy matter to reach a path running along the east side of Loch of the Lowes. This, a narrow path throughout its length, leads to a gate near the bridge across the linking Little Yarrow (1). Turn right at this point and follow the metalled roadway to Tibbie Shiels' Inn.

The strip of land on which Tibbie Shiels' Inn stands was formed after the last Ice Age (about 10,000 years ago) by the combined action of the Crosscleuch and Oxcleuch Burns depositing debris and sediment at a point where the then single loch shallowed. A little further east, Megget Water can be seen to be trying to do the same thing today. The lochs themselves are natural, and formed by glaciers which, at a point where Yarrow and Megget meet, combined forces to gouge an even deeper trench during the course of their retreat.

Continue past Tibbie Shiels' Inn to a gate, and on beyond the sailing club to another gate and stile, beyond which a good path leads into a small woodland of larch, pine and fir at the foot of March Sike, which is crossed by a wooden bridge (2). Eighteenth-century maps of this region show a road running along the south shore of St Mary's Loch, though there is scant evidence of it now. The lochside path that does remain continues its delightful course, a pleasure to walk, with the rounded heights of Watch Law, Henderland Hill, Capper Law and Kirkstead Hill across the loch for company. Below Capper Law is the site of St Mary's Chapel, in which William Wallace is said to have been appointed Warden of Scotland in 1297. Closer by, the conifered slopes of Bowerhope Law, are less attractive, and only serve to direct our attention to the picturesque

Resident mute swans on Loch of the Lowes

loch, which in summer is enhanced by the coloured sails of yachts.

At all times of the year both lochs are a haven for wild birds. Mallard, wigeon, tufted duck, goldeneye, oystercatchers, common sandpiper, great-crested and little grebe share the waters with a resident pair of mute swans, while in winter the morning air is often moved by the evocative sound of whooper swans in flight as they move south from their Arctic summer breeding grounds.

Further along the loch is the isolated farm of Bowerhope **(3)**, an old and venerable building dating from the early 1800s.

Beyond Bowerhope, an access track runs out to the road, below plantations of larch and birch. Across the loch, as the road is neared, can be seen journey's end, Dryhope Tower, a yellowing sixteenth-century peel tower that contrasts markedly in late sunlight to the more dismal grey of the surrounding farms.

At the eastern end of St Mary's Loch a bridge **(4)** takes us on across what is now Yarrow Water.

As soon as the Yarrow bridge is crossed, turn right to follow the north bank of the river to a footbridge over Dryhope Burn, and so on to a stile at the main road. Cross the road, go over a stile, and pursue a dyke up the edge of two fields to reach the track from Dryhope to Blackhouse.

Dryhope Tower is just a short way to the left.

The linear route ends at Dryhope Tower. A four-mile walk back along the road, here provided with ample verges, will return you to Chapelhope, or you could simply retrace your steps.

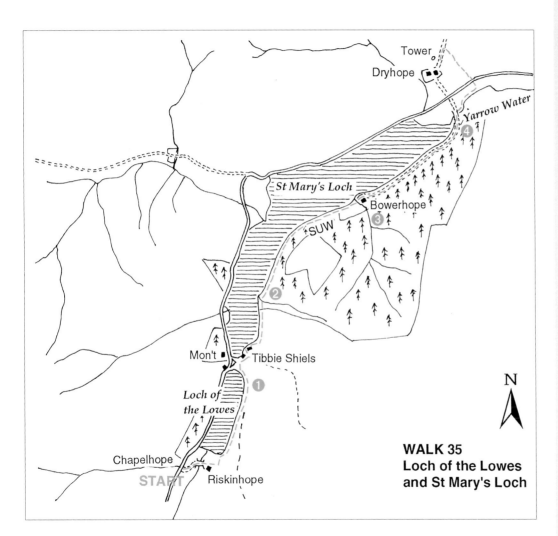

WALK 35
Loch of the Lowes and St Mary's Loch

N

FACT FILE

Map OS Landranger 1:50 000 Series Sheet 73: Peebles, Galashiels and surrounding area; Sheet 79: Hawick and Eskdale area
Start Chapelhope/Riskinhope GR 231190
Finish Dryhope Tower GR 267246
Length 8 km (5 miles)
Walking time 3 hours
Difficulty Easy lochside stroll

The route in brief

Start GR 231190. Leave A708 and follow farm road E to Riskinhope, then path NNE along E side of Loch of the Lowes to gate near bridge across Little Yarrow.
1 Turn R to Tibbie Shiels' Inn. Go past inn to gate, then past sailing club to gate and stile. Follow path N into woodland to bridge across March Sike.
2 Follow lochside path to Bowerhope.
3 Continue on path to bridge over Yarrow Water.
4 Cross bridge, then immediately go R along river bank to Dryhope Burn footbridge. Continue NW, crossing main road by stiles and following dyke along two field edges to reach Dryhope/Blackhouse track. Turn L for Dryhope Tower. Either retrace outward route or return SW via main road to start.

(Opposite) Tibbie Shiel's Inn, St Mary's Loch

143

FROM ETTRICK TO YARROW

You can make what you will of this walk. Starting in the Ettrick valley and calling a halt at Tibbie Shiels' Inn, if you can arrange for someone to pick you up; or reversing the walk; or perhaps starting at Tibbie Shiels and only going as far as the descent from the Southern Upland Way to Riskinhope, returning along Loch of the Lowes. The choice is yours. What is given here is a modest excursion on a fine summer's day, but something rather more demanding in, or immediately following, poor weather. It has the advantage of being able to adjust the length of your stay in the Yarrow valley according to the volume of summer visitors.

Parking is limited in the Ettrick valley, but it is usually possible to find room for a single car. If not, you could park in Ettrick itself and walk the mile or so down the road, passing en route the monument which stands on the site of the birthplace of the poet James Hogg, the 'Ettrick shepherd', and close friend of Walter Scott.

Leave the valley road by a stile opposite Scabcleuch Farm, where a Scottish Rights of Way signpost reads: 'Public Footpath to St Mary's Loch', and follow a path running steeply uphill on the west side of Scabcleuch Burn. At the top of the field, at a gate, ignore the rough road going left, but bear right, following the burn upstream **(1)**, its course enlivened by small cascades. This part of the crossing is pleasant, flanked by Scabcleuch Hill and Craig Hill, but once the upper reaches of the burn are gained the continuation to the abandoned farm at Riskinhope Hope can prove difficult in poor visibility. Stick closely to Scabcleuch Burn, avoiding the temptation of any paths heading away to the left. At the top of the burn, where the retrospective view is of Ettrick Pen and a rough and boggy col is reached, press on northwards to a fence at a stile beside a gate, with Peniestone Knowe immediately on your left **(2)**.

The fence, which extends from Peniestone Knowe to Rig Head (an extension of Ramsey Knowe) has two stiles over it. One bears a Scottish Rights of Way sign directing you over a stile and forward to Riskinhope and backward to Ettrick Kirk, while the other, to its left (west) serves the Southern Upland Way. Keep left after the SUW stile, following an indistinct path that improves as it runs along Peniestone Knowe – aim for a conspicuous tall pole with more signs on it.

The path now runs high above Whitehope Burn and arrives at a marked junction of paths about half a mile after the stile. More signs proliferate, one confirming the route of the SUW, the other, and the way we should go, is signposted 'Loch of the Lowes' **(3)**. This route quickly takes you across Pikestone Rig and down to the loch, reaching it either near Riskinhope Farm, or, by keeping right, along the flanks of Peat Hill, at a point two-thirds of the way down the loch **(4)**, from where Tibbie Shiels is easily reached.

The return journey is made by starting up the signposted farm track ('Hopehouse by the Captain's Road') that heads for Crosscleuch Farm from Tibbie Shiels, continuing on a broad, ascending track beyond a gate near the entrance to the farm. The Captain's Road is depicted on old maps as one of many drove roads linking Peebles with the lands to the south, though no one seems to have recorded who the Captain was. This fine track winds and climbs easily for some distance to meet the Berrybush Plantation at a cattle grid **(5)**.

At the entrance to the woodland the SUW leaves the track, descending to cross Moory Sike (not named on the 1:50 000 map) by a footbridge. Continue, climbing, to reach to a point where

---

The walk from Ettrick to Yarrow uses a path on the far side of St Mary's Loch

Map OS Landranger 1:50 000 Series Sheet 79: Hawick and Eskdale area
Start/Finish Scabcleuch, Ettrick valley GR 247144
Length 11 km (6.75 miles)
Walking time 2½–3 hours
Difficulty Moderate; some boggy sections

The route in brief

Start GR 247144. Cross stile opposite Scabcleuch Farm and follow path N uphill on W side of Scabcleuch Burn. At gate at top of field bear R, following burn upstream.
1 Stay close to burn. At top of burn (boggy col) continue N to fence and stile/gate to R of Peniestone Knowe.
2 Take the L of two fence stiles (SUW sign), following Peniestone Knowe path and heading for tall sign-pole. In about 800m meet path junction.
3 Follow 'Loch of the Lowes' path N across Pikestone Rig down to loch.
4 Follow lochside to Tibbie Shiels. Take 'Hopehouse by the Captain's Road' track, following SUW to Berrybush Plantation.
5 Leave SUW at woodland entrance, climbing track on R (S) to junction of paths. Leave Captain' Road for fire break, then stile signed 'To Riskinhope Hope only'. Follow path S to col between Earl's Hill and Fall Law, then descend and cross Crosscleuch Burn to reach Riskinhope Hope Farm.
6 Keep L of farm, climbing Pikestone Rig to rejoin outward route.
7 Retrace outward route to start.

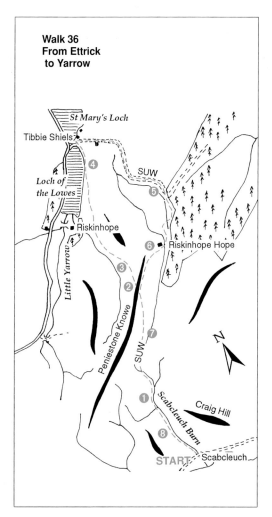

the Captain's Road is left as it pursues its journey across to Hopehouse, a traverse often made by Scott and Hogg.

A brief skirmish with a fire break leads to a stile beside a gate with a sign directing you 'To Riskinhope Hope only'. Press on, leaving the forest behind, to reach the col between Earl's Hill and Fall Law. From here descend to cross Crosscleuch Burn, the northerly extension of Whithope Burn, and so arrive at the sad ruins of Riskinhope Hope Farm **(6)**, a sheep farm, derelict now rather like the ring of conifers that surrounds it. ('Hope' in this context means a valley with a meandering stream, or a sheltered valley, and is encountered elsewhere in Britain, notably, but by no means exclusively, in the Peak District of Derbyshire.)

Keep to the left of the farm, and climb on to Pikestone Rig, high above Whitehope Burn, to rejoin, near a sheepfold **(7)**, the outward route which is followed back to Scabcleuch.

THE CHEVIOT HILLS
TANGLE GREEN

Straddling the border between Scotland and England, the Cheviot Hills form the highest ground in Britain's most northerly national park, Northumberland, and continue beyond, spilling down to the Teviot, the Tweed and the Till. The Cheviots do not compare to the daunting heights of the Highlands, or even the bolder summits of the Galloway Hills, but there is a calm and abiding restfulness, a gentle soughing of the wind as it constantly moves the swathes of grassland this way and that.

The Cheviot from the Border Gate (Clennell Street)

The Cheviot itself at 815 metres (2,674 feet) is significantly higher than most of the range, which consists of gently rolling hills cleft by steep-sided valleys.

The hill's modest overall elevation, and a sizeable collection of minor summits may tempt the unsuspecting walker to tackle more than they can manage, for the range can prove demanding and unforgiving. Peat, tussock grass and large stretches of damp moorland overlying granite feature largely among the Cheviots, though walking is never impossible, except perhaps on The Cheviot itself, the summit of which is a black quagmire after prolonged rain. But the worst excesses are confined to the highest ridges, leaving many of the valleys to provide walkers with idyllic conditions.

Little that is visible today betrays the group's volcanic origins, for rock outcrops are few and far between, and the scenery the product of huge glacial action that planed smooth the rugged countenance of the pre-Ice Age landscape.

This is a region that has seldom known peace. Inhabited first by Neolithic man, later by the Beaker folk and the Romans, and more recently by Norse invaders, it has always been a strategically important boundary. From the tenth century, the Cheviots were the battleground for a lengthy war of attrition that saw families on both sides of the border set against each other. The

The Cheviot, highest point of these fine hills, seen from Windy Rig

days of the border reivers were a notoriously undisciplined time, in spite of the efforts of many to impose discipline and a sense of order, and affected the whole of the border lands, both north and south. The convoluted arrangement of the Cheviot hills and valleys were ideally suited to those who sought to prosper at others' expense, and afforded countless avenues of retreat and concealment. Many of the hill paths and crossings that exist today originated in these troubled times. The whole region is awash with tradition, legend and folklore, and has a cultural heritage, of which it is fiercely proud.

The Cheviots can be approached successfully from either side of the border, and most of the summits reached in the walks that follow lie on the border line, or substantially in England. The range offers virtually limitless walking at every standard, with short circular walks, forest trails, high ridge-walks and long-distance routes. Central to this wealth of walking opportunity is the main ridge of The Cheviots, extending SW–NE, from Kielder to the Till at Wooler, the complete traverse of which is an energetic and exhilarating expedition. It is this ridge that to a large extent forms the present-day border.

The Ministry of Defence control much of the land between the Rede and Coquet rivers. When red flags or lamps are displayed around the perimeter of the land, it is in use as an artillery and infantry training area and should be avoided at all costs. You could be killed.

Elsewhere the land has been skilfully turned to farming. Early cultivation terraces and enclosures can still be traced on some of the hillsides, though much of the land today is used for the rearing of sheep, including the region's own breed the Cheviot. Walkers on many of the high tops will find the black faces of their woolly inhabitants peering quizzically at them.

Few roads cross the Cheviot in a north–south direction, only the weakness of Carter Bar allowing passages. Nor are the Cheviots as a whole circled by a continuous road network. As a result, there are large tracts of sparsely populated land dotted with isolated farms and villages. For those seeking solitude, the Cheviots have the answer.

Kelsocleuch, hidden among the green folds of the Cheviots

THE CHEVIOT

The Cheviot is the highest point of the whole range of the Cheviot Hills, and overtops its neighbour, Cairn Hill, by 38 metres (125 feet). Sadly, its position as monarch of the group is anything but regal, for its summit plateau is a massive peaty bog, formed because rainwater is unable to permeate the underlying granite, which prevents normal decomposition of surface heather and grass. On the other hand, The Cheviot is surrounded by some of the most attractive valleys in Britain, and walkers who choose their day carefully (during a prolonged dry spell, or on a freezing winter's day), will find that the bog which earns The Cheviot such an unenviable reputation is quite manageable.

The mountain was visited in 1728 by Daniel Defoe. Which approach he used is not clear, but that from the College valley is by far the finest.

College valley is a private valley to which consent for vehicle access is required. It is open to approximately 12 motor vehicles on any day except between the middle of April and the end of the May, when lambing is taking place. Permits may be obtained without charge from Sale and Partners, 18–20 Glendale Road, Wooler, Northumberland, NE71 6DW; remember to specify the dates on which you wish to walk.

The walk that follows effects a circular tour, and is best tackled from just north of Southernknowe, where the two valley roads meet. There is a hall here, beside which vehicles may be parked.

Walk down the roadway into the valley, as far as Mounthooly **(1)**, where a track runs on beside College Burn. In spring and early summer, the valley is alive with colour, as wild flowers clothe the landscape. Gradually, the track we are following deteriorates to a narrow path, and changes direction **(2)** to head for a massive corrie and gorge, known as the Hen Hole. It was formed during the Ice Age, and now boasts a damp and dank inner sanctum down which the stream cascades in a series of small falls.

From near the base of of Hen Hole we aim next for a conspicuous gash in the hillside to the south,

known as Red Cribs. The name derives from the colour of the soil, and the gap once used as 'a passage and hyeway for the theefe'. Once we gain Red Cribs, we can continue to the border fence, which leads us gently upwards to Auchope Cairn (3), and then on to a fence junction (GR 896194), where the border suddenly veers westwards (4). At this point we encounter, and must circumnavigate as best we can, the first of the peaty clutches of The Cheviot, following a line of rotting fence posts to Cairn Hill (5), where a more substantial fence then leads us on and up to the summit of The Cheviot (6).

The trig point on The Cheviot is surrounded by a morass of black peat, though recent pathworks avoid the worst of it. The peat is quite deep in places, and conceals the wreckage of a number of aircraft that came to grief during the Second World War.

From the summit we set off for our starting point by heading roughly northeast, along a fenceline, and descending over Scald Hill to a col above New Burn (7), a feeder of Harthope Burn to the east. Once this vague col is reached, we stay with the fence, and ascend slightly on to Broadhope Hill to reach a gate (8). Turning west here (the path is not clear), we meet an improving path to Goldscleugh (9), from where a good track runs out speedily to Southernknowe and the starting point near the hall.

The Cheviot, viewed from Russell's Cairn on the Windy Gyle

FACT FILE

Map OS Landranger 1:50 000 Series Sheet 74: Kelso; Sheet 80 Cheviot Hills and Kielder Forest area
Start/Finish College Valley Hall GR 888252
Length 19 km (12 miles)
Walking time Allow at least 6 hours
Difficulty A long, moderate walk with little difficulty. Even though there are good paths most of the way, and fences to serve as guides, a clear day is essential

The route in brief
Start GR 888252. Follow roadway SSW to Mounthooly.
1 Continue on track beside College Burn generally SSW, then change direction to ESE.
2 Head towards corrie and gorge (the Hen Hole). Then, aim for gash in hillside (Red Cribs). Once gained, continue to border fence. Follow fence to Auchope Cairn.
3 Continue to fence junction (GR 896194).
4 Leave border and follow fence posts to Cairn Hill.
5 Follow more substantial fence NE to The Cheviot's summit (NB avoid trig point if ground is wet).
6 Head NE along fenceline, over Scald Hill, to col above New Burn.
7 Stay with fence N on to Broadhope Hill and gate.
8 Turn W and follow unclear path to Goldscleugh.
9 Take good track back to Southernknowe and start.

START

WALK 37
The Cheviot

N

Southernknowe

Lambden Burn

Goldscleugh

Mounthooly

The Schil

College Burn

Scald Hill

Hen Hole

**THE
CHEVIOT**

Auchope Cairn

Cairn Hill

151

THE SCHIL

In spite of being more than 200 metres lower than The Cheviot, The Schil is a prominent landmark among this range of hills, not least because it is one of the few summits on which more than a scattering of rock outcrops occur; indeed, to reach the very tip of The Schil, some mild scrambling is involved.

This approach begins in Kirk Yetholm, one end of the Pennine Way, and largely follows the Anglo-Scottish border, crossing it on a number of occasions. The Schil lies a good 30 metres into Scotland, and is a worthy objective at any time of year, though a fine spring day would enrich the walk with a spread of wild flowers and the serenade of moorland and mountain birds.

Kirk Yetholm has a unique and fascinating story of its own, being a mecca for Border gypsies, and conveniently close to the border to move into English jurisdiction when the purpose suited. The gypsies had their own king, of course, the last being Charles Blyth Faa (d. 1802), drawn to his coronation in a coach pulled by six donkeys.

The Schil: a prominent landmark among the Cheviots

We begin from the Border Inn in Kirk Yetholm, following the ascending roadway opposite to cross a minor ridge that undulates southeastwards over Staerough Hill, Sunnyside Hill, Wildgoose Hill and Latchly Hill before reaching a fine, minor summit, The Curr. Shortly after crossing a cattle grid, we leave the road to ford Halter Burn (1), so gaining a broad track rising across the southern slopes of Green Humbleton, used in time gone by as the site of a hill fort with a commanding position overlooking the Bowmont valley.

Gradually we climb to meet the border, and at a gate (2) cross into England for a short distance to the col between White Law and its small companion to the west. The exact position of the border was for long periods of history uncertain, a boundary commission set up in 1222 admitting defeat. Later attempts to locate the border were also doomed to failure, and it was not until some time after the Union of the Crowns in 1603 that the issue began to be resolved.

Near White Law, another gate (3) permits a return to Scotland for a fine, airy traverse along Steer Rig to reach the broad col between The Curr and an elongated summit, Black Hag, at the head of Fleehope Burn. Here, at last, The Schil springs into view, a domed mound, set against the distant brooding bulk of The Cheviot.

At the top of Fleehope Burn (4), we return once

more to England for the final approach to The Schil, gained by re-crossing the border fence once we are level with its craggy topknot.

This attractive and rare appearance of granite, and the encircling spill of rocks and boulders, gives The Schil special appeal, enhanced by its distance from other heights. As a result there is an excellent panorama embracing a ring of alluring hills and valleys, and an uninterrupted view out to the North Sea, and northwest to the Ettrick and Tweedsmuir ranges.

An enjoyable return may be made down Curr Burn to Primsidemill in Bowmont valley, facing you with a pleasant road walk back to Kirk Yetholm. But we shall make our way back along the Alternative Pennine Way, the so-called bad weather option.

By retracing our steps **(5)** towards the col near The Curr, and diverting slightly from our outward route, we reach a gate leading down to the Halterburn valley **(6)**.

Halterburn valley is, particularly in its upper section, a relaxing place, where the remnants of former lives and homes gradually succumb to the passage of time and the attentions of wandering sheep. Bright-eyed primroses dot the landscape, on a warm and still day, lending to the pervading air of contentment.

Below Latchly Hill, as the path forks, we go right, dropping quickly to Old Halterburn **(7)** and Burnhead, where the minor road used on the onward stretch leads north to Halterburn before passing around Staerough Hill to return to Kirk Yetholm.

FACT FILE

Map OS Landranger 1:50 000 Series Sheet 74: Kelso
Start/Finish Kirk Yetholm GR 827282
Length 17 km (10.75 miles)
Walking time Allow 5 hours
Difficulty A moderate walk using the Pennine Way and its alternative

The route in brief

Start GR 827282. Climb roadway opposite Border Inn. Shortly after cattle grid leave road to ford Halter Burn.
1 Take broad track SE across Green Humbleton. Cross Anglo-Scottish border at gate.
2 Continue S to the W of White Law.
3 Re-cross border via gate. Traverse Steer Rig heading S to col between Black Hag and The Curr at the head of Fleehope Burn.
4 Cross border again to approach The Schil, re-crossing into Scotland at the highpoint.
5 Retrace steps, diverting slightly to gate leading down L to Halterburn valley.
6 Follow path N and W through valley until it forks after crossing stream.
7 Head N to regain minor road which is followed back to start.

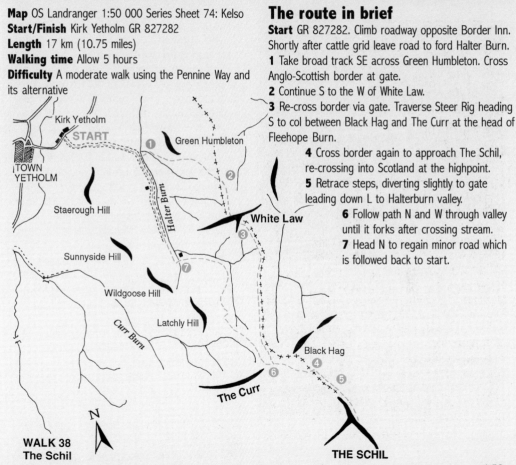

WALK 38
The Schil

153

WINDY GYLE

Viewed from a distance, Windy Gyle seems to have little distinction, appearing as a flat, uninteresting mound, yet it is the focal point of a number of rewarding circuits, some originating in England, some, as the present walk, confined almost totally to Scotland. It stands on both the border and the Pennine Way, at one of its more attractive points and is one of the highest points in the entire Borders Region. Walkers should bear in mind that it is not called 'Windy' Gyle without cause, and that there is little protection from the elements.

On a fine day the walk is quite delightful and uses some of the ancient cattle byways and reivers' highways that cover these hills. We begin in Cocklawfoot, heading south along a farm road beside Kelsocleuch Burn as far as the farm. Above the farm, to the south, stands a small plantation, and this is our objective, climbing gently, initially along the line of Back Burn, to reach the plantation. On arrival, a wide forest ride is discovered passing through the plantation, booby-trapped with half-concealed fallen branches, and calling for care and attention for a while. At the top of the ride we pass through a gate to gain the open hillside above **(1)**, following a path that becomes less distinct as we climb on to a narrowing grassy ridge known as Windy Rig. Before long we arrive at the border, meeting it at a gate **(2)**. Here we turn left (southeast), and climb easily to the trig pillar on Windy Gyle **(3)**, perched atop a massive spread of boulders, with smaller, untidy piles of stones and Pennine Waymarkers nearby. One such accumulation is known as Lord Russell's Cairn, and commemorates the luckless victim of 'a noteworthy piece of Border mischief'.

The summit is one of the best and most pleasurable vantage points in the Cheviot Hills, and a perfect spot for a short break. The view extends north across the Bowmont valley to the distant Tweed, and south into England, overlooking delightful Coquetdale, and the summits of Yarnspath Law and Bloodybush Edge to the east.

Our route continues northeastwards along the border fence to the Border Gate **(4)**, where an ancient drove road, Clennell Street, crosses the border. During the period of the Border

Summit cairn on Windy Gyle, possibly an ancient burial mound

Troubles, the Border Gate was often agreed upon as an acceptable place at which to hold Wardens' Courts, and was formerly known as Cocklawgate.

We descend, west of north from the Border Gate, flanking a minor rise called The Bank, and continuing to a gate. The broad ridge of Cock Law lies ahead, with our route winding about a little, eventually to pass through a small conifer plantation **(5)**. Beyond we meet a farm track dropping steeply to reach an old sycamore tree that is a conspicuous landmark near a farm gate. We go through the gate to another, crossing the farm yard to a wooden bridge, and so return to Cocklawfoot.

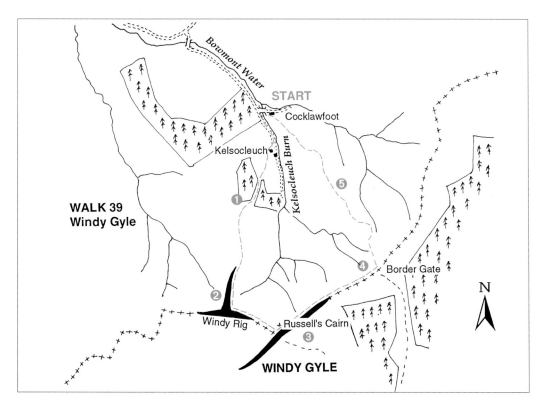

WALK 39
Windy Gyle

FACT FILE

Map OS Landranger 1:50 000 Series Sheet 80: Cheviot Hills and Kielder Forest area
Start/Finish Cocklawfoot GR 854186
Length 9.5 km (6 miles)
Walking time 4 hours
Difficulty Only moderately testing

The route in brief

Start GR 854186. Go S along farm road beside Kelsocleuch Burn to farm. Follow Back Burn to plantation, then forest ride to gate on to hillside.
1 Follow indistinct path S up Windy Rig to meet border at gate.
2 Turn L (SE) and climb Windy Gyle (trig pillar).
3 Follow border fence NE to the Border Gate.
4 Descend NW, flanking The Bank, to reach gate. Follow winding route, generally NW, eventually passing through conifer plantation.
5 Pick up farm track to gate (near sycamore tree). Go through gate, then another gate and cross farm yard to wooden bridge. Return to start.

MOZIE LAW, BEEFSTAND HILL AND LAMB HILL

Mozie Law, Beefstand Hill and Lamb Hill are relatively minor summits straddling the border, but provide a good excuse for a meandering walk composed of the perfect ingredients for relaxation.

As with the immediately preceding walks, the border line is used by the Pennine Way, and often sees a fair amount of pedestrian traffic heading for Kirk Yetholm. To the south the hills and moors spread amiably, and contrast noticeably with the tight-packed terrain to the north, where narrow valleys and undulating ridges tumble and twist towards the Tweed. It is by way of these ridges and valleys that our walk progresses, and makes use of an ancient drove road, The Street, which links the Bowmont valley with Coquetdale.

We begin in the quiet village of Hownam (pronounced 'Hoonam') on Kale Water, a popular place of retreat during the time of the Covenanter upheavals, when the remote valleys would have proved ideal for clandestine prayer meetings. The same nooks and crannies also provided concealed highways for marauding cattle thieves during the Border Troubles. These days everything is much quieter.

Car parking in Hownam is very limited, so please show consideration, and ensure you leave your vehicle in a safe and convenient place.

Begin by ascending a track opposite the last house on the right, and climb to a large white house (initially obscured) on the hillside (1). Turn right, through a gate to join The Street, and climb to a tattered plantation on the skyline (2). From here we press on eastwards, climbing easily to a

On the 'new' Pennine Way, across Mozie Law

junction by a gate in the dyke. Ignore the gate, and continue now southeast along The Street. Throughout its length The Street is generally easy to follow, though the regular use of these pastures by farmers occasionally creates tracks rather more prominent in one or two places than The Street itself, and potentially misleading. As Windy Law draws near look for a gate on the left **(3)**, and continue beyond it, following the line of a dyke and heading for Craik Moor, an obvious lump to your left.

These gentle slopes in springtime are alive with the purple and yellow of mountain pansies, while the hillsides resound to the call of curlew, golden plover and lapwing. As you cross Craik Moor an interest in Iron Age hill forts will draw you away for a moment to Blackbrough Hill, on which there is an especially fine example in a strategic position high above the Heatherhope valley.

At the head of Singingside Burn **(4)** the route deviates a little to pass through a couple of gates before resuming its upward line to the border. Unerringly we arrive at the border fence, and shortly we must turn right to reach the first summit, Mozie Law **(5)**, beyond which the fenceline will lead us on, first to Beefstand Hill and then Lamb Hill **(6)**, a lonely outpost amid a spread of boggy ground and tussock grass. The whole of this section in fact, frequently trodden by Pennine Wayfarers, is heathery and contains an abundance of peat hags and wet stretches, across which paving slabs and duckboards have been provided to make things easier. The extension of the walk to reach Lamb Hill is

FACT FILE

Map OS Landranger 1:50 000 Series Sheet 80: Cheviot Hills and Kielder Forest area
Start/Finish Hownam GR 779193
Length 19 km (12 miles)
Walking time 5 hours
Difficulty A delightful, quiet and straightforward walk

The route in brief

Start GR 779193. Ascend track opposite last house on R. Climb to large white house on hillside.
1 Turn R through gate. Climb The Street to a plantation. Continue E to junction in dyke (gate).
2 Ignore gate. Continue SE on The Street, watching for gate on L (NE) approaching Windy Law.
3 Beyond gate follow dyke SE towards Craik Moor on your L (hill fort nearby on Blackbrough Hill). Continue to head of Sunningdale Burn.
4 Route passes NE through two gates, then resumes SE upward line to border. Just after border fence, turn R (S) to Mozie Law summit.
5 Follow fenceline to Beefstand Hill and Lamb Hill (duckboards over boggy sections).
6 Return NE towards Beefstand Hill to gate at GR 815141.

7 Descend NW alongside fence towards tall cairn on Thorny Hill
(Callow Cairn). Descend E side of Thorny Hill, heading for dyke that runs on to Green Hill.
8 Continue NW past hill fort to valley road near Greenhill Farm.
9 Follow valley road back to start.

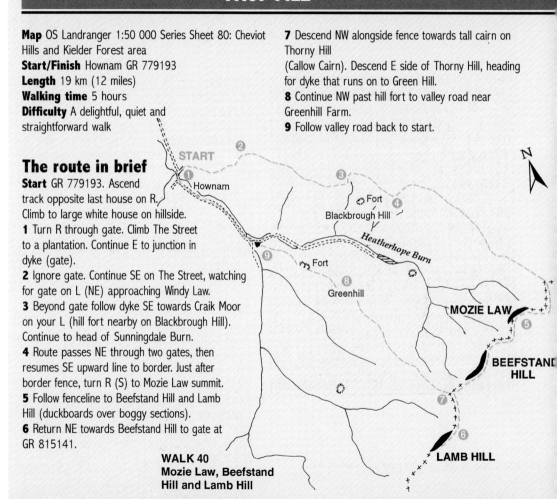

**WALK 40
Mozie Law, Beefstand
Hill and Lamb Hill**

optional (though it has been included in the distance), but, like Beefstand Hill, it provides a pleasing view of granite heartlands of The Cheviot some seven miles distant, and on a fine day is well worth the short deviation.

From Lamb Hill we need to return towards Beefstand Hill, aiming for a gate in the fence at GR 815141 **(7)**, from where we descend alongside another fence towards a very tall cairn on Thorny Hill (Callaw Cairn). The origins of this magnificent cairn seem to be lost in the mists of time, but it may well have been a burial place for Iron Age chieftains.

For a while the path remains indistinct, but soon improves as we reach the east side of Thorny Hill. Now begins a long a delightful descent, heading for a distant dyke that runs on to Green Hill **(8)**, and continuing ultimately to reach another hill fort in a commanding position overlooking Heatherhope Burn and Capehope Burn. The siting and the manner of construction of many of these forts and settlements, most of which date from about 500 BC, certainly seems defensive in nature rather than pastoral, suggestive of yet another troubled period in the history of these hills.

The onward path finally reaches the valley road near Greenhill Farm **(9)**, at the end of the Heatherhope valley, followed by a gentle stroll back to Hownam.

BIBLIOGRAPHY

Along the Southern Upland Way, Jimmie MacGregor (BBC Books, 1990)

The Border Country, Alan Hall (Cicerone Press, 1993)

The Border Hill Fort in The Southern Annual, 1963, R.K. Akers (The "Southern Reporter", 1963)

The Borders, F.R. Banks (B.T. Batsford Ltd., 1977)

Discovering the Historical Lowlands, Norman Hillson (Herbert Jenkins, 1958)

The Folklore of the Scottish Highlands, Anne Ross (B T Batsford Ltd, 1976)

Glen Trool: Forest Park Guide, ed. H.L. Edlin (HMSO, 1965)

Grey Mare's Tail: Management Plan 1992-1997 (National Trust for Scotland, 1992)

The Heart of Scotland, George Blake (B.T. Batsford Ltd., 1934, 3rd edition, 1951)

Lanarkshire: An Inventory of the Prehistoric and Roman Monuments (The Royal Commission on the Ancient Monuments of Scotland, 1978)

The Lowlands of Scotland: Edinburgh and the South, Maurice Lindsay (Robert Hale, 1977)

The Pentlands' Pocket Book, Albert Morris and James Bowman (Pentland Associates, 1990)

Pentland Walks, D G Moir (John Bartholomew & Son Ltd., 1977)

The Poetical Works of Sir Walter Scott, ed. J. Logie Robertson (Henry Frowde, 1906)

Portrait of the Border Country, Nigel Tranter (Robert Hale, 1972)

Portrait of the Burns Country, Hugh Douglas (Robert Hale, 1968)

Portrait of the Clyde, Jack House (Robert Hale, 1969, 2nd edition, 1975)

The Scottish Borderland - The Place and the People, Ed. Richard Allan and Isobel Candlish (The Border Country Life Association, 1988)

In Scotland Again, H.V. Morton (Methuen & Co. Ltd., 1933)

The Solway Firth, Brian Blake (Robert Hale, 1955, 3rd edition, 1982)

The Southern Uplands, Ken Andrew (SMC, 1972, with A A Thrippleton, and 2nd edition, 1992)

The Southern Upland Way, Ken Andrew (HMSO: Forestry Commission, 1984: 2 vols)

A Guide to the Southern Upland Way, David Williams (Constable, 1989)

The Steel Bonnets, George MacDonald Fraser (Collins Harvill, 1989)

The Story of Scotland: Nigel Tranter (Lochar Publishing, Moffat, 1991)

Walking the Scottish Border, Robert Langley (Robert Hale, 1976)

INDEX

Abbotsford, 105
Alba, 7
Anderson, Alexander, 104
Andrewhinney Hill, 138
Awful Hand, 16, 19–26

Back Hill of Bush, 38
Ballencleuch Law, 77–9
Battle of Rullion Green, 84
Battle of the Steps o'Trool, 19
Beefstand Hill, 156–8
Bell Craig, 138
Bell, David, 22
Benniguinea, 59–61
Benniner, 65–7
Birkhill, 138
Blackbrough Hill, 157
Blackhope Burn Round, 115–17
Bodesbeck Law, 134–5, 140
Bodesbeck Ridge, 138–140
Border, Anglo-Scottish, 152
Border Gate, 155
Border Troubles, 9, 110, 148, 154, 156
British watershed, 5
Broad Law, 107û9
Broughton Heights, 83, 90–1
Bruce's Stone, 19, 53
Bucccleuch Countryside Service, 70
Buchan Burn, 19, 27
Buchan, John, 31, 53, 103
Burns, Robert, 15, 27

Caerlaverock National National Reserve, 63
Cairngarroch, 47–9
Cairnsgarroch, 41–3
Cairnsmore of Carsphairn, 65–7
Cairnsmore of Dee, 59–61
Cairnsmore of Fleet, 56–8
Cairnsmore Range, 17, 65–7
Callaw Cairn, 158
Captain's Road, 144
Cargill, Rev. Donald, 123
Carlin's Cairn, 36
Carnirock Stone, 25
Castlelaw Hill, 84
Cheviot, The, 148, 150–1
Cheviot Hills, 147–58
Chapelgill Hill, 94–5
Charlie, Bonnie Prince, 73
Clatteringshaw Loch, 7, 53, 54
Clyde, River, 70
College Valley, 150
Coran of Portmark, 41–3
Corbetts, 13
Corserine, 36–8
Covenanters, see Wars of the Covenant
Craigencallie, 33, 47
Craiglee, 30
Cramalt Craig, 107–9
Criffel, 62–3
Crockett, Samuel Rutherford, 21, 22, 27, 59
Culsharg, 20, 28

Culter Fell, 94–5, 96
Culter Hills, 93–7
Culter Watershed, 96–7
Curleywee, 44

Daerhead, 78
Daer Reservoir, 7, 77
Dalveen Pass, 69
Debateable Land, The, 9
Dee, River, 33, 36, 54
deer stalking season, 12
Devil's Beef Tub, 110
Dob's Linn, 121
Dollar Law, 107–9
Donalds, 13
Donald's Cleuch Head, 123
Douglas's Cairn, 62
Dryhope Tower, 143
Dundreich, 86
Dungeon Hills, 17, 27–31
Dungeon of Buchan, 47
dykes, 10, 13
Ettrick Forest, 133
Ettrick Hills, 131–46
Ettrick Round, 136–7

Fallburn Fort, 99, 100

Gairland Burn, 27, 30
Galloway Forest, Park, 16
Galloway Hills, 5–26
Gathersnow Hill, 96

Gladhouse Reservoir, 83, 87
Glentress Forest, 83
Glen Trool, 19, 27, 30, 53
Gordon Arms, 104
Green Humbleton, 152
Green Lowther, 73–5
Green Well of Scotland, 41, 65
Grey Man of Merrick, 21, 28
Grey Mare's Tail, 106, 119
grouse shooting season, 12

Hart Fell, 110û13
Hen Hole, 150
Herman Law, 138
Hillshaw Head, 96
Hirendean Castle, 86
Hogg, James, 15, 104, 131, 144
Hownam, 156
Hudderstone, 97

James, King V, 93
James, King VI/I, 9
Jeffries Corse, 86

Kells Range, see Rhinns of Kells
King's Well, 42
Kirkhope, 77
Kirriereoch, 24

Lamachan Hill, 50
Lamb Hill, 156–8
lambing season, 12

Lapworth, Charles, 121, 138
Larg Hill, 50
Leadhills, 69
Loch Arron, 27
Lochcraig Head, 127–9
Loch Dee, 44
Loch Doon, 27, 42
Loch Dungeon, 38
Loch Enoch, 21, 27
Loch Harrow, 36
Loch Kindar, 62
Loch Neldricken, 27
Loch of the Lowes, 7, 141–3
Loch Skeen, 119
Loch Trool, 7, 53
Loch Valley, 27, 31
Lowther Hill, 73–5
Lowther Hills, 69–79
Lumps of Garryhorn, 42

Manor Hills, 106, 107–9
March Burn, 36
McAdam, John Loudon, 106
Meaul, 41–3
Megget Stone, 107
Melrose, 105
Mennock Pass, 69

Meikle Millyea, 33–5
Merrick The, 19, 27
Mid Craig, 123–5
Millfore, 47
Minnigaff Hills, 16, 44–55
Moffat, 106
Moffat Hills, 106, 110–30
Moorfoot Hills, 81, 86–9
Mozie Law, 156–8
Mullwharchar, 27
Munros, 13
Murder Hole, 22, 27
Murray, Professor Alexander, 58

Nieve of the Spit, 20

Peebles, 105
Pentland Hills, 81, 84–5
Picts, 7
Polharrow Glen, 36

Raiders' Road, 59
Ramsey, Allan, 69
Rhinns of Kells, 17, 32–43
Rights of Way, 12
Rig of Jarkness, 30
Robert the Bruce, 7, 19, 36, 42, 47

Rodger Law, 77–9
Rowantree Junction, 22
Ruskin, John, 105

Scald Law, 85
Scaut Hill, 98–9
Schil, The, 152–3
Scottish Mountaineering Club, 121
Scott, Walter, 15, 19, 81, 104, 105, 110
Shalloch on Minnoch, 22
Silver Flowe, 36, 44
Solway Hills, 17, 56–63
Southern Upland Fault, 5, 16
Southern Upland Way, 33, 54, 73, 134,
    137, 144
South Esk, River, 83
South Esk Watershed, 86–7
St Mary's Loch, 7, 104, 141–3
Street, The, 156
Sweetheart Abbey, 62

Talla Linn, 107
Talla Reservoir, 107
Talla Water, 107, 127–9
Tarfessock, 22, 24
Taylor, John, 69
Thick Cleuch Moss, 77–8

Threipmuir Reservoir, 81
Tibbie Shiels, 104
Tibbie Shiels' Inn, 104, 141
Tinto Hills, 93, 98–101
Trahenna Hill, 90–1
Traquair House, 105
Turnhouse Hill, 84
Tweed, River, 7
Tweedsmuir Hills, 103–30

Union of the Crowns, 9

Wallace, William, 133, 141
Wanlockhead, 69
Wars of the Covenant, 9, 41, 73, 103, 107
Battle of Rullion Green, 84
The Covenant, 9
Dempster, John, 41
Hunter, John, 110
The Killing Times, 10
Watch Knowe, 119
Wedder Law, 77–9
West Kip, 85
White Coomb, 115, 119, 123–5
White Lochan of Drigmorn, 47–8
Windlestraw Law, 83, 88–9
Windy Gyle, 154–5
Woodhead Lead Mine, 41